Digital Labour, Society and the Politics of Sensibilities

Adrian Scribano • Pedro Lisdero
Editors

Digital Labour, Society and the Politics of Sensibilities

palgrave
macmillan

Editors
Adrian Scribano
CONICET
Buenos Aires, Argentina

Pedro Lisdero
CONICET
Córdoba, Argentina

ISBN 978-3-030-12308-6   ISBN 978-3-030-12306-2 (eBook)
https://doi.org/10.1007/978-3-030-12306-2

Library of Congress Control Number: 2019931001

Cover image © Alex Linch / shutterstock.com

This Palgrave Macmillan imprint is published by the registered company Springer Nature Switzerland AG.
The registered company address is: Gewerbestrasse 11, 6330 Cham, Switzerland

Foreword

I am very delighted to see Adrian Scribano and Pedro Lisdero publishing *Digital Labour, Society and the Politics of Sensibilities* with Palgrave Macmillan. Although I was not able to contribute with my own chapter, I have tried to support the project as much as I can from the beginning onwards. This foreword gives me the opportunity to reflect on some developments within the field the book aims to cover. In the following, I would like to bring your attention to the ongoing research and debates in the fields of the gig economy, digital labour and Big Data analytics.

Firstly, in a similar way as the emergence of social media was mainly a reaction to the explosion of the dot-com bubble around 2000, online sharing platforms such as Airbnb, Uber and Deliveroo are often discussed as a reaction to the global financial crisis in 2008 in order to find new strategies of capital accumulation. These online sharing platforms can be considered as a new business model trying to commodify the idea of sharing in neoliberal times and individualized cultures. The companies tend to avoid taxes, create a new low-wage economy with precarious working and living conditions for the digital workers and weaken local economies. However, as a response to the gig economy, the idea of platform co-operativism has emerged that questions the exploitative logic of the capitalist digital platforms by advocating a change of ownership and solidarity in the twenty-first-century information society.

Secondly, there has recently been a lot of academic interest around the notions of value creation and digital labour in the context of digital media and technologies. Scholars have been discussing how far online activities of users are value creating and can be considered as work tasks (digital

labour debate). Besides this, a lot of research is at the moment being conducted that takes into account a global view on digital media and technologies by focusing on the international division of digital labour. Due to
the imperialist character of digital capitalism, new inner colonies of exploitation are created: miners in Congo extracting minerals that are essential
in the manufacture of a variety of electronic devices, assembly line workers
at Foxconn with inhuman working conditions, IT workers in the Indian
software industry and Call Centre workers in parts of Eastern Europe.

Thirdly, Big Data has become the new buzzword in the arena of digital
media and technologies. For the processing of Big Data, some sort of
software (including codes and algorithms) and hardware (including servers and data centres) are required, resulting into new global social and
ecological challenges. The emergence of Big Data and cloud computing
can be considered in the context of the neoliberal fetish of quantification
and the belief in providing technological fixes to social problems. The
algorithmic logic of Big Data analytics reinforces the instrumental and
administrative understanding of society. Equally, data centres, which con-
sist of servers that are able to store Big Data, use electricity for power and
cooling on a permanent basis that causes new ecological problems in digital capitalism. Big Data and cloud computing also strengthen the idea of
outsourcing IT labour to the cloud and bring new forms of deskilled
labour.

Finally, a critical theory and political economy approach to digital
media and technologies deals with questions and concepts of, to name but
a few, ownership, labour, commodity, fetishism, ideology and alienation.
Those concepts are still highly relevant for any theory and political praxis
that is interested in establishing a commons-based information society
that benefits the many, not the few. While the aforementioned developments impact civil society on a global scale, the visible research is mainly
conducted in the Global North such as the US and the UK. This collection will undoubtedly serve as a fresh and inspiring contribution by going
beyond the Anglo-American tradition and including perspectives and case
studies from many parts of the world. I am sure this book has the potential
to reach out widely.

University of Stirling   Thomas Allmer
Stirling, UK
November 2018

ACKNOWLEDGEMENT

This book is fully dedicated to our families for their love and patience as always. To the authors who contributed passionately to this project, as well as the staff of Palgrave Macmillan, especially Anca Pusca and Katelyn Zingg for their generous support. In this way, we appreciate the work and time of the reviewers who made a substantial contribution with their observations. We must underline the editing work carried out by Majid Yar, with his usual kindness and excellence. Surely, we have not exhausted in this book all the connections between Digital Labour, Society 4.0 and Politics of the Sensibilities, but we are sure that the critical discussion of these topics should remain a central axis of the social sciences.

PROLOGUE: EMOTIONS, LABOUR AND SOCIETY 4.0

The *digital revolution*, or third industrial revolution, occurred in the second half of the twentieth century (Scholz 2013). The consequence of this was the automation of work technologies devices, with the insertion of computers, the massive use of the Internet, the development of microprocessors and high-tech communications impacting on society in a universal way, modifying the ways of life of ordinary citizens (Beck et al. 1994).

The fourth industrial revolution, also called *disruptive technology*, is being expanded and consolidated in the twentieth century (Bower and Christensen 1995). It is a technological revolution that has been changing the everyday ways and styles of life of the common man. This so-called disruptive technology, among other possible paths, is characterized primarily by the connection between technologies (Skobelev and Borovik 2017). These technologies bring together the physical, digital and biological sphere, with direct consequences for the ways of living, of relating to other people and things and of working for the common person (Ford 2016; Edwards and Ramirez 2016). This process has been called, also, Society 4.0.

Society 4.0 can be defined as the new societies whose sociability has been generated, on the one hand, by the new changes in cultural and political-economic policy that have been produced in the globalized contemporary world since the late 1970s, especially with the advent of the productive restructuring generated by the new logic of financial capital. Created too, on the other hand, by the policy of devaluation of labour as a fundamental category of profit generation of capitalism, which has been expanding vigorously since the beginning of the twenty-first century, with the consolidation and advancement of the digital age (Steiner and Dixon 2012; Wellman 2011).

This new model of society, which has developed rapidly in the last decades, especially in Western societies, has been causing profound historical changes in the cultural, social and economic planes with consequences of great impact in all Western countries, and among all globalized nations. The main characteristics of these changes are (1) the advancement of digital base technology, with a strong impact on employment policy through automation, (2) increased financial speculation (money generating money), (3) mass unemployment, resulting in an army of cheap and subservient labour, especially among developing societies, and (4) the policy of devastation of forest reserves, causing immediate impacts on the environment.

This book has the main aim of debating the consequences of the advance of this new social form, Society 4.0—through the relationship between work and sensibilities in the digital age—from a multidisciplinary perspective. This book discusses, among other things, the changes in the world of work in the context of the digital age and, alongside this, the consequences of the digital age in the current process of social structuring and transformations.

The set of chapters in this book traces a tense picture of the connections between labour and society in the present times. It builds an analytical framework that seeks to understand the uncertainties, risks, expectations and weaknesses of the contemporary everyday person, and the possible forms of conflict and struggle for recognition in an arduous battle of sensibilities.

The chapters that compose the *Politics of Sensibilities* organize a broad view of issues of unparalleled importance for understanding the paths taken by emerging sensibilities in an era of insecurity and risk. In a century of ever more fragile frontiers and a harder and more exclusionary economic policy, the basic guarantees of the rights of the common man are threatened and become more and more weak and shattered by the demolishing action of neoliberalism in consolidation.

The chapters in this book reflect this anxious, distressing and harrowing moment in today's Western world. This is what Scribano called the *new neocolonial religion* (Scribano 2017).

One of the central effects of relationships between Society 4.0, digital work and the social structuring process, according to the editors of this book, is the change in the politics of sensibilities. Policies of sensibilities are understood as the set of cognitive-affective social practices directed to the production, management and reproduction of horizons of action, disposition and cognition.

This book, thus reviewing the literature on the new social processes under way in the globalized world and in the formation of societies 4.0, detects the lack of studies and research on how the politics of sensibilities is being altered by the current configuration of societies and digital labour, and makes it the central object of its analysis. Additionally, it examines the substantial changes that have greatly altered the lives of individuals, groups and society in general. The chapters present, in this way, the aim to broaden the scope of discussion and reflect on the changes mentioned as an essential background for understanding globalized society in the digital age.

This book contains discussions that are at the forefront of intellectual and academic thinking, and of the cultural, social, political and economic concerns of the present time. The themes discussed here are directly or indirectly present in the debates between common person and in the public arenas of contemporary politicians, intellectuals and academics, as well as in their sombre and/or utopian prospects for the future of societies, whether by the way uncertainty and risk, or by the possible paths of resistance and social transformation.

Scribano and Lisdero, in the organization of this book, gave priority to a multidisciplinary perspective on a set of social practices that modify the meanings of everyday interactions, especially those that dispose and affect the world of work. This book as a whole, according to the editors, combines two types of contributions: on the one hand, there are chapters devoted to understanding the changes in labour in the context of the *digital age*; and, on the other hand, there are those which aim to understand, debate and point out the consequences of these transformations in the current processes of social structuring in the contemporary Western world.

These two types of contribution run through this book and make it denser in understanding the context of *planetary massification* of new information and communication technologies (ICTs). Such technologies are oriented to the restructuring of labour environments and the worlds of everyday life; that is, the precariousness and flexibility of the world of work, and the policies of deterritorialization and social control, as well as the policies of emotion and sensibilities embedded in the inscriptions of digital spaces, in the forms of fear, risks and uncertainties, on the one hand, and the uses and practices of the digitized space and its strategies for the redefinition of perceptions through the digital look, on the other.

The authors who have contributed to this book seek to explore the politics of sensibilities felt as absent in the current analysis of the connections between Society 4.0 and digital labour. In their chapters, they review the impact of connectivity and communication on Society 4.0, and of the transformations in the forms of border management. Likewise, the articles reflect on the ways in which fear and terror have appeared in the virtual world.

They also discuss the ways in which time and space are redefined in the context of access to "digital territories", as well as the socio-productive implications of the accelerated process of outsourcing in the creative and software industries, as examples of changes in the politics of sensibilities. This book brings important and original contributions to the disciplines of applied social sciences and social sciences.

This book is composed of two parts. The first deals with the *Politics of Sensibilities and Society 4.0*; the second part, in turn, deals with the broad thematic of *Politics of Sensibilities and Digital Labour*. The broad scope outlined by the contributions of the various authors present in this book, thus, traces an open and innovative view of the relationship between labour and sensibilities in this neoliberal era.

This book has multidisciplinary and international appeal. Besides the editors of this book, Argentines Adrian Scribano and Pedro Lisdero, the contributing authors of this book are Maximiliano E. Korstanje (Argentina), Francisco Osorio (Chile), Juan A. Roche Cárcel (Spain), Sergio Martínez Luna (Spain), Zhang Jingting (China), Mustafa Berkay Aydın (Turkey) and Çağdaş Ceyhan (Turkey).

In this context, this book aims to provide a multidisciplinary perspective on the transformations in social practices that modify the meaning of everyday interactions and especially those that affect the world of labour.

This book is composed of two types of texts: some dedicated to exploring the modifications of labour in the context of the "digital age" and others to point out the consequences of those transformations in the current social structuration processes. In the aforementioned context, the two lines that are configured are transversally stressed in this book: one connected with precarity/uncertainty and another related to the gaze/vision, two lines that, in the context of the planetary massiveness of the new information and communication technologies, restructure horizons and atmospheres for work and daily life.

On the one hand, we have the precariousness and flexibility, deterritorialization and immaterial control, risk and uncertainty, emotionalization and politics of the sensibilities fit in the inscription surface that implies the digital. On the other hand, there are the visual uses of the digitized space, the virtualized practices of terror and fear, the strategies of redefining perceptions through the gaze, the transformation of borders into observation edges, and the constitution of a digital gaze.

This book unfolds across ten chapters concepts that are articulated through a central concern: to point out the connections between the current social transformations and the effects of the impacts that come from the interrelations (or not) between digital work and politics of sensibilities in a *digital age*. Chapter 1, written by Adrian Scribano, serves as a general introduction to the other chapters. In this chapter, Scribano presents the current contents of the research on Society 4.0, digital work and politics of sensibilities, which seek to provide the reader with a clear vision of how the three fields explored in this book are connected to each other. The proposal is to understand the transformations of current society through the articulation of the three fields of study, allowing an understanding of the politics of sensibilities from the perspective of the sociology of bodies/emotions.

As already indicated above, this book is divided into two parts. The first part, *Politics of Sensibilities and Society 4.0*, contains a total of five chapters.

In Chap. 2, written by Adrian Scribano and Pedro Lisdero, and entitled "Digital Gaze and Visual Experience", the authors try to address the relationship between *digital life* and *images*, seeking to question the potential of social research, related to two facts: the expansion of social relations mediated by ICTs, where *images* constitute the central *tension* in relation to the purpose, and the format of the interactions. It aims to explore the contributions made by the study of social sensibilities to a critique of the political economy of "look 4.0"; to this end they explore some debates about the relationship between the image, photography and the Internet. They conclude the article by offering elements for a critique of the political economy of the eye, highlighting the conditions of reception of the images and the implications of seeing-feeling-actions in the current structuring context.

The next chapter (Chap. 3), "Work and Sensibilities: Commodification and Processes of Expropriation Around Digital Labour" is also written by Adrian Scribano and Pedro Lisdero. In this chapter, the authors demonstrate how the expansion of the phenomena that link work to new media has resulted in the emergence of debates that cross different areas of knowledge. They show how the notion of digital work not only has revitalized discussions around critical communication studies but has also been relevant to investigations into the metamorphosis of work relationships and even into studies of everyday life. This chapter explores some contributions from the sociology of the body/emotions to understand practices associated with digital work in the context of ICT, when addressing issues emerging from these insights. In this way, the authors (i) explore theoretical debates around the definition of digital work, in order to underline the importance of redefining forms of exploitation in relation to related practices; (ii) develop arguments from the perspective of the sociology of bodies and emotions, which allow us to understand the extent to which technological mediation linked to the expansion of ICTs constitutes a reconfiguration of "sense politics"; (iii) finally, they analyse cases of workers in ICT industries that allow them to connect their daily experiences with certain mechanisms of expropriation and mercantilization of the vitality of the bodies.

In Chap. 4, "Location and Data Visualisation Culture in Chile", Francisco Osorio aims to reflect on the social and cultural consequences of living under a constant system of spatial and temporal location. The paradigmatic example is the maps that Google creates daily, which makes it possible to know the location of an individual during any time of the day or any place that the same individual visits during the week, among other aspects. This phenomenon, although it has existed for several decades, continues to evolve and the consequences that it brings to the form of social relationship between people who use this technology are still unclear.

Chapter 5, entitled "Borders and Archives Under the New Conditions of Digital Visuality", by Sergio Martínez Luna, presents and discusses a relevant issue for the comprehension of the contemporary visuality, woven by the new digital devices of surveillance and control at the border between the physical and the technological, or between embodied human perception and the technological look of artefacts. This question concerns how this articulation is rearranged within today's contemporary visuality and the logic of digital visual technologies, given the imperatives of surveillance, mobility and total visualization.

In Chap. 6, "The Society 4.0, Internet, Tourism and the War on Terror", Maximiliano E. Korstanje examines how September 11 marked the end of an era. According to the author, the surveys agree that the attacks on the

World Trade Center have changed international and geopolitical relations like never before. The author highlights the accelerating changes in organizational culture after 9/11. He concluded his analysis by stating that while technology creates a more open society, terrorism closes the frontiers to strangers, affecting one of the key values of Western civilization: hospitality.

The second part, *Politics of Sensibilities and Digital Labour*, contains the rest of the chapters, totalling four contributions. The first of these, Chap. 7, entitled "Labour, Body, and Social Conflict: The 'Digital Smile' and Emotional Work in Call Centres", is written by Pedro Lisdero. In this chapter, the author reflects on the reconfiguration of a series of flexible processes oriented to expropriate and commercialize the cognitive and affective corporal energies of workers. In this sense, the chapter aims to investigate some contributions from the sociology of the body and emotions to understand the expressions of social conflict associated with new work scenarios, as a "sensitive" space from which to understand processes of social structuration.

In Chap. 8, written by Zhang Jingting and entitled "'Sharing Economy, Sharing Emotions' in the Society 4.0: A Study of the Consumption and Sensibilities in the Digital Era in China", the author focuses on the development of the sharing economy in China. Why has China, a country with a population of 1.3 billion, experienced a boom of the sharing economy from the year 2016? In order to understand this, the author explores briefly notions such as "HE" (Harmony) and "Tian Xia" (All Under Heaven) in the Chinese traditional culture, on the one hand. On the other hand, the author discusses how these shared products (from bikes to basketballs) change people's daily lives and guide their emotions. The author investigates the politics of sensibilities applied through consumption in Society 4.0, which is related closely with the virtual world or the mobile world. What is the situation of social mass media in China, as compared with other countries at a global level? And, last but not least, he analyses some relevant works about the prediction of the development of Society 4.0 and China's influence as a leading global force.

In Chap. 9, entitled "The Invisible Face of Digital Labour in Turkey: Working Conditions, Practices and Expectations", Mustafa Berkay Aydın and Çağdaş Ceyhan try to understand the working conditions of the software sector in relation to employees. In this respect, the authors conducted 14 in-depth interviews with employees in the software sector in Ankara and İstanbul. The main questions of the research concern how employees define their working conditions, what employees think about forming a union and where software sector employees place themselves in respect of digital labour in general. Employees' major issues are those of flexible working hours, temporary projects and working on a project basis. Software industry employees clearly reveal some characteristics of precarity, particularly in terms of its emotional aspects. Precarious work has become a common form of labour in Turkey since the early 2000s. Although the software sector has an educated and qualified workforce in Turkey, the working conditions exhibit precarious working qualities. This study examines the precarious working conditions in the digital labour market in Turkey for the first time.

In the final contribution, Chap. 10, entitled "An Approach to Creative Work in the Global Economy of Risk and Uncertainty", Juan A. Roche Cárcel begins the chapter by stating that there seems to have been an enthronement of creativity as an emerging topic in the field of social sciences, its empowerment as a nearly absolute energy, which might lead us to think that it would constitute a useful response to overcoming the work crisis, and even to endow this activity with prestige and take it to the place where it should really belong. Following this, he states that the aim of his account is to confirm whether or not creative work has achieved such aims; whether it has actually pursued them; whether or not, in addition to generating fast and large profits for the creators and firms that have hired them, it has become a powerful force both regarding social cohesion and the globalization of economy, of society and of democracy and its values. The author, in seeking to meet the aforementioned aims, divides the chapter into four sections. The first one, meant as a general introduction, is followed by Section "The Crisis of Work in Late Modern Society", where he tries to define work, to frame it within the negative perception that the West has traditionally had about it, additionally synthesizing the two models by means of which our civilization strives to provide employment and finally summarizes the characteristics of work at present. As for Section "Creative Work in the New Global Economy", it focuses on creative work in the context of the global economy and, inside it, he places the emphasis on defining what creativity and the global economy are, on describing the most essential features of cities and creative industries, and how the latter are causing new inequalities. Lastly, with Section "Final Reflections", the author offers some final reflections aimed at analysing the main traits currently assumed by creative work.

This book thus presents itself as an important critical reflection on contemporary neoliberal politics. Its importance lies in the exploration of various dimensions of Society 4.0 in its relations with the politics of sensibility and of the body, as well as through its role in the possible adjustments of nations to the technological rhythm assumed by neoliberalism. The reflections contained in this book hail from countries as diverse as Argentina, Chile, Italy, Spain, Turkey and China, allowing the reader to enter, on the one hand, into the ways in which Society 4.0 has been shaping new forms of oppression and psychological and social suffering in the process of adapting these societies to the neoliberal politics of contemporary capitalism. And, on the other hand, it warns the reader of the dangerous relations of neoliberalism with the policies of sensitivity directed at ordinary people in daily life. This is a book that can be read by the everyday person who is interested in the current discussions of culture, politics and society in the contemporary world.

Likewise, this volume should be of great interest to academic readers, educated professionals and undergraduate or postgraduate students, in addition to general readers. It is a must-have work on every shelf of private or public libraries and serves as the background needed for discussions of the risky paths wrought by new advances in society in this increasingly digital and globalized age.

This is a book that must undoubtedly be on the shelf of contemporary scholars and practitioners for their ambitious exploration of social relations in an era of radical transformation; by its critical view of the resurgence of neoliberalism and its creation of heavy labour in a spectacular and sacrificial way; and by its denunciation of the structuring and construction of a moral (and cultural) economy that ignores the ethics, values and elementary rights of individuals in contemporary society.

Mauro Guilherme Pinheiro Koury

REFERENCES

Beck, U., Giddens, A., & Lash, S. (1994). *Reflexive Modernization.* Cambridge: Polity Press.

Bower, J. L., & Christensen, C. M. (1995). Disruptive Technologies: Catching the Wave. *Harvard Business Review, 73*(1), 43–53.

Edwards, P., & Ramirez, P. (2016). When Should Workers Embrace or Resist New Technology? *New Technology, Work and Employment, 31*(2), 99–113.

Ford, M. (2016). *Rise of the Robots: Technology and the Threat of a Jobless Future.* New York: Basic Books.

Scholz, T. (Ed.). (2013). *Digital Labor: The Internet as Playground and Factory.* New York: Routledge.

Scribano, A. (2017). *Normalization, Enjoyment and Bodies/Emotions: Argentine Sensibilities.* New York: Nova Science Publishers.

Skobelev, P. O., & Borovik, S. Y. (2017). On the Way from Industry 4.0 to Industry 5.0: from Digital Manufacturing to Digital Society. *International Scientific Journal* "Industry 4.0", *2*(6), 307–311.

Steiner, C., & Dixon, W. (2012). *Automate This: How Algorithms Came to Rule Our World.* New York: Portfolio.

Wellman, B. (2011). Community Networks Online. In L. Keeble (Ed.), *The Rise of Networked Individualism.* London: Taylor & Francis.

CONTENTS

Notes on Contributors

Thomas Allmer studied media and communication and political science at the University of Salzburg, Austria, and the Victoria University, Melbourne, Australia. After he had finished his PhD in 2014, he started as Lecturer in Social Justice at the University of Edinburgh, Scotland, UK. Since 2016, he has been Lecturer in Digital Media at the University of Stirling, Scotland, UK. He is also a member of the Unified Theory of Information Research Group, Austria. His publications include *Towards a Critical Theory of Surveillance in Informational Capitalism* (2012) and *Critical Theory and Social Media: Between Emancipation and Commodification* (2015).

Mustafa Berkay Aydın holds a bachelor's degree in Sociology from Ankara University, Ankara, Turkey, and a PhD in Sociology from Middle East Technical University, Ankara, Turkey. He is a researcher at Uludağ University, Bursa, Turkey. His areas of interest are digital sociology, sociology of sport, applied sociology, political sociology, justice, migration and sociology of work. He has some publications to his credit in these areas.

Çağdaş Ceyhan holds a bachelor's degree in Journalism from Ankara University, Ankara, Turkey, and PhD in Journalism from Anadolu University, Eskişehir, Turkey. At present, he is a researcher at Anadolu University, Eskişehir, Turkey. His interests include social movements, sociology of sport, sport journalism, data-driven journalism, alternative media and digital ethnography. He has published some works in these areas.

Zhang Jingting holds bachelor's and master's degrees in Spanish Literature from Shanghai International Studies University and PhD in Sociology from the University of Buenos Aires, Argentina. Zhang is a postdoctoral candidate of the project "Emotions and consumptions in the digital era in China" under the guidance of Adrian Scribano in the Gino Germani Research Institute, University of Buenos Aires. She is a member of the Group of Studies on Sociology of Emotions and Bodies (GESEC) in the Gino Germani Research Institute, University of Buenos Aires, and the Centre for Sociological Research and Studies (CIES).

Maximiliano E. Korstanje is a leading and global cultural theorist specialized in terrorism, mobilities and tourism. Korstanje serves as a senior researcher at the University of Palermo (Economics Department), Buenos Aires, Argentina, and editor-in-chief of *International Journal of Safety and Security in Tourism and Hospitality*. Besides, he was a visiting professor at CERS (Centre for Ethnicity and Racism Studies) in the University of Leeds, UK, University Institute of Tourism and Sustainable Economic Development (TIDES) in the University of Las Palmas de Gran Canaria, Spain, and the University of Habana, Cuba. In 2016, he was included as Scientific Editor for Studies and Perspective in Tourism (CIET) and as honorary member of the Scientific Council of Research and Investigation hosted by UDET (University of Tourism Specialities, Quito, Ecuador). With more than 1200 publications, including 30 books, Korstanje is a book series editor of Advances in Hospitality, Tourism and Service Industries for IGI Global, US, the foreign faculty member of Mexican Academy of Tourism Research, Mexico, as well as foreign member of the Tourism Crisis Management Institute, University of Florida, US. In 2018, his biography was selected to be part of the roster of Alfred Nelson Marquis Lifetime Achievement Award (Marquis Who's Who). Korstanje has been awarded as Editor-in-Chief Emeritus for the *International Journal of Cyber Warfare and Terrorism*. At present, he works as an active advisor and reviewer of different editorial projects for the most leading academic publishers such as Elsevier, Routledge, Palgrave Macmillan, Cambridge Scholar Publishing, Edward Elgar, CABI, Nova Science Publishers and IGI Global among others. His latest book is *The Challenges of Democracy in the War on Terror* (UK).

Pedro Lisdero holds a bachelor's degree in Sociology (U. Siglo XXI, Córdoba, Argentina) and PhD in Social Studies of Latin America (Center for Advanced Studies—National University of Córdoba). Lisdero is a researcher at the National Scientific and Technological Research Council

(CONICET, Argentina), Co-director of the Program of Studies on Collective Action and Social Conflict of Center for Research and Studies on Cultures and Societies (CONICET and National University of Córdoba—UNC), and a researcher at the Centre for Sociological Research and Studies (CIES, Argentina). In addition, he is an assistant professor and Chair "General Sociology" at the National University of Villa Maria (UNVM), Director of Sociological Studies Editora (ESEditora—CIES), and a member of the editorial team of RELACES, RELMIS, and Onteaiken.

Sergio Martínez Luna holds a PhD in Humanities from Carlos III University (Madrid). Since 2015 he has been Professor in Cultural Theory at Carlos III University. He was a visiting scholar at the Institute of Cultural Inquiry (ICON) at Utrecht University in 2017. He was a member of the R&D Research Project: Culturas materiales, Culturas epistémicas, Standards, Prácticas cognitivas y conocimiento (2013–2017). He is part of the R&D Research Project funded by the Spanish Ministry of Economy and Innovation: Imágenes, Acción y Poder (Zaragoza University). He is also a member of iViCON: Fundación Imagen Contemporánea y Estudios Visuales, Santiago de Chile. His publications include articles in journals such as *Third Text: Critical Perspectives on Contemporary Art and Culture, Artnodes, Escritura e Imagen, Laocoonte, Fedro, Campo de relámpagos, Revista de Antropología Iberoamericana (AIBR)*.

Francisco Osorio is a social anthropologist from the University of Chile, editor of *Cinta de Moebio* (*Moebius Strip*) www.moebio.uchile.cl, a journal devoted to epistemology of social sciences in Latin America. He was a Fulbright Scholar (1999) at the Annenberg School for Communication, University of Pennsylvania. Osorio was an honorary visiting fellow at the Anthropology Department, University of Manchester (2007–2010) and a postdoctoral research fellow at the Communication Computing Research Centre at Sheffield Hallam University (2011). His experience as editor started in 1997 creating the first online journal in the area of philosophy and social sciences in Latin America, run from the Social Science Faculty (FACSO) at University of Chile (www.facso.uchile.cl).

Mauro Guilherme Pinheiro Koury is an anthropologist, specializing in anthropology of emotions, urban anthropology and anthropology of the image. He is an associate professor and a researcher at the Graduate Program in Anthropology at the Federal University of Paraíba, Brazil. He is the chief editor of the journals such as *RBSE Brazilian Journal of*

Sociology of Emotion, Urban Sociabilities, Journal of Anthropology and Sociology and the *Editions of GREM*. Koury leads two research groups at the Federal University of Paraíba: the GREM Research Group on Anthropology and Sociology of Emotions, and the GREI Interdisciplinary Group on Image Studies. Koury has more than 200 publications to his credit in the form of articles and chapters of books and more than 20 books on urban anthropology, image and emotions.

Juan A. Roche Cárcel is Professor of Sociology of Culture and Arts at the University of Alicante. Among his latest publications include, as author: *Entre el Monte de Apolo y la vid de Dioniso. Naturaleza, Dioses y Sociedad en la arquitectura teatral de la Grecia Antigua* (Anthropos, 2017); and *La Sociedad Evanescente* (Anthropos, 2009); *The Vanishing Society* (2013); as editor, *Espacios y tiempos inciertos de la cultura* (Anthropos, 2007); *La Sociología como una de las Bellas Artes. La influencia del arte y de la literatura en el pensamiento sociológico* (2012); and *Transitions. The Fragility of Democracy* (2016). He is the author of numerous articles in national, European, Latin American and North American specialized journals and coordinator of monographs from Spain, Argentina, Brazil and Colombia, among which, *Revista Política y Sociedad, Arte y Poder* (n° 46, 2007); *Papers. Revista de Sociología, Cultura y migraciones* (n° 94, 2009); *Res Publica. Revista de Ideas Políticas, Transiciones. La fragilidad de la democracia* (n° 30, año 16, 2013); *Res Publica. Revista de Ideas Políticas, Cuerpo y poder en la Grecia Antigua* (2016); *Política y Sociedad, El Saber Social de los griegos antiguos. Homenaje a Gómez Arboleya* (2016); *Culturas* (UNL, Argentina), *Cine y sociedad* (2017). He has been a research coordinator in the Culture and Arts area of the ESA (European Association of Sociology) and Vice President of the AESCA (Spanish Association of Sociology of Culture and the Arts). He is or has been a visiting professor of, among others, the National University of the Littoral and University of Buenos Aires (Argentina), the Pontificia Javeriana de Cali (Colombia), the Federal University of Pelotas (Brazil) and the University of Guanajuato (Mexico). He is the co-director of the collection of Social Sciences, Globalizations, at the Anthropos publishing house (Barcelona).

Adrian Scribano is Director of the Centre for Sociological Research and Studies (CIES estudiosociologicos.org) and Principal Researcher at the National Scientific and Technological Research Council, Argentina. He is also the Director of the *Latin American Journal of Studies on Bodies,*

Emotions and Society and the Study Group on Sociology of Emotions and Bodies, in the Gino Germani Research Institute, Faculty of Social Sciences, University of Buenos Aires. He also serves as Coordinator of the 26 Working Group on Bodies and Emotions of the Latin American Association of Sociology (ALAS) and as Vice-President of the Thematic Group 08 Society and Emotions of the International Sociological Association (ISA).

LIST OF FIGURES

CHAPTER 1

Introduction: Politics of Sensibilities, Society 4.0 and Digital Labour

Adrian Scribano

The predatory expansion of capitalism on a planetary scale has generated a rapid, complex and massive articulation between the features of so-called Society 4.0, digital labour[1] and a political economy of morality. Some of the features of the transformations taking place in this current social structuration process include the expansion of the revolution 4.0 and its

[1] As Fuchs (2014) states, in English it is necessary to make a semantic differentiation between "work" and "labour". In this regard, he adopts an expression that Engels formulates in a footnote in Marx's *Capital*: "The English language has the advantage of possessing two separate words for these two different aspects of labour. Labour which creates use-values and is qualitatively determined is called 'work' as opposed to 'labour'; labour which creates value and is only measured quantitatively is called 'labour', as opposed to 'work'" (Marx 1867: 138) (in Fuchs 2014: 26). From here, Fuchs uses this distinction for discerning digital work for digital labour: "Labour is a necessarily alienated form of work, in which humans do not control and own the means and results of production. It is a historic form of the organization of work in class societies. Work in contrast is a much more general concept common to all societies. It is a process, in which humans make use of technologies for transforming nature and society in such a way that goods and services are created that satisfy human needs" (Fuchs 2014: 26–27). In the chapters of this book written by myself, in collaboration with Lisdero, and the one written by Lisdero alone, the distinction made by Fuchs has been (in general) taken into account.

A. Scribano (✉)
CONICET, Buenos Aires, Argentina

© The Author(s) 2019
A. Scribano, P. Lisdero (eds.), *Digital Labour, Society and the Politics of Sensibilities*, https://doi.org/10.1007/978-3-030-12306-2_1

1

impact on productivity and labour, the massification of a political economy of morality based on non-truth, the growing number of refugees and
migrants around the world, military tensions and wars of a multilateral
nature.

The modifications in work and its consequences in the social structure
are central axes of the history of humanity: the crossing between production, needs, goods, models of work organization and wealth distribution
systems have been, are and will be the constituent axes of societal forms.

In the same vein, it is possible to understand how technological transformations have involved modifications in work and in social relations as a
whole. These technological changes imply, in one way or another, varia-
tions in the mode by which people relate to time, space, shortage and
satisfaction.

In the described context it is easy to understand how and why the
expansion of digital labour comes about in the context of the massification
of the modifications produced by the digitalization of society, generating
consequences in the politics of sensibilities.

The digital society brings together the expansion of Industry 4.0 (and
digital labour) with the wide spread and globalization of digital consumption. It is in this intersection/convergence that "new/diverse" features of
the politics of sensibilities are elaborated.

> The digital economy is expanding in several ways. Global production of ICT
> goods and services now amounts to an estimated 6.5 per cent of global gross
> domestic product (GDP), and some 100 million people are employed in the
> ICT services sector alone. Exports of ICT services grew by 40 per cent
> between 2010 and 2015. Worldwide e-commerce sales in 2015 reached
> $25.3 trillion, 90 per cent of which were in the form of business-to-business
> e-commerce and 10 per cent in the form of business-to-consumer (B2C)
> sales. UNCTAD estimates that cross-border B2C e-commerce was worth
> about $189 billion in 2015, which corresponds to 7 per cent of total B2C
> e-commerce. Sales of robots are at the highest level ever, worldwide ship-
> ments of three-dimensional printers more than doubled in 2016, to over
> 450,000, and are expected to reach 6.7 million in 2020. And by 2019, the
> volume of global Internet traffic is expected to increase 66 times from what
> it was in 2005. (UNCTAD 2017: xiii)

To paraphrase what Montesquieu said about the connection between
trade and capitalism through digital commerce and mercantilization,

consuming is softened and sweetened. The politics of digital sensibility promises instant consumption without conflict, taking for granted the thousands of people "behind the scenes" that make those sensations possible.

> The role that social media plays in the lives of its users has evolved. Digital consumers are now almost as likely to say they use social to follow the news as they are to identify it as a platform for keeping in touch with friends (40% vs 41%). Almost 4 in 10 internet users say they are following their favorite brands on social, while 1 in 4 are following brands from which they are thinking of making a purchase from. Influencer marketing makes the most impact among 16–24s, but even among this age group it's just 18% who say they find new brands via celebrity or influencer endorsements. Social commerce is gaining traction primarily in the research and brand interaction stages of the purchase journey. But when it comes to the final purchase, the appetite to do so in these platforms remains low and most are moving to a retail site to do so. (Global Web Index 2018: 4)

As we have already argued above, it is in this scenario that the planet is experiencing a process of social metamorphosis on a global scale. One of the consequences and central effects of the relationships between Society 4.0, digital labour and the social structuration process are the changes in the politics of sensibilities. And if we know that these politics "are understood as the set of cognitive-affective social practices tending to the production, management and reproduction of horizons of action, disposition and cognition" (Scribano 2017: 244) to reflect on the changes mentioned is essential to understand the current situation of society.

In this context we detect that in the existing literature there is a lack of attention to and research about how the politics of sensibilities is being altered by the current situation of Society 4.0, given that digital labour implies substantial changes in the lives of individuals, groups and society in general (Fig. 1.1). Just as an example, this implies that we also have to analyse how the situation of the geometries of the bodies, the grammar of actions, the politics of the bodies/emotions in relation to what is the digital era, digital platforms, teleworking and so on now modify day-to-day life.

In this book we choose to deepen the study of the politics of the sensibilities since it is an unknown perspective in the current analysis of the connections between Society 4.0 and digital labour.

From a general point of view the book involves reviewing the impact of digitization (and digitalization), connectivity and communication of

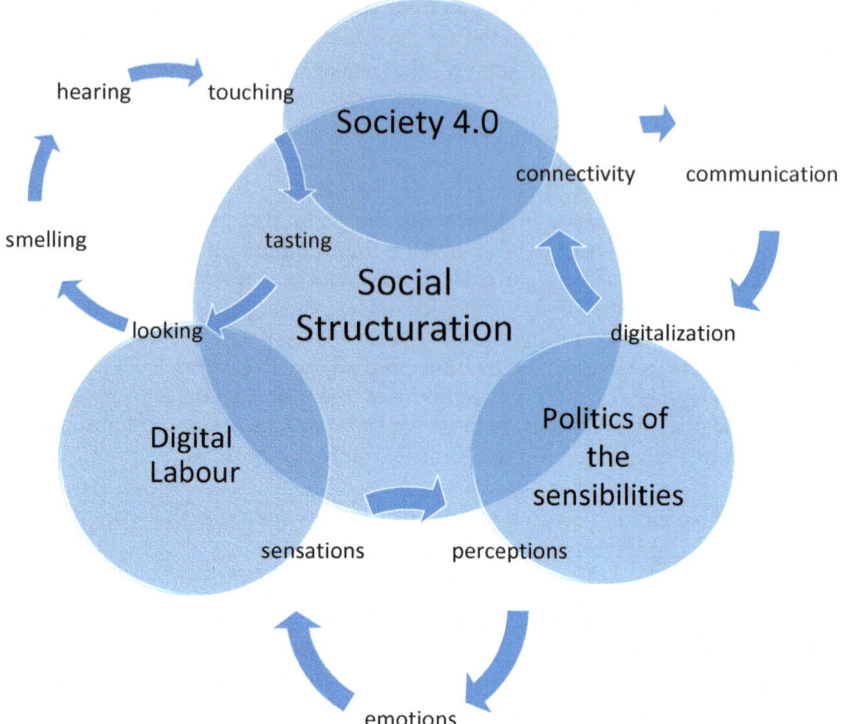

Fig. 1.1   Politics of sensibilities, Society 4.0 and digital labour

Society 4.0 in the transformations of modes of managing borders; the ways that fear and terror appear in and through the virtual world; the ways of redefining time and space in the context of access to "digital territories"; and the socio-productive implications of outsourcing, in the creative and software industries, as examples of the alterations in the politics of the sensibilities.

Every form of work and especially digital work involves certain ways of managing at least two spheres of the world: those connected with the senses (hearing, touching, tasting, looking and smelling) and those that articulate perceptions, sensations and emotions. The politics of sensibilities are developed from, among other factors, the states of these two spheres.

SOCIETY 4.0

The mobile/digital revolution implies transformations in the management of labour and vice versa, and under the umbrella of these modifications are developing new politics of sensibilities.

One of the most important aspects of the advent of companies 4.0 is the rapid development of social networks and the enormous growth of their commercialization and commercial value. In this framework, the interactions between the face-to-face social world, the virtual world and the "mobile" world of cell phones and tablets have grown exponentially. As Simply Measured claims in its 2017 report:

> Social media spending is expected to rise to 17.3 billion by 2019 (Statista). The allocation of funds to marketing analytics is expected to see a massive increase within the next few years, according to the CMO Survey. In 2017, marketing analytics consumes just 4.6% of marketing budgets. This number could jump to almost 22% by 2020.... (Simply Measured 2017: 12)

In this context, Scott Fallon, VP Marketing of the company holds:

> The expected rise in social media budgets is based on bringing social more fully into the marketing mix. Today, too many companies view social media as a siloed activity. That view is dying. Social will get more budget as more companies realize that social signals have to be attended to during the customer lifecycle. Social activity has been too long ignored from an attribution standpoint. Social channels will soon be sales channels. (Simply Measured 2017: 12)

Many authors argue that we are facing the Fourth Industrial Revolution, and that this can be characterized by the consolidation of at least three factors: (a) the appearance of Big Data as a resource for social diagnosis, (b) the Gig Economy as evidence of the growth of deinstitutionalization and, (c) the Internet of Things (IoT) as a new form of production and "management of sensibilities".

For its part, the use of Big Data analysis implies: 1. material surveillance of massive amounts of information about people and societies; 2. Internet, social networks and mobile interaction as a space for search, construction, management and distribution of information; 3. the digital dependence of the most dynamic sectors of the "real" economy; 4. changes in the management of work and appropriation of the benefits of capital; and 5. the intimate relationship between the depredation of environmental assets and computer/digital assets.

In relation to the Gig Economy, it is possible to notice as central features: 1. flexibility in the modalities of coordination of action; 2. transformations in resources to guarantee competences; 3. the contingency of temporary and spatial links between the consumer and the producer; and 4. the transformation of the means of payment for services and goods.

On the other hand, the Internet of Things brings with it the following consequences: 1. a new kind of "do it yourself" paradigm; 2. the redefinitions of proximity/distance between the product and the producer; and 3. changes in the relationship between "materials"/sensation.

The increasingly important weight of "The Cloud" as a virtual space for production, storage, management and distribution of information must be added. Indeed, among the many factors that converge for the modification of the modes of work management, knowledge and production at present, the cloud is the most important one. This is so, since (a) it is a virtual space designed to improve collaborative work, (b) it allows to obviate the inequalities of access to expensive hardware and (c) to promote a more "agile" information management.

Another feature of the connection between Society 4.0 and labour is the so-called sharing economy, as maintained by Parente and his colleagues:

> The popularized "sharing economy" term has been used frequently to describe different organizations that connect users/renters and owner/providers through consumer-to-consumer (C2C) (e.g., Uber, Airbnb) or business-to-consumer (B2C) platforms, allowing rentals in more flexible, social interactive terms (e.g., Zipcar, WeWork). (Parente et al. 2018: 53)

"Collaborative consumption" and the "access-based economy" are other ways to identify a set of economics interactions based on the Internet as platform and implies countless social transformations. One of these changes is the new and stronger role of consumption and consumers in shaping economic interactions. In some way, these interactions modify the practices of having, possessing and using under the influence of the Internet and the time-space resignification that this implies. The perceptions about what it means to be an owner are confronted by the "experiences of using".

In the aftermath of the global financial crisis beginning in 2008, consumers sought other means of gaining access to products and services aside from the burdens of ownership. A new economic model, known as the sharing economy or collaborative consumption, emerged which integrated collaboration, technology, and the desire to be more efficient with products and services. (Davidson et al. 2017: 364)

The aforementioned processes intersect and interact with the expansion of the redefinition of institutions, as in the case of Uber, where one can observe a flexibilization, "liberalization" and resignification of state controls. In the same direction, it is possible to verify the growing impact of Artificial Intelligence in its different applications such as chatbots, robots, drones and other objects/processes linked to the IoT and the modifications that this involves for everyday life.

In this Society 4.0, there is an important transformation of the political economy of morality, the politics of sensibilities and the political economy of the truth associated with it. The structure of the political economy of morality accompanies the changes in the political economy of truth. It modifies the set of processes accepted to produce the truth, the criteria to accept a perception as true and the specialized areas to "guarantee" the truth.

The processes to obtain the truth move away from the traditional scientific procedures and move towards logics articulated around sensibilities and emotion. From the different forms of empathy, perception and sensations of "capture", through intelligent regimes of emotional regulation, to alternative spiritualities, all these are crossed and articulated as possible ways of reaching the truth. Thus, socioneurology, informative layout of haptic systems, fuzzy logic, body/machine interfaces, nanotechnology, genetic design and artificial intelligence are some of the scientific procedures of the twenty-first century that "help" new ways of obtaining the truth.

As instruments designed to "see things happening", drones "stretch" the current paradigm of sensibility, playing the role of witnesses that reproduce reality from a distance.

What is sustained up to now is more complex if we bear in mind that Society 4.0, among many other things, has transformed the potential of communicating through photographs, videos and audios expressed in terms of cell phones and smartphones. What also brings its use as a technique to record, portray and interpret the world, as argued by Lansen and García (2015) in their study of photography, self-pornography and social networks:

Contemporary digital photography practices are remediating sociality, embodiment and subjectivity, especially with the convergence of digital cameras, mobile phones and social networks (...) Playfulness and experimentation are common features of camera phones and digital camera usage, which are similarly found in their uses for erotic purposes. These changes are made possible by the ease of digital production and the low cost of production for individuals. (Lansén and García 2015: 717)

From the different forms of empathy, perception and sensations of "capture", through intelligent regimes of emotional regulation, to alternative spiritualities, all these are crossed and articulated as possible ways of reaching "the truth" and/or "new sensibilities states".

Precariousness, massification, instantaneity and digitization of daily life are practices that consolidate the era of a new "politics of touching" and diverse "politics of seeing", and work is a space where these processes are rapidly and strongly evident. In the scenery of the globalization of normalized societies in the immediate enjoyment through consumption, the processes of classification and qualification of touch are modified, thus a renewed "politics of touching" assembles different (and diverse) geometries of the bodies deployed in virtual environments and by digital resources. In the same vein the proximity and distance between gaze, seeing and observing are transformed on the digital horizon. From 3D effects, passing for augmented reality, to the arrival of drones in daily life, we see modification and the appearance of a new form of "politics of seeing". Both the new "politics of touching" and diverse "politics of seeing" have a central impact in redefining the "world of work": "new" environments, resources, processes and goals have been created and with them the labour and workforce are transformed.

Digital Labour[2]

Work/labour as a practice that transforms the world, as an action to obtain money and/or action to obtain results, has been modified. Currently, the deep predatory practices of environmental assets, genetic manipulation, the intensive use of endocrine disruptors and the application of nanotechnology create a scenario of rapid and complex transformations. These

[2] In Chap. 3, "Work and Sensibilities: Commodification and Processes of Expropriation Around Digital Labour", an approximation of the state of the art about digital labour is outlined in a deeper way.

modifications testify that the work of human beings modifies their environment and themselves. The double content of work as an action implies a specific way to perceive, construct and manage the world and these involve the elaboration of politics of sensibilities.

Among different perspectives, Society 4.0 is now associated with Industry 4.0, and this is a new step in the digitization of the manufacturing sector, driven by four clusters: (a) more data managed by industrial companies, (b) powerful and cheap computers, (c) analytical capacity and (d) improvements in the interactions between people and machines, robots and 3D printers. In this way, the reduction in costs, the improvements in production lines and the use of new databases are some of the central results that derive from such characteristics.

A broad and heterogeneous field of research is developing a prolific discussion around what is usually defined as "digital labour", "virtual work", "online work", among other expressions. The differences included in these definitions imply in turn the complexity of the debate in terms of what we could initially define from the transformations in the "world of work" linked to the growing incorporation of new ICTs, and particularly, the impact of the Internet.

Complexity and overlapping are two processes that characterize the world to which the distances and proximities between work and social life refer, as understood by Scholz,

'The digital' does not sum up our entire condition. The essence of technology is not solely technological. But without falling for the fallacious rhetoric of 'Twitter revolutions' digital media have also been instrumental for social movements worldwide. It is time to rethink well-worn conceptions of the digital divide by acknowledging the unprecedented global turn in online sociability. While the 2 billion Internet users are indeed a global minority, the 5 billion people and their families who use cell phones are not. Facebook is becoming available on cell phones all across Africa, and it should be understood that digital labour is not just a predicament for the privileged few. Our silence will not save us from the tyranny of digital labor. (Scholz 2013: 10)

Alluding to the complexity of the field and definitions, Huws points out that:

The topic of online work sits at the intersection of a wide range of different academic disciplines and fields of interest, each of which has addressed it from a different perspective, often using different terminology. Since the 1980s, sociologists, psychologists and business analysts have studied 'tele-working', 'eWork' or 'networking'; students of media and communications studies have looked at 'digital labour' or 'creative labour', economic geographers have examined the delocalisation of work and new patterns of agglomeration and clustering, organisational theorists have analysed the role of ICT-enabled offshore outsourcing and policy-makers have fretted about the employment implications of the development of a 'knowledge-based', 'information' or 'networked' economy. More recently, attention has been drawn to new forms of 'virtual' or 'digital' labour, such as 'crowdsourcing' using online platforms such as oDesk or eLance (Caraway 2010) or Amazon's Mechanical Turk (Kittur et al. 2013). (Huws 2016: 6)

The author also points out how this complex body of studies has contributed to generating new questions:

It has also been asked whether distinctions can continue to be drawn between production and consumption, whose putative merger is encapsulated in terms such as 'playbour' (Kücklich 2005) 'prosumption' (Toffler 1980; Tapscott 1995; Ritzer and Jurgenson 2010; Comor 2010), and 'co-creation' (Prahalad and Ramaswamy 2000; Banks and Humphreys 2008), and whether it is in fact Internet users whose unpaid labour produces the value that is harvested by companies such as Google and Facebook. (Huws 2016: 7)

It is in this context that the articulation of the aforementioned views and discussions about the new forms of B2C or C2C economies becomes relevant. Consume and produce, consumer and producer imply positions and conditions in social relationships that involve new sensibilities.

From a complementary perspective, Fuchs and Sandoval characterize the field of emerging debates around "digital labour" (in its first phase) as a concentrated space on Facebook, YouTube and Twitter. Thus, they express that

authors have for example discussed the usefulness of Karl Marx's labour theory of value (Fuchs 2010, 2012b; Arvidsson and Colleoni 2012; Scholz 2013), how the notion of alienation shall be used in the context of digital labour (Andrejevic 2012; Fisher 2012), or if and how Dallas Smythe's concept of audience labour can be used for understanding digital labour (for an overview discussion see Fuchs 2012a). (Fuchs and Sandoval 2014: 487)

For these authors, the complexity of the debate is related to the heterogeneity of labour experiences that entail diverse labour organization arrangements, different labour environments and a wide array of contractual relationships, among others. However, a linking thread of this puzzle is that all pieces contribute to the existence and expansion of ICTs and, simultaneously, large corporations of this sector benefit from them. In turn, the variety of digital labour forms can be organized into three categories: agricultural, industrial and informational. The latter refers to the informational labour in the domain of digital media production, that is, workers who create digital content whose relationships and forms can be characterized in terms of how they access work (online/offline), the technologies used for production (digital/non-digital), the products created and how consumption is distributed. In this respect, the mere existence of these work positions/workers suggest questions about the impact of digitalization/computerization of human activity; that is, the social consequences associated with the connections between digital media technologies and emerging forms of work. In this sense, the "mobile/digital revolution" applied to the "world of work" has influenced both value assessments and the transformation of valorization processes through which the individual is connected to the informational context. The transformations of the "experiences" of work together with the changes in the management of emotions in the digital society imply modifications in the politics of the sensibilities and vice versa. Sensibilities of a mobile/digital world that influence and are influenced by the experiences of digital labour are dependent on the state of the politics of sensibilities.

Politics of Sensibilities

We live in an "emotional world" as revealed global Gallup study on emotions:

> Averaging the 'yes' responses to the 10 questions that make up the Positive and Negative Experience Indexes provides a picture of the most and least emotional societies worldwide. Ecuador, El Salvador and Liberia top the list of the most emotional countries in the world in 2016. On average, nearly six in 10 residents in each of these countries reported experiencing positive or negative emotions the previous day. Countries with ties to Russia and the former Soviet Union again largely dominate the list of countries at the other end of the spectrum, where fewer than four in 10 residents reported experi-

encing any of these feelings. Percentages range from a high of 60% in Ecuador to a low of 37% in Belarus. (Gallup 2017: 9)

In a study "suggestively" called "Skills for Social Progress. The Power of Social and Emotional Skills", the OECD links emotional skills and development, revealing that emotions are objects of intervention on the part of states and the market.

As "skills beget skills", early interventions in social and emotional skills can play an important role in efficiently raising skills and reducing educational, labour market and social disparities. (OECD 2015: 14)

In this context, as we have expressed in our most recent works (Scribano 2017, 2018), the following are the interpretive nodes of the social structuration processes today:

(a) The current situation of the Global South in particular, and of the planet in general, is characterized by (1) a great process of depredation of common goods especially that of the corporal/emotional energy, (2) the consolidation of social bearability mechanisms and devices for the regulation of sensations on a planetary scale and (3) an immense repressive machinery that has been elaborated on the basis of fear and violence.

(b) In the context of the situation described, a "new neo-colonial religion" has been developed whose dogmas of faith are mimetic consumption, resignation and humanitarianism/solidarism. The above-mentioned dogmas connect with the massification of a "sociodicy of frustration" that obliterates disruptive practices and reproduces the consolidation of the present political economy of morality.

(c) Within the framework displayed above, it is possible to note the consolidation of normalized societies in the "immediate enjoyment" through consumption that imply the consecration of a sacrificial and spectacularized structure of a cultural economy for global emotionalization.

(d) In respect of the breakdown of the neo-colonial religion, there is a set of interstitial practices (love, reciprocity, joy) that deny the truth regime of the political economy of morality and which, in turn, are inscribed in the context of a set of disruptive practices such as collective "interdictions" and topologies of rejection.

To understand much of what is expressed in this introduction, we must articulate the schematic diagnosis with the following conceptual instruments regarding our approach to a sociology of bodies/emotions.

Social agents know the world through their bodies. Perceptions, sensations and emotions build a tripod that allows us to understand where sensibilities are founded. Thus, a set of impressions impact in the ways subjects "exchange" with the socio-environmental context. Such impressions of objects, phenomenon, processes and other agents structure the perceptions that subjects accumulate and reproduce. Perception, from this perspective, constitutes a naturalized way of organizing the set of impressions that are given in an agent.

This weaving of impressions configures the sensations that "produce" what can be called the internal and external world: social, subjective and "natural" worlds. Such configurations are formed in a dialectic tension between impressions, perceptions and their results that give sensations the "meaning" of a surplus or excess. Therefore, it puts them closer and beyond such dialectic.

Sensations, as a result and as antecedent of perceptions, locate emotions as an effect of the processes of adjudication and correspondence between perceptions and sensations. Emotions, understood as the consequences of sensations, can be seen as a puzzle that becomes action and effect of feeling something or feeling oneself. Emotions are rooted in the "state of feeling" the world that allows sustaining perceptions. These are associated with socially constructed forms of sensations.

At the same time, organic and social senses also enable what seems unique and unrepeatable as are individual sensations and elaborate the "un-perceived work" of incorporating social elements turned into emotions.

Sensations, as a result and antecedent of perceptions, give way to emotions which can be seen as the manifestation of the action and effect of feelings. They are rooted in the states of feeling the world that build perceptions associated with socially constructed forms of sensations.

Consequently, the politics of bodies (i.e., the strategies that a society accepts in order to offer a response to the social availability of individuals) is a chapter—and not the least important chapter—in the instruction manual of power. These strategies are tied and "strengthened" by the politics of emotions that tend to regulate the construction of social sensibility.

Politics of emotions require regulating and make bearable the conditions under which social order is produced and reproduced. In this context, we understand that social bearability mechanisms are structured around a set of practices that have become embodied and that are oriented towards a systematic avoidance of social conflict.

The forms of sociability and experience are strained and twisted as if contained in a Moebius strip along with the sensibilities that arise from regulatory devices and the aforementioned mechanisms. The need to distinguish and link the possible relationships between sociability, experience and social sensibilities becomes crucial at this point. Sociability is a way of expressing the means by which agents live and coexist interactively. Experience is a way of expressing the meaning gained while being in physical proximity with others, as a result of experiencing the dialogue between the individual body, the social body and the subjective body. For the body to be able to reproduce experience and sociability, it is necessary that bodily energy is an object of production and consumption. Such energy can be understood as the necessary force to preserve the state of "natural" affairs in a systemic functioning. At the same time, the social energy shown through the social body is based on bodily energy, and refers to the allocation processes of such energy as the basis of the conditions of movement and action.

Thus, sensations are distributed according to the specific forms of bodily capital; and the body's impact on sociability and experience shows a distinction between body-image, body-skin and body-movement.

Social sensibilities are continually updating the emotional schemes that arise from the accepted and acceptable norms of sensations. They are just a little long or short of the interrelationships between sociability and experience. Sensibilities are shaped and reshaped by contingent and structural overlaps of diverse forms of connection/disconnection among various ways of producing and reproducing the politics of the bodies/emotions.

As has already been said, the politics of sensibilities are understood as the set of cognitive-affective social practices tending to the production, management and reproduction of horizons of action, disposition and cognition (Scribano 2017: 244). These horizons refer to (1) the organization of daily life (day-to-day, wakesleep, food/abstinence etc.), (2) information to sort preferences and values (adequate/inadequate, acceptable/unacceptable, bearable/unbearable) and (3) parameters for time/space management (displacement/location, walls/bridges; enjoyment). Interstitial practices nest in the inadvertent folds of the naturalized, naturalizing surface of the politics of the bodies and the emotions of neo-colonial religion. They are disruptions in the context of normativity.

In this framework, it is possible to understand how the digitalization of the world coexists with the emotionalization of the processes of domination and of everyday life. We are facing a social system that is globalized by producing/buying/selling emotions in and through the media, social networks and the Internet. In this sense it is probable to understand what it is possible to call the emergence of "sensibilities of platform".

The book connects nine edges of an indeterminate geometry of current work processes and their impacts on the politics of sensibilities: (1) Leisure/Tourism/Terror, (2) Border/Interface/"Surveiller", (3) Georeferencing/Location/Visualization, (4) Creativity/Uncertainty/Risk, (5) Observe/Look/Conflict, (6) Precarity/Monitoring/Punish, (7) Sharing/Expropriation/Sensibilities, (8) Seeing/Feeling/Looking and (9) Flexibility/Expectation/Fragility.

There are nine sides that are interwoven possibilities and limitations in some renewed ways to release/repress the creative energy of human beings, and are just some examples of how the inhabitants of this planet are living the twenty-first century. These are some of the possible paths to investigate the connections between working and society, which are nowadays involved in the battle of sensibilities.

We live in a virtual/digitally connected world shaped by the technological transformations of the last 10 years. Internet and mobile telephony are two vectors that set the stage for three strong changes in the politics of the sensibilities: (a) the organization of the day/night unlinked to the experience of the subjects that experience it, (b) the modification of the sensations of classification and (c) valuations on world modifications.

Each society has a preponderant way of managing work and this constitutes a central axis of the politics of sensibilities. Society 4.0 implies the massification of digital labour and with it the "sensibilities of platform".

A "sensibilities of platform" emerges in this Society 4.0 that is immediate in three senses: (a) in the vehicle in which the action resides (it is the feeling of always being "on line"), (b) it is a society that "is during use", "between", "in passing" and (c) is pure presentification (here/now). Much of digital labour has the same characteristics and, in this direction, the political economy of morality consecrates this way of "feeling the world".

It is from the "immediate" that appear some of the connections between the digitalization of society and the consolidation processes of normalized societies in the immediate enjoyment through consumption. The ephemerality of enjoyment resembles what many authors associate with digital labour as disruptive or creative destruction. The immediate is similar to an "on demand" platform strategy.

In this context, perhaps "in the course", "in this action becoming permanently", in this idea of the immediate and ephemeral, we should interpellate the world with silence. An act of listening where one person feels the other in a different way. Silence is the starting point of dialogue as a matrix of knowledge and life becomes personal interaction.

REFERENCES

Andrejevic, M. (2012). Exploitation in the Data Mine. In C. Fuchs, K. Boersma, A. Albrechtslund, & M. Sandoval (Eds.), *Internet and Surveillance. The Challenges of Web 2.0 and Social Media* (pp. 71–88). New York: Routledge.

Arvidsson, A., & Colleoni, E. (2012). Value in Informational Capitalism and on the Internet. *The Information Society, 28*(3), 135–150.

Banks, J., & Humphreys, S. (2008). The Labor of User Co-creators. *Convergence, 14*(4), 401–418.

Caraway, B. (2010). Online Labour Markets: An Inquiry into oDesk Providers. *Work Organisation, Labour and Globalisation, 4*(2), 111–125.

Comor, E. (2010). Digital Prosumption and Alienation. *Ephemera, 10*(3/4), 439–454.

Davidson, A., Reza Habibi, M., & Larochec, M. (2017). Materialism and the Sharing Economy: A Cross-Cultural Study of American and Indian Consumers. *Journal of Business Research, 82*, 364–372.

Fisher, E. (2012). How Less Alienation Creates More Exploitation. *tripleC: Communication, Capitalism & Critique, 10*(2), 171–183.

Fuchs, C. (2010). Labor in Informational Capitalism and on the Internet. *The Information Society, 26*(3), 179–196.

Fuchs, C. (2012a). Dallas Smythe Today. The Audience Commodity, the Digital Labour Debate, Marxist Political Economy and Critical Theory. Prolegomena to a Digital Labour Theory of Value. *tripleC: Communication, Capitalism & Critique, 10*(2), 692–740.

Fuchs, C. (2012b). With or Without Marx? With or Without capitalism? A Rejoinder to Adam Arvidsson and Eleanor Colleoni. *tripleC: Communication, Capitalism & Critique, 10*(2), 633–645.

Fuchs, C. (2014). *Digital Labour and Karl Marx*. New York: Routledge.

Fuchs, C., & Sandoval, M. (2014). Digital Workers of the World Unite! A Framework for Critically Theorising and Analysing Digital Labour. *TripleC, 12*(2), 486–563.

Gallup. (2017). Global Emotions Report. Gallup, Inc. https://news.gallup.com/reports/212648/gallup-global-emotions-report-2017.aspx?ays=n#aspnet Form

Global Web Index. (2018). Social Global Web Index's Flagship Report on the Latest Trends in Social Media. H1 2018. www.globalwebindex

Huws, U. (2016). Working Online, Living Offline: Labour in the Internet Age. *Work Organisation, Labour & Globalisation, 7*(1), 1–11.

Kittur, A., Nickerson, J. V., Bernstein, M. S., Gerber, E. M., Shaw, A., Zimmerman, J., Lease, M., & Horton, J. J. (2013). The Future of Crowd Work. *CSCW '13*, 1301–1318. https://doi.org/10.1145/2441776.2441923.

Kücklich, J. (2005). Precarious Playbour: Modders and the Digital Games Industry. *The Fibreculture Journal, 5.* Retrieved from February 27, 2018 http://five.fibreculturejournal.org/fcj-025-precarious-playbour-modders-and-the-digital-games-industry/

Lansen, A., & García, A. (2015). "...But I Haven't Got a Body to Show": Self-Pornification and Male Mixed Feelings in Digitally Mediated Seduction Practices. *Sexualities, 18*(5/6), 714–730.

Marx, K. (1867). *Capital: Vol I.* London: Penguin.

OECD. (2015). *Skills for Social Progress: The Power of Social and Emotional Skills, OECD Skills Studies.* OECD Publishing. https://doi.org/10.1787/9789264226159-en.

Parente, R. C., Geleilate, J. M. G., & Rong, K. (2018). The Sharing Economy Globalization Phenomenon: A Research Agenda. *Journal of International Management, 24,* 52–64.

Prahalad, C. K., & Ramaswamy, V. (2000). Co-opting Customer Competence. *Harvard Business Review, 78,* 79–87.

Ritzer, G., & Jurgenson, N. (2010). Production, Consumption, Prosumption. *Journal of Consumer Culture, 10*(1), 13–36.

Scholz, T. (2013). *Digital Labor. The Internet as Playground and Factory.* New York: Routledge.

Scribano, A. (2017). *Normalization, Enjoyment and Bodies/Emotions: Argentines Sensibilities.* New York: Nova Science Publications.

Scribano, A. (2018). *Politics and Emotions.* Houston: Studium Press.

Simply Measured. (2017). The State of Social Marketing. 2017 Annual Report. (Online): Extraído el 30 de noviembre de 2017 desde: https://get.simplymeasured.com/rs/135-YGJ-288/images/SM_StateOfSocial-2017.pdf

Tapscott, D. (1995). *The Digital Economy: Promise and Peril in the Age of Networked Intelligence.* New York: McGraw-Hill.

Toffler, A. (1980). *The Third Wave.* New York: Bantam Books.

UNCTAD. (2017). *Information Economy Report 2017. Digitalization, Trade and Development.* Geneva: United Nations.

PART I

Politics of Sensibilities and Society 4.0

CHAPTER 2

Digital Gaze and Visual Experience

Adrian Scribano and Pedro Lisdero

INTRODUCTION

In the early twentieth century, Small wrote in the *American Journal of Sociology* about the potential ambiguity between having "a sociological point of view" without making reference to facts and how relationships among human beings recursively affect their own understanding. He expressed concretely:

> The individual of today is being modified by his contacts with other individuals, and by his contacts with today's institutions. Tomorrow's individuals will not be wholly the causes or the effects of tomorrow's institutions. Each is both cause and effect of the other. (…) Perhaps there is no phrase which is used with more vagueness of meaning than the phrase "the social point of view", or "the sociological point of view". Everybody who is intelligent

A first version of this chapter was published in Scribano, A. y Lisdero, P. (2018) "Experiencia visual e Investigación Social: hacia una crítica de la economía política de la mirada digital". *Religación. Revista de Ciencias Sociales y Humanidades*, 9(3), 165–181.

A. Scribano (✉)
CONICET, Buenos Aires, Argentina

P. Lisdero
CONICET, Córdoba, Argentina

© The Author(s) 2019
A. Scribano, P. Lisdero (eds.), *Digital Labour, Society and the Politics of Sensibilities*, https://doi.org/10.1007/978-3-030-12306-2_2

today supposes himself to be first "scientific" and second "sociological" in his mental attitude. We need not now discuss what is involved in the "scientific" attitude, but under this title, the "social fact", we may note some of the marks of the sociological attitude toward the world. The use of this appears in the consideration just dwelt upon that the sociologists are trying to focalize within one field of vision all the activities that are going on among people, so that men and women who get the benefit of this outlook may see their own lives in their actual relation to all the lives around them. The sociological outlook is a position chosen for the deliberate purpose of placing each of us in his relations to all the rest, so that the meaning of each one's part in the complicated whole may appear. (Small 1900: 785)

A hundred and eighteen years later, it is necessary to revisit the problems of a "politics of looking" on the one hand, and on the other, the modifications in human interaction.

The debates we present here are inscribed in a research trajectory that tries to problematize the role that knowledge about the social plays in processes of structuring in contemporary societies. Elsewhere, we have developed some analyses that are relevant to the challenges faced by the social sciences at the dawn of a new millennium, highlighting the peculiarities of the contexts that are called "Global South" (Scribano 2012, 2015), and elaborating on the strengths of certain strategies that, based on the expressive and creative components of the experiences of subjects, propose a critique of the understanding of social problems (Scribano 2013, 2016a). In addition, we have explored the "expansion" that digital life has had on those structuring processes as well as the potency and possible intersections between social research and "digital media" (Scribano 2017a, b; Scribano and Dhers 2013; De Sena and Lisdero 2014). Finally, we have looked into the convergence between photography-image-video and sociology as a fertile field in which society expresses, with the particular texture of "the visual", the specificity of "the social" these days (Lisdero 2017a, b; Scribano and De Sena 2013; Scribano 2013, 2016b).

Bearing in mind that trajectory, here we intend to deal with the converging relationship between "digital life" and "images" in order to make our research practices reflective, that is to say, to challenge ourselves, to question ourselves about the conditions and potentialities of social research related to two facts that characterize our times: the expansion of social relations mediated by ICTs, in which "images" constitute a central "tension" in relation to the goal, and the shape of the interactions.

Linking this work with some previous debates, our goal is to explore the contributions made by the study of social sensibilities for a critique of the political economy of the "look 4.0".

With that aim in mind, we have opted for the following argumentative strategy. Firstly, we will carry out a preliminary exploration of some debates on the relationship between photography-image and the Internet, from which some relevant dimensions of the experience lived by millions of subjects will emerge. Secondly, we will trace several cues in order to problematize the "global/local structuring" of contemporary knowledge practices. This will make it possible to reflect upon the role of sensibilities in knowledge processes. Thirdly, we will emphasize the importance of making the "politics of looking" critical as a condition for research practice, and we will advocate for the notion of "visual experience" on the basis of a critique of the extended forms of understanding "the visual". Fourthly and lastly, we will offer some considerations about the contents of a critique of the political economy of looking, highlighting the reception conditions of the images and the implications of the actions of seeing-feeling-looking in the current structuring contexts.

Towards a Criticism of the Politics of the Look 4.0

Even though photography and sociology share roots in the history of reflexivity processes of modern societies, there is still in our times a certain disconnection that arouses considerable interest. As Bericat (2011: 114) says, there seems to be a contradiction between, on the one hand, a social world plagued by images, and on the other, a sociology that is "blind" in relation to a key element in the lives of human beings. The author, thus, poses the following question:

> (…) given the vital relevance that images have acquired, we should ask ourselves, with Mitchell, what does it mean for societies that human beings are visual beings (Mitchell 2005: 244). People have eyes with which they look at the world and social sciences cannot continue to ignore what people see with their eyes. (Bericat 2011: 115; our translation)

Approaching the intersections of photography-image and sociology in an exhaustive way would certainly be a task that lies beyond the scope of this chapter. We have made some references to them elsewhere (Lisdero 2017b);

in this respect, we would like to bring back here the idea that this relationship features something more than a mere temporal coincidence; early on, it has involved establishing "bridges" between the tasks of a social analyst and of a photographer. Thus, the place of visual reflection stands out in the works by E. Goffman (1976), D. Harper (1998), Becker (1974), Wagner (1979), Collier (1967), Bateson and Mead (1942) among others. What is important here is to highlight that, for these authors' arguments, image does not constitute a mere illustration of the obvious, but a systematic procedure involved in the wider research process.

In this context, the emergence of a "Visual Sociology" turns out to be the expression of a growing—though insufficient—historical convergence. A first approach to this field could be characterized as the use of photography and video for the purposes of studying society and its visual artefacts (Harper 1998), highlighting two specific components: images as social products and their capacity to "enable us to see" certain specific conditions. On the basis of the conception of the "Visual datum", there is an attempt to contemplate the whole society as a seen reality, to consider how "seeing is enabled" and how it is looked at by its members (Maresca and Meyer 2015: 36–39).

However, image and photography in society acquire a significantly different place with the emergence and the massification of digital photography and the Internet. Karina and Schwarz claim:

> The advent of new digital image technologies enables, among other things, their omnipresence in the daily life of the population in a large portion of the planet. Digital cameras and the mobile phones equipped with them, as well as webcams, and the so-called social networks have transformed the practice of photography as well as what can be photographed, the meanings, uses and social functions of photography (…). (2016: 70; our translation)

> Image has found ways to spread and have presence in human experience through different media; one of them is the digital medium and the Internet in particular (…) Digital systems mediate in the understanding of the world through an interface modality in which two technological communication devices take a central role: the screen and the technical interface. The latter manifests the transformation of the culture based on writing, on the logo-centric narrative structures and physical contexts into a digital culture oriented towards what is visual, sensory, retroactive, non-linear and apparently immaterial (…). (2016: 60; our translation)

The transformations that the authors detect in the emergence of Societies 4.0 have brought about the use of this specific combination of photography and the Internet as a means to record, portray and interpret the world, as is claimed by Lansén and García (2015) in their study about photography, self-pornography and social networks:

> Contemporary digital photography practices are remediating sociality, embodiment and subjectivity, especially with the convergence of digital cameras, mobile phones and social networks (...) The ubiquity of cameras and the growing display and exchange of pictures online reveal changes in the uses and meanings of everyday photographic practices. Playfulness and experimentation are common features of camera phones and digital camera usage, which are similarly found in their uses for erotic purposes. These changes are made possible by the ease of digital production and the low cost of production for individuals. (Lansén and García 2015: 717)

These worlds in transformation, these technological possibilities, and the redefinition of the cognitive skills necessary to experience a plurality of life worlds enhanced by the materiality of each one of them present the social sciences with a number of challenges. One of them involves inquiring again about the specificity of the visual in research practices. In relation to that, Renobell highlights a particular element pertaining to the relationship between image and Society 4.0:

> Professional visualities of the mass media are on a par with household or private images. The professional eye participates in the amateur eye in a network of social issuers. The styles overlap and different visualities emerge. (Renobell 2005: 4; our translation)

To this author, this partially sets up a new stage of "visual thinking", which he calls "hypervisuality":

> From a historical perspective, three key moments can be highlighted in the change of social visualities: the emergence of the printing press, the emergence of photography and the mass media y the emergence of the Internet. Each one of these changes has added a new dimension to visuality. (...) A new stage in visual thinking is reached, whose highest point is the definition of photographic hypervisuality as a new visual process of the modern era. (Renobell 2005: 4–6; our translation)

Hypervisuality is characterized by (among other elements) the following:

- A multiplicity of senders, media, receivers, authors and channels (as opposed to the uniform visuality of modernity, and the ambiguous and complex one of postmodernity).
- Communicational values and immediacy (as opposed to the ideological values of modernity, and the consumerist values of postmodernity).
- Hypervisual and hypermedia expression (as opposed to the pre-eminence of the modern word and the postmodern image).
- The representation of hyper-realities is sought (when the modern word seeks to convince, and the postmodern image to seduce) (Renobell 2005: 7; our translation).

The notion of reality itself and the technical mediation are what is at stake as a common ground for the discussion around image, the Internet and social sciences. If photography itself was used to constitute an epistemic category at the dawn of modernity, it was because it was a category of thought different from the relationship among sign, time, space, the real, the subject and the doing (Dubois 1986). It is in part this specificity upon which virtual sociology stands in order to stake a claim to the potency of the visual. But it is also this relationship that is disrupted in the constitution of Societies 4.0.

That is to say, the indexicality associated with photography (i.e. its capacity to capture, freeze a moment and offer the possibility of "re-living it" upon seeing it) overlaps with a new aspect in face of the mediation of the digital technologies strengthened by the Internet. If, following Peirce, the sign can be approached in terms of something that stands for something else in somebody's perception, and photography appeared in modernity as the physical trace perceived in the act of seeing: What is the specificity of the trace, its texture, when all experience is processed through "zeroes" and "ones"? Where is the specificity of the "physical connection" in the passage from "light-sensitive film" associated with a photographic act of the "modern eye" to "the digital technology" linked to the eye 4.0 that produces/spreads images on/through the Net?

The technical dimension of the construction of an image, the digital camera, tries to emulate the mechanical work of the eye from which photography originated in an expansion process of the body-prosthesis in the world. However, in the amplified experience of photography together with the Internet, the mediation of technique becomes more complex, the Internet is not simply a sound box of a digital "click"; instead, the Net has a twofold operation: first, we must acknowledge that the Web is already present in the social object that is captured, and at the same time, this does not constitute a "means"; instead the image itself is modified and acquires specific senses of its own on/through the Internet. All of this redirects the old idea of "physical connexion" underlying the notion of photography-trace towards a new state of complexity: the possible connexions between "digital image" and "reality 4.0". As a result, the debates over the realism of photography or even its link with an indexicality process must be reconsidered (would it be possible to talk about a double indexicality, one pertaining to photography and the other to the Net?)

Undoubtedly, what is key here is the eye as the underlying layer of these transformations, and looking as a field of action and dispute of perception. Evidently, besides the rationality of images or of the media, we need to extend the contextualization of knowledge practices towards the rationality of the "sensibilities" in order to understand the possibilities in which the possible "looks" are inscribed.

Sensibilities and Social Knowledge Practices

A reflection about knowledge processes should acknowledge that those of us who are living the complex beginning of the twenty-first century are experiencing a phenomenal series of transformations that, despite being evident, are not easy to interpret. This complexity emerges when we ascertain a fact that defines the scene of our contemporaneity: we face a world in constant transformation, which is evident in the mutation of social practices with a growing global impact.

The above-mentioned scene also involves a series of changes linked to public policies: from the internationalization of public infrastructure and labour market and the redefinition of benefits and beneficiaries of welfare policies at a multinational level, to the reconfiguration of the concept of democratic citizenship itself (Scribano and Korstanje 2017).

Another relevant feature of this complex global scene is the metamorphosis of the "world of work", that is, the transformations in the forms it takes and the changes in transnational management. Phenomena like "uberization", the emergence of "platform economies", the digitalization of productive life, marketing through social media, the convergence of work and training in the digital space and so on reveal a turbulent present in which the notion of work/workers has to be reconsidered necessarily at a global scale.

To the transformations we have just mentioned and which are related to the state (public policies) and the (labour) market as central components of the emergence and consolidation of the social world in the nineteenth and twentieth centuries, we have to add and highlight the implications of the mutation in the processes of individuation, of subjectivity and identity constitution.

The multiplication and worsening of discrimination and social abomination are barely a hint to this dimension, which can be observed in, among others, the racializing segregation of migrants, poverty, human trafficking and the growth of urban marginalization around the world.

In our research, we have also observed that said transformations involve a complex range of practices associated with particular emotion regimes, politics of sensibilities associated with specific ways of elaborating perceptions, all of which leads to socially producing sensation management processes. These become a central component in the process of global structuring because they reconfigure the way in which social conflict is tied to processes of continuity-change in our societies. In a "porous" and extended way, though with particular spatializations in each specific context, these processes "go unnoticed" and shape consensus and the integration of societies. They are specific practices linked to the shaping of the social ways of being in the world, and thus, qualitatively transforming modes of standardization, the coordination of action, among other central components of modern life.

Thus, the complexity of our days could be characterized by the expansion of societies with standardized practices of immediate enjoyment through consumption where a phenomenon of internationalization of emotionalization (Scribano 2017c) is extended, which runs through public policies, processes of discrimination and work. On the basis of these axes, it is possible to reconstruct new geometries where the grammars of actions are associated with the game of proximities and distances that redefine the subjects' own constitution, their associations (collectives) and the state itself (Scribano 2015).

This image made up of at least some of the brushstrokes that we can briefly reconstruct here becomes an interesting starting point to reflect upon the knowledge processes structured as condition/consequence of this scenario. For the perspective we would like to develop here, it is especially important to highlight the connections between epistemology and emotions (Scribano 2012).

One of the possible ways of scrutinizing these connections involves exploring the relationship among "word", "knowledge" and "sensibilities" in phenomena that cut across the contemporary life world such as "work 4.0". It becomes evident that "virtual spaces" and, consequently, our work experience become accessible to us "in" and "through" specific politics of sensing: that is to say, "adequate" ways of touching, seeing and hearing.

Knowing becomes an extension of the sensibilities that are globally commodified. In the world 4.0, expert knowledge, the scientist and knowledge about everyday life intersect and intertwine in daily experiences. An epistemology of social sciences that tries to improve the capacities to know the world should incorporate the different modalities of reflexivity that make up the diverse modulations between knowing and sensing. Thus, the relationship between truth and language must be reconnected beyond that dualism in the framework of a dialectics between knowing, sensing and saying.

On the other hand, another important aspect is that the twenty-first century is a century without "present". That is, if the twentieth century placed the "present" centre stage, today that idea is associated with at least two bands of a Moebius strip: on one side, existence, occurrence and situation from the perspective of the sensing subject; on the other side, what is highlighted is indetermination, contingency and the unsayable from the perspective of the cognizant subject. These days, that band is a spiralling movement which opens in a direction where immediacy unfolds between the present and the "here/now". What is instantaneous, sudden and imminent structures a life lived with no intermediaries, or anything that gets in the way, an iterative "now" without mediation or delay. The "modern" present used to need circumstances, (pre)occupations-in-time, dedication; it was shaped as an updated past and a future made now. The present of the diverse forms of existentialism (Sartre, Mounier, Levinas etc.), of the multiple facets of discursivism (Ranciere, Derrida, Laclau etc.) and of the multiple facets of so-called postmodernism was a here/now that was constitutive/maker of the immediacy that is blurred, which is lost, which vanishes in the "now", in the disconnections, in what suddenly emerges—it is a present that is experienced as "that-in-which-we-are". Leaving the present behind, linking the imminent with the sudden through the instantaneous, there emerges the consolidation of the triumph of catallactics (in the sense of Hayek): the market. This experience, summarized in the expression "I do not know what I want... but I want it now", takes value away from the present. Thus, it becomes evident that there is a mutation of a political economy of morality that results from the impact of the twentieth-century synaesthesia and aphasia like pastors of the neo-colonial religion.

These modifications become central when it comes to thinking/re-thinking social research the way Charles Cooley did at the end of the nineteenth century:

> It is clear that one who attempts to study precisely things that are changing must have a great deal to do with measures of change. Now, almost all those phenomena of society with which the statistician is chiefly interested are in constant motion, cannot be caught and pinned down permanently in one place, but must be taken on the wing and their velocity measured. Next to their present position their direction and velocity are the most important things to be known about them, since these alone give us any power to forecast future positions. (Cooley 1893: 285)

How is change measured when the idea of present is transformed? In what sense do social relations change if the horizon is what is immediate? How do we locate/describe subjects' positions and conditions that are "constantly changing"?

The motto "live the present" needs a set of sensations anchored to the here/now, immediacy can do without such ties, sensing-once-and-again is the best way to just sense that one senses "definitely" nothing.

This has theoretical/epistemic/methodological consequences, among which we can point out that the notion of stage gets blurred and loses value, the experience of what it means to produce is re-problematized and the view of what means-ends signifies is re-elaborated.

In principle, from evolutionism and developmentalism, to the variants of the revolutions (be it as affirmation or as negation), the twentieth century can be explained through the notion of stage, phase and/or period, which has essentially changed. This eradication has procedural consequences because the notion of step, stage and sequence is altered in "methodological" terms.

On the other hand, the radicalization of immediacy threatens the very notion of production: changing the processes of commodification of time (of the nineteenth and twentieth centuries), transforming the before/after producing "logic" and consecrating the experience of "in between" as an autonomous experience of the process of doing/elaborating things/practices. This has important implications when it comes to re-thinking the productive matrix of our methodological "doings", or our narration practices and publication demands. But in addition, these Moebius strips among what is imminent, sudden and instantaneous challenge the teleological action underlying the instrumental logic of means-ends, it redefines it in its instantiations, in its connections and in its iterations. The spontaneity and naturalized version of the irreversible connection between "a" vehicle for "a" goal gets blurred, and so does its radical relativistic version: there is no predetermined means for a particular end. It is through this that the structure of social inquiry itself, as we practice it, is challenged and threatened by the modifications of social practices themselves.

These components of social structuration processes of knowledge practices in our societies are particularly relevant for thinking about the relationship among image and Internet research that we problematize here. As was said before, it is key to understand in what sense what we have described as "structural properties" of the ways of being in our societies constitute central elements of the "politics of looking" that affect social scientists. In the following section, we propose a critique of the "accepted ways" of treating "the visual" in social research.

The Look of/in the Social Sciences: The "Visual Experience"

We are interested in understanding "the politics of looking" not only as part of our object of study, but also because it enables us to reflect upon some assumptions that constitute the conditions for a strategy of research on/with the visual. In this sense, we share with Becker our reflections about the specificity of the visual, the specific texture of the information that would be linked to what we previously referred to as "visual datum".

The author believes that images do not refer to the text nor are they explained by it; instead, they constitute (and are thus presented in social media) as a dimension/level in itself. The images that we are interested in do not become (only) a confirmation of the real. On the contrary, the implication of the experience in/with the digital image mediated by the Internet makes the "fantasy" of the "representation of the real" more complex, breaking a "model of knowledge" specifically anchored to a series of assumptions closer to an empirical context of the sciences, and opening the field to a multiplicity of questions: what does the texture of this particular register (visual and virtual) inform? In what sense does the game of the interjections assumed in the virtual implication subject-photography constitute in itself rich information about the phenomenon to be studied? Which are the possible guarantees that we can propose in a systematic process of analysis of these registers? This aperture to the ambiguity (Becker 2002) imbued in photography-digital-image in the Web, far from becoming an obstacle for research, can embody the potentiality for this type of specific "data".

In the same direction, we must acknowledge that diverse authors have postulated a particular feature of sensibility that accompanies the global development of capitalist society. Said feature becomes understandable due to what the "use" of photography tells us about the "politics of looking" that is dynamically shaped from the creation and massification of the camera (from Benjamin, Sontag, Bourdieu, Dubois, among many others) and its now digital metamorphosis on/by the Web. In order to frame this discussion, we take up John Berger's (1998) observations about the relationship among eye, camera and "reality" to understand the action of looking in the development of modern society:

> We had to wait, however, until the 20th century and the period between the great wars for photography to become the dominant and most "natural" way of referring to appearances. It was then that it substituted the world as immediate testimony. It was in this period that people believed in photography as the most transparent, direct method to access reality (…) However, this was a brief moment. That "truthfulness" of the new medium gave way to its deliberate use as a propaganda instrument (…) instead of offering new options, its use and its "reading" gradually became habitual, a part of modern perception itself that has not been examined. (1998: 32; our translation)

> A capitalist society requires a culture based on images. It needs to provide large amounts of fun in order to stimulate people to buy and anesthetize the wounds inflicted by class, race and sex. And it needs to gather an unlimited amount of information in order to exploit natural resources better, increase productivity, maintain the order, make war and generate work for bureaucrats. The camera, which can subjectify reality as much as it can objectify it, is the ideal instrument to satisfy those needs and to strengthen them. Cameras define reality in two ways that are essential for the operation of advanced industrial society: as a show (for the masses) and as a surveillance object (for leaders). The production of images facilitates, in addition, a leading ideology. Social change is substituted for a change in the images. (1998: 35; our translation)

Here we are interested in making explicit the conditions in which a specific practice of knowledge is inscribed, that is, in proposing an opportunity to reflect about the tensions and implications among "the eye, what is seen and the look". Modernity somehow implied that experiencing cities is related to enthroning the sense of sight in the construction of a "look" in which the "eye" constitutes the surface of inscription of these social processes. However, we are not interested in the biological processes involved in the senses; instead, our focus is placed on sight as a historical and social configuration, particularly associated with the ways in which subjects sense (and feel). Following Berger's text, the subjects' environment constitutes a reality that "can be seen", and is therefore liable to be shaped as a "visual datum". Nevertheless, we must acknowledge that "said look" is inscribed in a specific regime of sensibilities: it is the socially adequate way of regulating the flow and exchange of subjects with other subjects, their material and symbolic environment, and themselves. It is not difficult to imagine that the emergence of the Internet has made this relationship more complex.

The perception that is located closer to "the look" that constructs the "visual datum" must be inscribed in specific regimes of sensibilities challenging the empiricist feature that is imbued with the "datum" as a reality that exists independently of the eye that looks. Thus, a space for critical reflexion opens up to deal with the notions associated with the "representation of what is real" that usually runs through common sense; due to this, it is necessary to explore the possible connections between perception and the units of sense that are our object of inquiry. Thus, establishing some analytical keys about these regimes contributes to enriching the process of making theoretical and methodological decisions for research in/from the visual on/through the Net.

On the basis of the idea that the subjects' as well as the researcher's "looks" are inscribed in enclosed regimes of sensibilities, we propose to shift from the notion of "visual datum" to the conception of what Scribano has proposed about the *units of experiencing*.

In fact, challenging the notions of units of observation and analysis, the author sketches a concept that is adequate to clarify the processes of observation, recording and analysis of social sensibilities, emphasizing the urgency of re-directing the researcher's perception to a *hiatus* that opens between analysis and observation (Scribano 2011: 72).

In his proposal, focusing on sensibilities involves understanding that:

> Perceptions, sensations and emotions constitute a tripod that allows us to understand where sensibilities are founded. Social agents know the world through their bodies, through a set of impressions that have an impact on the ways in which they have "exchanges" with the socio-environmental con-text. Thus, objects, phenomena, processes and other agents structure their perceptions, conceived as naturalized ways of organizing a set of impressions. That

scheme shapes the sensations that the agents experience on the bases of what can be called the inner and the outer world, the social, subjective and "natural" world, recreating a dialectics between impression and perception, from which the "sense" of surplus sensations – closer or further – results. As a result and as an antecedent of perceptions, these sensations give way to emotions as an effect of the allocation processes and the correspondence between perceptions and sensations. Emotions can be seen as a puzzle that becomes the action and effect of sensing or of feeling, and therefore, they get entrenched in the states of feeling the world that enable the transmission of the perceptions associated with socially constructed forms of sensations. (Scribano 2008a: 210)

This critique of perception (in whose theoretical background we can recognize the expected objectives and results) is oriented to register: (a) the space of interaction linked to showing, showing (us) and showing (oneself); (b) the complexity of the dramaturgical situation (Goffman); (c) how, from where, whom and what the registered expressions tell; (d) the capacity to register "silences" (absences); and (e) the expressive weave between the experienced sensations and the emotions (Scribano 2011: 23). If the *units of experiencing* are perceived in the process by which "(...) what the subjects *feel*, what the subjects do to manifest what they *feel*, and what is *felt* by the subjects who receive/look/share what is made, are assembled (disassembled) (...)" (Scribano 2013: 81), then the *visual experiences* constitute an effort to limit said process to what has historically been defined as the "sense of sight". The specificity of "the visual" mediated by the Internet abandons the ascetic appearance of the datum, hence emphasizing that its particular "texture" becomes relevant precisely because it implies the porous relationship between perception and sensation.

It is on the basis of this complexity that an experience of/with "the visual" on the Internet could strengthen "what the image communicates", inquiries "what is absent from the image", and emphasizes "what the image manifests" (Scribano 2008b: 256).

Conclusions: Re-thinking the Visual and the Virtual in Society 4.0

What we call "political economy" of "the look 4.0" is related to a global phase of humankind in which our senses converge (in a way that is different from how they had up to this point) with the world of technology in search for "assistance/orthopaedic aids" to say what is real and how we experience it. The old pre-eminence of the eye—and the sense of sight—in our modern society is restructured in relation to the complexities that we have reconstructed in this chapter. It is in this context that it becomes relevant to highlight the content of the practices that are changing our ways of producing sociabilities, experiences and sensibilities in order to be able to map possible roads for our future research practices.

The first issue that we would like to emphasize is related to the receptivity conditions of images in our societies. These days, from telephones to heaters, all sorts of "devices" surrounding us are or can be digital. We are immersed in a process that is called "revolution 4.0", and that is strongly associated with what we call *touch culture*.

The social forms of immediacy entail specific spaces in which conditions of particular experiences are taken for granted and sociabilities are presupposed. What is immediate is a special kind of "here-now" that redefines the present.

Conditions of productivity and commodification of the sensations converge in a common "pre-origin" that gets elaborated into "using-the-body" to relate to instruments/machines/devices. In this context, social practices acquire the texture of the materiality of the body/emotion, the density of sensation and the natural processing of the senses. The social ways of connecting oneself with the world have been transferred to the hands, fingers and fingertips: firstly, with our communication instruments, but also with payment systems, entertainment systems and cooking and cleaning devices and so on. We literally spend our lives pressing buttons, sliding, touching and "clicking".

Social relations have shifted towards a metaphor of "touching", "clicking" and interacting with instruments. Subjects express themselves sliding, pressing sensitive parts of devices and thus, more than being able to see or do, it is necessary to "be able to touch".

This is an approximation to what is real which redefines the accesses to the world even though it does not eliminate "the know-how" and the "know-what". We are in a post-cyborg era in which the line between the superfluous, the prosthetic and the extension gets diluted with the "friendliness" of the interfaces to buy/enjoy. "Being able to touch", more than a skill, is a condition of cognitive/affective possibility of being in the world.

The twenty-first century will be a century of "touching" and the social sciences will have to redefine themselves in terms of their inquiry strategies and ontological discussions. In these contexts, actor, agent, subject and author will be reconfigured and consequently their public positioning will be modified as well.

Image and "the logics of looking" are not immune to these transformations; on the contrary, they are framed in these re-definitions of what *seeing-sensing-touching* implies. This is *the second issue* that we would like to highlight.

The photography-digital image that we have made reference to in this chapter emerged in a context of technological and productive convulsions of institutional sliding and of resurgence of the importance of the hand as the organ that is connected to thinking.

Seeing-feeling-oneself starts with a touch-looking-at-oneself. Today (more than ever?) image is an intersubjective production that acquires features of an instantiated practice at the moment of acquiring the production made for those who see themselves. While we produce an image, we touch the surfaces of devices that we need to look at in order to see-ourselves-feeling what we want to know and let others know.

Today, to see is to touch, feeling what is seen. Fingertips come into contact with the screen(s), the glass is pressed when a decision is made, and when the fingertips slide, they surf the menu of options that the previous selection made available. When we see a photograph, we touch it, at times in an almost imperceptible way, but most of the times with that moment of monitoring that stops incorrectness: the unwanted *like*, the incorrect *upload*, the wrong *stalking*.

In this manner of interaction, human beings are elaborating a grammar of vision as a code that is closer to us than the word. The digital image on the Web is a proposal to have an experience that involves getting immersed in a scene that goes through the sensitivity and sensing of publishing images with our hands.

The production of the digital image on/through the Web is guided by capturing, not photographing, looking for a capture—not a photo—trying to convey an experience—not an object—in a massive and radically self-produced way. It is a synthesis of a scopic regime which, on the basis of what is old, produces "new" consequences. Even though all images try to convey experiences, images on/through the Internet are based on the quality of "portraying" something and they use that as a starting point.

Are the transformations in our scopic regime transformations in our value system? If all aesthetic transformations correspond to certain ethics and, in turn, certain politics, then the answer may be that they are. Accepting that we are "feeling-thinking" beings (in the sense of Fals Borda) leads us to wonder about our "video-touching" condition as producers of sensibilities that enable us to know/sense the world. The challenge for the social sciences of societies normalized in the immediate enjoyment through consumption in the context of the revolution 4.0 still is how to connect/disconnect science and politics.

REFERENCES

Bateson, G., & Mead, M. (1942). *Balinese Character. A Photographic Analysis.* New York: Academy of Sciences.

Becker, H. (1974). Photography and Sociology. *Studies in the Anthropology of Visual Communication, 1*(1), 3–26.

Becker, H. (2002). Visual Evidence: A Seventh Man, the Specified Generalization, and the Work of the Reader. *Visual Studies, 17*(1), 3–11.

Berger, J. (1998). *Mirar.* Buenos Aires: Ediciones de la Flor.

Bericat Alastuey, E. (2011). Imagen y conocimiento: Retos epistemológicos de la sociología visual. *EMPIRIA. Revista de Metodología de las Ciencias Sociales, 22*, 113–140.

Collier, J. (1967). *Visual Anthropology. Photography as a Research Method.* Nueva York: Rinehart and Winston.

Cooley, C. (1893). Observations on the Measure of Change. *American Statistical Association New Series, 2*, 285–292.

De Sena, A., & Lisdero, P. (2014). Etnografía Virtual: aportes para su discusión y diseño. In A. De Sena (Ed.), *Caminos cualitativos: aportes para la investigación en Ciencias Sociales.* CABA: CICCUS.

Dubois, P. (1986). *El acto fotográfico: de la representación a la recepción.* Barcelona: Paidós.

Goffman, E. (1976). Gender Advertisements. *Studies in the Anthropology of Visual Communication, 3*(2), 209–213.

Harper, D. (1998). *Les vagabonds du Nord-Ouesr américain.* París: L'Harmattan.

Karina, P., & Schwarz, N. (2016). Fotografías en el espacio virtual: aspectos éticos y epistemico-metodológicos de su análisis en Ciencias Sociales. *Discursos Fotográficos, 12*(20), 63–81.

Lansén, A., & García, A. (2015). '…But I Haven't Got a Body to Show': Self-pornification and Male Mixed Feelings in Digitally Mediated Seduction Practices. *Sexualities, 18*(5/6), 714–730.

Lisdero, P. (2017a). Desde las nubes… Sistematización de una estrategia teórico metodológica visual. *Revista Latinoamericana de Metodología de la Investigación Social – ReLMIS, 13*(7), 69–90.

Lisdero, P. (2017b). Conflicto social y sensibilidades. Un análisis a partir de las imágenes/observaciones de los saqueos de diciembre de 2013 en la ciudad de Córdoba (Argentina). In G. Vergara & A. De Sena (Eds.), *Geometrías Sociales* (pp. 65–90). Buenos Aires: Estudios Sociológicos Editora.

Maresca, S., & Meyer, M. (2015). *Compendio de fotografía para uso de sociólogos.* Barcelona: Edicions Bellaterra.

Mitchell, W. J. T. (2005). An Interview with W. J. T. Mitchell. In M. Dikovitskaya (Ed.), *Visual Culture: The Study of the Visual After the Cultural Turn* (pp. 238–257). Cambridge: MIT Press.

Renobell, V. (2005, September 1). Hipervisualidad. La imagen fotográfica en la sociedad del conocimento y de la comunicación digital. UOC Papers. Revista sobre la sociedad del conocimiento, Barcelona.

Scribano, A. (2008a). Sensaciones, conflicto y cuerpo en Argentina después del 2001. *Espacio Abierto, 17*(2), 205–230.

Scribano, A. (2008b). *El proceso de investigación social cualitativo.* Buenos Aires: Prometeo.

Scribano, A. (2011). Vigotsky, Bhaskar y Thom: Huellas para la comprensión (y fundamentación) de las Unidades de Experienciación. *ReLMIS, 1*(1), 21–35.

Scribano, A. (2012). *Teorías Sociales del Sur: una mirada post-independentista.* Buenos Aires/Córdoba: ESEditora, Universidas.

Scribano, A. (2013). *Encuentros Creativos Expresivos. Una metodología para estudiar sensibilidades.* Buenos Aires: ESEditora.

Scribano, A. (2015). Comienzo del Siglo XXI y Ciencias Sociales: Un rompecabezas posible. *Polis, 14*(41), 1–11.

Scribano, A. (2016a). *Investigación social basada en la Creatividad/Expresividad.* Buenos Aires: ESEditora.

Scribano, A. (2016b). Cuerpos-en-expresión: una mirada para su análisis. In M. Valderrama & C. Gaona (Eds.), *Artes y Culturas* (pp. 250–267). Madrid: McGraw-Hill Education.

Scribano, A. (2017a). Miradas cotidianas. El uso de Whatsapp como experiencia de investigación social. *ReLMIS, 13*(7), 8–22.

Scribano, A. (2017b). Instaimagen: mirar tocando para sentir. Dossier—Las razones y las Emociones de las Imágenes‖ /Dossiê—As razões e as emoções das imagens. *RBSE Revista Brasileira de Sociologia da Emoção, 16*(47), 45–55.

Scribano, A. (2017c). *Normalization, Enjoyment and Bodies/Emotions: Argentine Sensibilities.* New York: Nova Science.

Scribano, A., & De Sena, A. (2013). La Argentina desalojada: un camino para el recuerdo de las represiones silenciadas. *Boletín Onteaiken, 16*, 58–79.

Scribano, A., & Dhers, V. (2013). Latin America: Body, Memory and Cyberspace. *Global South Sephis E-Magazine, 9*(2), 26–34.

Scribano, A., & Korstanje, M. E. (2017). Emotions and Epistemology: A Path for Reconsideration in the 21st Century. *International Journal of Human Rights and Constitutional Studies, 5*(2), 111–129.

Small, A. W. (1900). The Scope of Sociology. III. The Problems of Sociology. *American Journal of Sociology, 5*(6), 778–813.

Wagner, J. (Ed.). (1979). *Images of information. Still Photography in the Social Sciences.* Beverly Hills/London: Sage.

CHAPTER 3

Work and Sensibilities: Commodification and Processes of Expropriation Around Digital Labour

Adrian Scribano and Pedro Lisdero

INTRODUCTION

Connections between revolution 4.0, labour and the current process of social structuring involve transformations in practices and conceptualizations of the "world of work". In this context, for example, the notion of digital labour has revitalized discussions around critical communication studies, but it has also been relevant to inquiries on the metamorphosis of work relationships, and even in studies of everyday life in the context of Society 4.0. Addressing questions emerging from those insights, this chapter explores some contributions from the sociology of the

A. Scribano (✉)
CONICET, Buenos Aires, Argentina

P. Lisdero
CONICET, Córdoba, Argentina

© The Author(s) 2019   39
A. Scribano, P. Lisdero (eds.), *Digital Labour, Society and the Politics of Sensibilities*, https://doi.org/10.1007/978-3-030-12306-2_3

body/emotions for understanding the practices and politics of sensibilities associated with digital labour.[1]

To do this, this chapter (i) explores various theoretical debates around the definition of digital labour, in order to underline the relevance of redefining forms of exploitation regarding related practices, (ii) develops arguments from the perspective of the sociology of bodies/emotions, which allows us to understand in what sense the technological mediation linked to the expansion of ICTs constitutes a reconfiguration of "the politics of the senses" (look, see, observe, touch etc.) and (iii) analyses cases of workers in ICT industries (based on testimonies and records of virtual ethnography) that allow us to connect their daily experience with certain mechanisms of expropriation and commodification of the vitality of bodies.

DIGITAL LABOUR: A CRITICAL APPROXIMATION FROM A SOCIOLOGY OF SENSIBILITIES

From the results of the multiple investigations carried out on the transformations of the "world of work" in the last 20 years, we cannot ignore the "global/local" component that goes through these phenomena. Behind these findings, some tensions can be recognized, as a reflexivity of practical knowledge that seeks to understand the complexity that the current "metamorphosis" implies.

Thus, a first demarcation on the discussions that underlie the effort to understand work in the context of a global map in reconfiguration is linked to at least four initial tensions. First, the various investigations seem to realize that the complex "global/local" realities of work require for their understanding efforts that transcend the fragmentation of rigid disciplinary approaches, locked in their own questions. Quite the contrary, the radicality that involves thinking these objects, such as "digital labour", demands a break with the "horizon" of the frames that defined labour in the nineteenth and twentieth centuries.

This leads us to the second dimension we wanted to highlight, and that is part of a debate that has persisted throughout historical discussions of "work": the definition of the "worker". Thus, the current theoretical

---

[1] Some assumptions, characteristics and implications of Society 4.0 and politics of sensibilities have been developed in Chap. 1: "Introduction: politics of sensibilities, society 4.0 and digital labour".

disputes about his character, specificity, contours, customs and so on are connected with the problematization of the relationship between the following: the transformations of/in the world of global/local work, the deep metamorphosis of the conditions that shape the daily lives of subjects, and the emergence of "the body" as a surface of registration and territory for these tensions.

This understanding cannot ignore, in turn, the impacts that are caused by the different modes of accumulation upon marginalization (of the unemployed and underemployed) and the various forms of spoliation of heterogeneous masses of workers—which forms a division between employable bodies and a number of bodies deemed superfluous for the purposes of work. Thus, the third dimension to underline is linked to specifically reconfiguring historical mechanisms that lead to the commodification of vitality, its relation to the specific forms of work organization capabilities that are demanded, and "balance" in the metabolic processes of expansion of a capitalist global/local society.

Finally, the last tension to note is associated with the way in which global production networks are developed concurrently in relation to a set of (emerging/latent) conflicts, which brings us back to the question about the links between changes in the daily lives of thousands of subjects and current processes of social restructuring on a global scale. Such conflicts demand to be understood from a perspective that surpasses the false micro-macro antinomy (reconfiguring dimensions such as space/time), redefines the conditions of work reproduction and rethinks the forms/ uses (valorization processes) of bodies.

The disciplinary transpositions that redefine workers' expropriations and various conflicts mark a field of reflection for the "global labour" that is contextualized in the first two decades of the century. These tensions draw the outline of a series of specific work practices that are in some way paradigmatic of the transformations underway. Such is the case of what we call "Digital Labour", understood at least in an introductory way—as a series of openings depending on the expansion of ICT practices involving a set of "productive" relations concocted in and from digital platforms that "enhance" the "collaborative" features of interactions.

Digital labour studies have encompassed a variety of definitions and problem areas. We could point out how the complex group of studies about digital labour has contributed to generating new questions on the characteristics and the reach of the transformations underway. In a schematic way, we could summarize the contributions in three axes: (a) the discussions around the objects of exploitation, (b) the discussions about labour relations and the surfaces in which they register (time/space coordinates of productive interactions) and (c) the debates around the constitution of the subjects of work.

(a) An important part of the literature recovers some debates around the Marxist theory of value (Fuchs 2014; Fumagalli 2015; Dyer-Witheford 2015; Morini and Fumagalli 2010) and interrogate whether it still applies to work carried out on the Internet, and whether the relationship of labour to capital can any longer be modelled using traditional concepts of value creation at the point of production (Huws 2016). Other questions in this regard are associated with the notion of alienation applied to the context of digital labour (Andrejevic 2012; Fisher 2012; Fisher and Fuchs 2015), or from another point of view, valuation processes linked to the notion of "reputation" (Heam 2010) and "bio-work" (Morini and Fumagalli 2010). Some strands of this debate lead to the redefinition of contemporary capitalism as the permanent search for new dimensions of the social and the vital, which are absorbed and commodified, increasingly incorporating the vital faculties of the human being into the process of capitalist accumulation.

Thus, we arrive at the definition of "cognitive capitalism" (Vercellone 2006) as a new configuration that identifies in knowledge and space (geographical and virtual) specific commodities on which the new dynamics of labour and accumulation are based (Fumagalli 2015). Finally, from other perspectives, the idea of the increasing commodification of audiences (audience commodity) is the starting point from which the redefinition of digital labour is based, closely associated with the expansion of "communicative capital" (Nixon 2015). While the concept of "audience labour" (Smythe 1977) could refer to the political economy of "analogue age" communication, the literature emphasizes the ability to commodify audiences to paradigmatic scales based on the expansion of digital media, particularly the task of providing specific and stratified messages made possible by the expansion of the conjunction of the Internet and the mobile phone. The configuration of audience labour as exploitation associated with a specific accumulation mode allows us to understand digital labour as one of the ways in which Internet-related corporations elevate the creation of surplus value, reconfiguring a focused political economy around audience labour (Nixon 2015; Fuchs 2014).

(b) The scope of the paradigmatic changes that digital work implies at the level of the daily experience of subjects implies rethinking the limits of categories that structured the times/spaces of work in the last century. In this way, the discussion around the notion of "Prosumption" finds in the debate about digital labour a horizon that exceeds the formulations initially made by Toffler (1980) to problematize the progressive diffusion of the dividing lines between producer and consumer in the context of new economic and political forms of the last decades of the twentieth century. Instead, several authors are involved in investigating the relationship between digital work and prosumption (Olivier and O'Neil 2015), establishing that the expansion of the Internet facilitates the erasure of the barriers that traditionally divided production with consumption, proposing the idea of a "prosumer capitalism" (Ritzer and Jurgenson 2010). In an analogous logic, the literature also shows the limitations of the classical divisions between productive/leisure spaces to define digital labour. Thus, the developments about the notions of "Playbour/Gamebour" (Play + labour/Game + labour) (Arwid 2015) emphasize the diffusion of the times/spaces of "leisure" and "work" in the activities increasingly mediated by the Internet. Linked to the above, some studies highlight in the definition of Digital Labour a strong criticism of "free labour" (Terranova 2013; Kosnik 2013) deployed by users of social networks. That is, unpaid labour, which is not strictly regulated in some kind of contract-employment, and which is freely given. Based on the concept of "Gamification", McKenzie (2013) establishes a critique of the extended logic in the Internet, from which people are able to do things without paying in exchange for symbolic rewards. What is put into play here is a kind of "participation" on the basis of which various companies base their source of value. The cooperative practices (Meil and Kirov 2017) make up a central part of the "online" experience, which some authors have analysed from the notions of "entrepreneurs" (Michailidou and Kostala 2016), or from the implications of cooperative work in the framework of cognitive labour, as in the Mechanical Turk (Aytes 2013). From a different perspective, the idea of a "platform capitalism" also puts at the centre of analysis the cooperative dimension linked to the coordination of the action mediated by the Internet. This notion implies the following: (a) the penetrating expansion of a "network", governed by anonymous and inaccessible algorithms, oriented to the selection of information and people based on market criteria; (b) concentration and industrialization of the information infrastructure, where cloud computing (technology in the network that elaborates, archives and memorizes data) becomes a platform for the management of people and services on a global scale; (c) through the processes of profiling and Data Mining/Big Data (techniques and knowledge methodologies from the automatic or semi-automatic processing of large amounts of data) it is easy to perform the accumulative and systematic collection of data; (d) all of which leads to the constitution of an infrastructural environment—a platform—that mediates human interaction by metabolizing sociability in production processes and the accumulation of digital value (Armano et al. 2017: 9–10). Although the expansion of the business process of outsourcing (BPO), whose beginnings can be traced back to the final decades of the last century, already implied a transnational connectivity in the transfer of data, the process of "digital labour platforms" made possible by the expansion of the network is qualitatively different. In addition to the aforementioned characteristics, this process enables workers/clients to post jobs and workers to bid on them, without the intervention of the organizations that formally mediated the BPO (Graham et al. 2017: 3). Thus, the emerging "sharing economy" includes, among others, platforms such as Upwork, ODesk, Guru, Amazon Mechanical Turk and Uber (Irani 2015; Cingolani 2016), also defined as work "crowdsourcing" (Cherry 2011; Berg 2016; Bergvall-Kåreborn and Howcroft 2014) emphasizing the idea of organizing work payment through online work exchanges (Huws 2015).

(c) Finally, the discussion about social class also goes through the debate about digital labour. Huws (2013, 2014) highlights, in discussion about the existence of a "cybertariat", a productive form based on the intensification of the dependence of capital on a globalized and feminized work force, associated with routine work, neotaylorization, and on occasions unpaid work, among others. For his part, Dyer-Witheford (2015) emphasizes the need to think, within the framework of cybernetic expansion, a definition of the proletariat that implies certain continuities with "precariousness" as a characteristic inherent in its condition. And in this direction, although Dyer-Witheford coincides with Huws regarding the emerging characteristic of these workers, he also makes certain nuances about the conditions of global capitalism, traversed by primitive forms of accumulation, mainly in the Global South—which require us to think in the same range the coexistence of "cyborgs" and "slaves" (Dyer-Witheford 2015). This is a growing concern in a field of studies that seeks to find categories to bring together the multiple experiences contained in the category of digital labour. In this direction, Fuchs and Sandoval (2015) highlight that heterogeneity of labour experiences that entail diverse work organization, different work environments and a wide array of contractual relationships, among others. From this perspective, digital labour includes all those workers involved in the production chains of the digital commodity: both the miner who obtains lithium in almost slavery conditions, and the programmers who experience flexible working conditions. In order to characterize the diverse expressions of these forms of work, Fuchs and Sandoval (2015) propose a series of criteria (see Fig. 3.1) that include the form of the concurrence between workers and employers, as well as the characteristics in which the necessary interactions for production are established, distinguishing in the experience between those who use (or do not use) the Internet for economic purposes. In addition, following this scheme, the tools can be digital or non-digital, as well as the distribution and consumption of the products achieved with these activities. While these, as well as the object on which they work, can be digital, non-digital, or combine both characteristics.

Following this scheme for an operational definition, Fuchs and Sandoval (2015) identify a list that includes 1728 possible forms of digital informational labour, that is, they cover the possible expressions of the digital informational workforce that interact with specific production relationships. However, there is the question about the requirement of a minimum number of criteria previously presented so that an experience can be considered as digital labour.

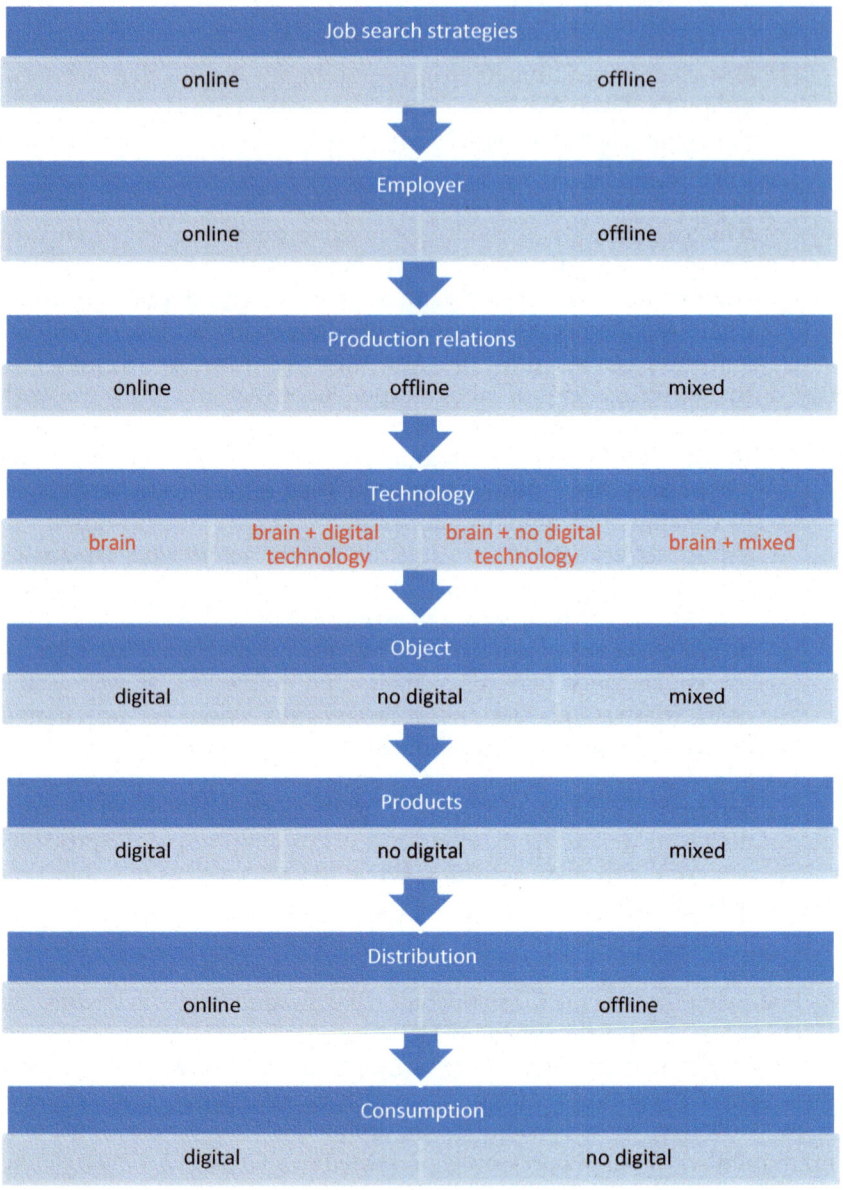

Fig. 3.1 Informational digital workers. (Own elaboration based on Fuchs and Sandoval 2015)

In summary, beyond the important contributions that these different perspectives make about the complexity of digital labour, it is interesting to note that the need to resolve the different discussions outlined is inextricably linked to the concern to redefine the broader structuration process in which the work experiences in question are inscribed ("cognitive capitalism", "platform capitalism", "sharing economy",[2] "prosumer capitalism", among others). It is in this sense the perspective we want to propose, about a sociology of sensibilities, seeks precisely to focus on the mediations-connections between the different dilemmas posed (see Fig. 3.2).

In other words, starting from the discussion about the body/emotions linked to digital labour, this perspective seeks to establish the mediations between the vitality of bodies and emotions as an object of exploitation. It tries to inquire about the redefinition of corporality associated with the

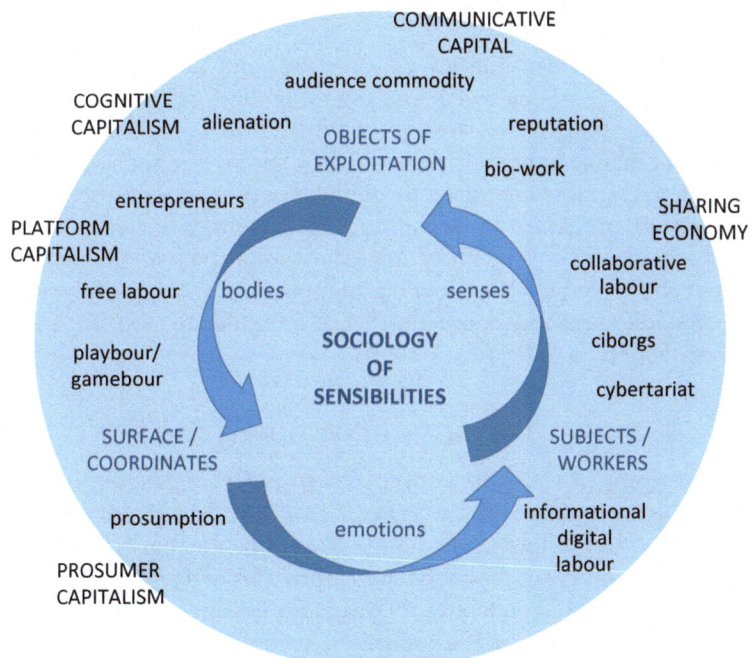

Fig. 3.2 Digital labour/sociology of sensibilities. (Own elaboration)

[2] For a gaze on sharing economy see in this book Chap. 8: "Sharing economy, sharing emotions in the Society 4.0. A study of the consumption and sensibilities in the Digital Era in China".

surface where digital devices/technologies are deployed, seeking the connection between these elements and the processes of accumulation and reproduction of the capitalist structures of Society 4.0.

In this sense it is interesting to note that when reflecting on the use of technology on that classification scheme, the authors associate informational labour with the "use of the brain", so that beyond the possible combinations with digital technologies or the non-digital, this always intervenes in the process. It is perhaps at this point that we can begin to rethink the definition of digital labour, questioning this naturalized relationship between brain and information, for which we propose to recover some contributions from a sociology of sensibilities.

Thus, by complexing the questions and the understanding of the uses of the body beyond the Cartesian split body/mind, we propose to put as a centre of reflection the sensibilities constructed as conditions and result of the interaction between body-working conditions and digital technologies.

The politics of sensibilities can be thought of as an articulation-mediation between Society 4.0 and digital labour, that is, as the result of the questions about which are the cognitive-affective practices linked to production, management and reproduction of the horizons of action, disposition and cognition required by digital labour. From this perspective, it is necessary to understand in what sense the advent of Society 4.0 relies on the management (intervention and transformation) of the senses, and therefore, how digital labour involves significant reshaping of the management of bodies/emotions aimed at capturing and metabolizing the vital energies of subjects and social systems.

KNOWING TOUCH AND POLITICS OF THE SENSES

From our point of view, the central axis to reflect on these "digital relationships" is to understand the changes from the standpoint of operating surfaces. One of the important points is vehicles for registration on these surfaces: eyes, fingers and ears. There is thus a triangle of expropriation of surplus instantiated in watching, playing and listening, as these senses are reconfigured in our societies. Consider, to contextualize this metamorphosis, the implication of the expansion of "touch" as technological mediation through the daily lives of millions of people from relatively "short time" ago. This mediation is, from the perspective that come up, a reconfiguration of the "politics of the senses" whose implications must be weighed regarding social structuring processes a global scale.

Thus, we consider that humans know, build and rebuild the world in and through our bodies and emotions. The most elemental form of alluded contact is the social construction of the connections between sensory impressions, perceptions and sensations. Through their bodies, social agents impact through a set of impressions in the forms of "exchange" with the socio-environmental context. Thus, objects, phenomena, processes and other agents structure perceptions, understood as naturalized ways of organizing the set of impressions. This framework configures the sensations that agents "make" of what can be designated as the internal and external world, the social, subjective and "natural" world, thus recreating a dialectic between impression and perception, which results in the "sense" of surplus—more here and beyond—of the sensations. The social production of sensations implies a modulation of the senses: smell, taste, touch, hearing and sight only to mention those that we might call "primaries". After thousands of years on the planet human beings are the only species that can design, create, manage, reproduce (and commodify) the aforementioned senses.

The systemic intervention on the senses has generated specific a politics about them; there is an expropriation and depredation of the senses. The capacities for use of the senses are distributed not only in diverse ways but also in an unequal way.

Geometries of bodies and grammars of actions are organized largely by the influence of the politics of the senses. The proximity and distances between the social agents imply the social value of the smell, the proper forms of the touch, the acceptable ways of listening, the standards of the look and the appetizing taste, and these are the components of a politics of the senses.

A politics of hearing implies how we configure a map of the environment, what are the components of equilibrium with the real, and a modality for classifying situations. From the record industry, through the massive access to information, to the balance between demand/supply versus bureaucracy are the sociabilities of the constructed listening modalities.

A politics of taste is based on the "between" generated by taste, food and stress hunger/enjoyment. In today's global contemporary world, eating has become an experience of hunger for millions and enjoyment for the few. From the author's food, through the mass media dedicated to the "kitchen", the academic formalization of the craft of cooking, up to the products offered as gourmet, eating and enjoying converge in the notion of "having an experience".

A politics of the look involves the connection between seeing, looking and observing. Seeing refers to perceiving objects by the eyes through the action of light; looking is to direct the sight to an object, taking it into consideration, and observing involves the action of examining carefully. Each phase of structuration social processes has its specific scopic regime.

The politics of smell implies a classification system of subjects and environments guided by olfactory sensations that are based on multiple distinctions that establish moral values. This establishes an odour detection threshold and with it a minimum of proximity and distance with other people and environments. The industry for body scents, flavouring for clothes and perfumes for the home, are some of the main objects of the huge business of smell.

The politics of touch refers to the articulation and disarticulation between proximity/distance with other bodies, the sensory possibilities through the hand and the skin (in general) and the social values of touching. Making contact through the body with others is an object of design, construction and management, especially in the context of the Society 4.0. In other words, at this time in the global structuration processes, there are inaugurated renewed conditions of receptivity relationships with others (social relationship) and the other (as a close person): the culture of touch. But appointed by a sense colonized by the "overlapping of the senses", this culture of touching and touch is a "different" way of inhabiting the world.

Phones, heaters, air conditioners, car locks, refrigerators, televisions, computers, tablets are all or can be, at present, digital objects. In www. macstories.net/ managed by Federico Vittici you can read about, the already old, Iphone 7 and its haptic system:

> The haptic feedback provides tactile feedback, such as a touch that draws attention and reinforces both actions the events. While many interface elements provided by the system (for example, switches, switches and controllers) automatically provide haptic feedback, you can use generators feedback to add their own feedback to views and custom controls. (www.macstories. net 2016)

As we suggested, we are engaged in a process that has been called Society 4.0 and it is strongly associated with what we call "era of touch".

In this direction, a major puzzle of the twenty-first century revolves around sensibilities:

1. Brain, nutrients, endocrine disruptors, "nano" and genomic life management are the central edges of the material conditions of life in the twenty-first century, social ways to produce, concentrate and play with power.
2. The social forms of the immediate entail specific surfaces where particular experiential conditions are assumed and sociabilities are supposed. The immediate is a special "here-now" that redefines the present.
3. The conditions of productivity and the commodification of sensations are united in a common "pre-origin" that is elaborated in the "use-the-body" to relate to the instruments/machines/apparatuses.

Social practices take the texture of the materiality of the body/emotion, feeling density and processuality of the senses. Social ways of connecting with the world have moved to the hands, fingers and the fingertips, first with communication tools, but also with the means of payment, entertainment centres and apparatus for cooking and cleaning. We live literally pressing keys, sliding, touching and "clicking"; our day-to-day life is filled with cell phones, credit cards, transport payment cards, cookers, microwaves and so on, which have been intertwined between social classes, genders, ethnicities and ages.

In societies that paradoxically are spectacularized yet reconcentrated individually, which excite "all" but are limited to the closest, are companies that redefine the politics of touch, the conditions of the rules/rules of play, of touching and being touched. It is precisely here that it makes sense to ask about the politics of sensibilities, as that set of cognitive-affective social practices tending to the production, management and reproduction of horizons of action, disposition and cognition (Scribano 2017).

The politics of sensibilities involve politics of the senses: hearing, sight, touch, taste and smell. All politics of the senses are activities in order to resolve situations (sensu Thomas), to be successful in the social presentation of the person (sensu Goffman), and develop knowledge at hand (sensu Schütz) that subjects use, and it is in the context of these politics that touch becomes relevant.

Social relationships have been modified in accordance with a metaphor of "the press a button", pressing "play", touching the screen, clicking on a point to interact with the instruments and also with people. They express moving subjects, plunging sensitive parts of the apparatus, and in order to see or do more with this action, they have to "know how play". This is the actual approach, if it does not eliminate the "know how" and "know what" (typical of the disputes of the twentieth century), redefines access to world. The Social Bot Era is a space-time where the borderline between the superfluous, the prostheses and the "extensions" is diluted within the "friendliness" of the interfaces to buy/enjoy. In this context, "touching" more than a skill is a condition of cognitive/affective possibility of "being in the world".

COMMODIFICATION AND EXPROPRIATION AROUND DIGITAL LABOUR FROM THE STANDPOINT OF A SOCIOLOGY OF SENSIBILITIES

A consequence of the previously described transformations refers to the update of surplus expropriation mechanisms as a spiralling process connecting what is produced as sight, elaborated as touch and executed as listening. In this section, we explore some dimensions of such expropriation process based on the experiences of young workers in Call Centres in Argentina. We will present data obtained though in-depth interviews and virtual ethnography field notes.[3]

The lived experiences of youths become paradigmatic of the reflections we present here in two ways. First, because the expansion of the Call Centres sector, especially in the global South, condenses a gamut of trends inherent to restructuration of capitalist production. The production of informational services on an industrial scale is a privileged field for observing the contradictions and ambivalences of contemporary work in general (Braga 2009). In addition, youths employed in companies within this sector are also the protagonists of the ever more intense "digital life" in these countries: the numbers that confirm the expansion of Internet (in terms of

[3] The data used in this article was gathered as part of a research project funded by CONICET: since 2007 we have been engaged in and completed, at least, more than 20 interviews with members of organizations linked to the sector in the city of Córdoba, Argentina, and a virtual ethnographic gathering of data from blogs, Facebook profiles and Web sites of the work organizations linked to Call Centres.

family and personal connections through smartphones), the exponential growth of social network profiles (Facebook, Instagram etc.), and the conflictive presence of numerous workers' groups who "activate" through these networks, as a whole, constitute relevant data that link the experiences of these subjects to the emergence of a sociability implied in "living in network". In other words, the experience of Call Centre workers is a valid way to problematize the linkages between expropriation, sensibilities and digital labour/life.

In this direction, and in the context of the interactions deployed from the expansion referred to in the digital revolution, eyes, sight, a glance or a friendly environment are all developed and reproduced in a habitus "of-being-in-network".

In this way, concurrently with the expansion of Internet-mediated interactions, we observe the advent of a phenomenal development of digital technologies aimed at "rendering productive" the elaboration-circulation-sale of information. Systems that operate regulating the "conversation" of Call Centre (CC) operators—that is, demarcating the quality standards that translate the speaking ability into an informational service—have a distinct nature and texture. We could thus mention the complex organizational technology that sets the disposition of teamwork, quality manuals and "problem-response trees", among other elements that guide the discursive reactions of CC operators, to the headsets, computers and information systems that "command" every interaction (with the client, supervisors, external companies that conduct quality control etc.). However, the balance that this multiple configuration of elements has for workers' everyday life is linked to the configuration of an environment that, as we just said, entangles the sense of the action of "looking at the screen".

(...) the system cannot corroborate that you hang up calls, but they appear as hung up by the clients, they lost signal or any other reason. The only manner in which [the company] can verify the hanging up of calls is through screen monitoring. (Interview 12: Call Centre Worker)

(...) You have reception desk assistants (specific form to be logged in) that enables you getting the call through. When the conversation ends, you have two systems: a digital one that you seen in the computer, or a database (....) When you finish the communication, you can allow the client to hang up, without touching anything the communication remains in standby. It remains there accumulating minutes allowing you to enable you to get settled (...). (Interview 09: Call Centre Worker)

From the CC operators' voice, "looking" in the digital workplace is not only "reading" instructions on the screen, but subjects are also "seen", they are monitored (controlled). Seeing entails the ability to "join" (log into) the (digital) system, deploying a set of capabilities, where the screen is not only a mark in the unidirectional communication flow (to see or be seen), and the "eye" is not only an instrument of perception. Screen, eye and action are redefined in/through the digital labour.

Extending this relationship, we could establish that looking, seeing and observing, connection and resetting, articulate what for them was indicated in social research. It is then possible, following this distinction, to analyse the realization of an "optical profit", which is nothing more and nothing less than the "on work" eye as part of the body, as visual system and as the subject's environment. The screen as visual field, as the eye surface intervention, in turn becomes the iterative set of relationships that allow the expropriation of knowledge, that is, "human" skills/abilities/capabilities.

To advance further in these discussions, we could appeal to the etymologies of the terms used to problematize digital labour, drawing on certain clues:

I. The first of these leads us back to the relationship between "View = admire = laugh." Here, look corresponds to admire and admired, because you look so striking. It looks and is looking toward a place, a process object, an agent, a human being, yet one sees itself is directed. In looking there, a quantum reflexivity look that captures (and catches) a funny and perceptive field slowly. Why "you look" is also akin to the "laugh" or taken as object of the process that is given me, lightly but seductively, and connects with something that calls me (why I get involved in what I see). This relationship is evident in one of the expressive forms of conflict in the CC sector, such as the enormous quantity of "memes" that different work unions distribute through social networks. As it can be observed both in the content of the memes and in the words of interviewed workers, the "visual" element of the mobilisation strategy is related to the expanded disposition where the production-dissemination and appropriation of those images are registered in the space where the looking-laughing widens the (self) perception of what the sectoral conflict implies for society.

(...) A guy had a website back then, with animations, it was really good. And he started searching for information in the Internet about the managers. We found information to mock them, so to speak, to bolster the struggle. We did demonstrations outside the company, with *pintadas* (graphic expression). We talked to the neighbours, for example, we left leaflets in bakeries, so that local neighbours could know what was going on therein. That was cool, because in that area there are many buildings, and we tagged the streets with the website, so people visited the site to see what was going on and cracked up, and greeted us. (Interview 10: Call Centre Worker)

As such, if the expansion of labour in CC takes place without any criticism of the working conditions in the sector, "digital humour" opens up the possibility of a reflective gaze that highlights the activity in its context, widening the perceptual horizon.

Nevertheless, this practice of looking is a human skill, and once commodified, it transforms but also reproduces environments. That is, when I look I am producing distraction, relaxation and fun. Here "look" is linked to entertainment and business. Going back to the situation of CC workers, despite the fact that social networks and "memes" have contributed to breaking the perceptive frontiers of the "benefits" of "working in a CC", thereby opening space for the emergence of work union collective identities in the sector, "digital actions" have however concentrated almost all protest energies of these subjects. Therefore, in terms of body dispositions, an exploited worker at his/her work desk directs the attention in "looking at the screen" just as much as it is done by the one protesting while sat down in his/her home, in front of the laptop, or "activating" through Facebook profiles. Virtual channels are thus the privileged means to—in the form of spectacle/business—process visual capabilities in a comfortable and pleasant manner, both the productive and the surplus capabilities.

II. It becomes another track from the relationship between "View = know = witness". With this game it involves "seeing" as that which lies on the potential of the "presence as knowing", seeing and witnessing what I'm getting, is constituted as a knowing being. Thus, "see" is an area that in the experience of the web disembodies. It is a presence that makes us know without the "need" to put flesh and bones, becoming a renewed way of knowing eyeless the present.

Thus, for instance, the life experiences of emerging work union forms in the Call Centre sector reveal the aforementioned redefinition between looking, knowing and being. A female worker who participates in a work union that manages without face-to-face meetings affirms:

> We have met (in face-to-face meetings) in the last 9 months (...). The organisation operates by twitter, by email, mouth of word, the ladies goad, tweet, post in Facebook (...). This is beautiful. We are organising ourselves... we will use against the company the very same tools the company used against us. (Interview 12: Call Centre Worker)

The certainty of the existence of an "us" as a testimony of an incipient collective body does without the interaction "face-to-face" as the traditional field where individual biographies blend in a collective story. Instead, "being" is linked to the everyday life that, mediated by social networks, enables subjects to "recognize themselves" as members of the collective. "Seeing" a post in Facebook or a tweet or an email is for them a knowledge action that confirms the presence/existence of others with whom they have never met "face-to-face", with whom they have never shared a co-presence space, and whose only materiality is translated in the combination of zeros and ones in their particular impression in/from "the visual".

Seeing/me/you/us on Internet, it is a "testimony without organs" that supports a radical relocation and enables instant, simultaneous and overlapping bodies/emotions that are not in "co-presence" spoliation. This relocation is a product that is expensive, which only few can afford and that many produce without charging.

> III. Finally, the third track is linked to the relationship between "Note = retain = register". There is then, in watching a game of "interlacing in the register", that is, a way to capture keeping in memory. The observer constructs a period of time, recorded in such a way that "sees" an event structure arranged for another time/space: for after update.

In the experience of Call Centre workers, the aim of having a "chat" with a client (either by telephone or Internet-based platforms) as well as what the eye seeks in the "system"/software that regulates the interaction, is structured "at full speed" to be processed in the time-space of effectiveness:

(...) I felt a lot of pressure in the eyes, especially because I was in front of the computer for long hours (...). You are useful only as long as you are effective (...). (Interview 12: Call Centre Worker)

(E: how did you realise that you learned the profession of Call Centre operator?)

I: With the speed: the speed with applications, having various windows [simultaneously], the visual quickness. When I realised that I could speak with the client and, while listening to him, opening several windows and checking the number, controlling the used minutes with the deducted minutes, because they are different applications, these are different windows in the same system (...). That explains the feeling when you call [a Call Centre] that they are not listening to you. They are not listening to you, [the operator] is trying to detect –as you are doing right now. You are looking for my answer, I am a chatterbox, you are searching for something and when you feel that I mention it, you adjust, then readjust and ask again, until you find the answer, so to speak. (Interview 12: Call Centre Worker)

The observer is a registrant, retainer and "buffer", while "observing" becomes a quest that has identified the sought on "watch". All this comes as a production process where "digital life" is linked to capturing the experience of an event.

These approaches to looking, seeing and observing allow us to read the commodification and practices of expropriation in the virtual world. Thus, it stands first a dialectic of the skill of human beings to intuit the real and produce through the eye. Secondly, a process of spiralling tensions between design, production and distribution of events, and through this the view is established. Lastly, superimposed commodification thus establishes the ability to perform an overall record through the virtual observation.

CONCLUDING NOTES

Initially, we could argue that the evidence shows that, in the context of the Society 4.0, sensibilities have been transformed in the privileged space of profit production and capitalist exploitation.

Digital labour articulating/disarticulating the seeing, touching and listening puts perception chains assembled in and through senses at the centre of a set of actions to create, manage, reproduce and appropriate the surplus of digital practices.

In this context, modalities of politics of sensibilities are created in a way that coincide with digital forms of labour generation and management: labour produces sensations in which the commodity logic and the metamorphosis of twenty-first-century fetishism are engraved.

The current capitalist emphasis on design, production, management, reproduction and dissemination of sensations impacts on work modalities as well as the content and volume of possible expropriation.

Politics of sensibilities are immersed in a set of geometries of the bodies and grammar of actions that suffer significant metamorphosis in the framework of digital labour: the notion of proximity with the produced is redefined, relationships with other workers are modified, bonds with clients/demanders are restructured, hierarchical vehicles and forms are transformed, among other phenomena.

REFERENCES

Andrejevic, M. (2012). Exploitation in the Data Mine. In C. Fuchs, B. Kees, A. Anders, & M. Sandoval (Eds.), *Internet and Surveillance: The Challenges of Web 2.0 and Social Media* (pp. 71–88). New York: Routledge.

Armano, E., Murgia, A., & Teli, M. (2017). *Plataform capitalism e confini del lavoro negli spazi digitali*. Milan: Mimesis.

Arwid, L. (2015). A Contribution to a Critique of the Concept Playbour. In E. Fisher & C. Fuchs (Eds.), *Reconsidering Value and Labour in the Digital Age* (pp. 63–79). Westminster: Palgrave Macmillan.

Aytes, A. (2013). Return of the Crowds: Mechanical Turk and Neoliberal States of Exception. In T. Scholz (Ed.), *Digital Labor. The Internet as Playground and Factory* (pp. 100–124). New York: Routledge.

Berg, J. (2016). *Inclusive Labour Markets, Labour Relations and Working Conditions Branch*. Conditions of Work and Employment Series, No. 74. Geneva: International Labour Office.

Bergvall-Kåreborn, B., & Howcroft, D. (2014). Amazon Mechanical Turk and the Commodification of Labour. *New Technology, Work and Employment, 29*(3), 213–223.

Braga, R. (2009). A vigança de Braverman: o infotaylorismo como contratempo. In R. Antunes & R. Braga (Eds.), *Infoproletários. Degradaçao real do trabalho virtual* (pp. 59–88). São Paulo: Boitempo.

Cherry, M. (2011). A Taxonomy of Virtual Work. *Georgia Law Review, 45*(4), 954–1009.

Cingolani, P. (2016). Capitalismo de plataforma: nuevas tecnologías de la comunicación e internacionalización del trabajo. *Boletín Onteaiken, 22*, 42–47.

Dyer-Witheford, N. (2015). *Cyber-proletariat. Global Labour in the Digital Vortex*. London: Pluto Press.

Fisher, E. (2012). How Less Alienation Creates More Exploitation? Audience Labour on Social Network Sites. *tripleC: Communication, Capitalism & Critique-Journal for a Global Sustainable Information Society, 10*(2), 171–183.

Fisher, E., & Fuchs, C. (Eds.). (2015). *Reconsidering Value and Labour in the Digital Age*. Westminster: Palgrave Macmillan.

Fuchs, C. (2014). *Digital Labour and Karl Marx*. London: Routledge.

Fuchs, C., & Sandoval, M. (2015). Digital Workers of the World Unite! A Framework for Critically Theorising and Analysing Digital Labour. *TripleC, 12*(2), 486–563.

Fumagalli, A. (2015). The Concept of Subsumption of Labour to Capital: Towards Life Subsumption in Bio-cognitive Capitalism. In E. Fisher & C. Fuchs (Eds.), *Reconsidering Value and Labour in the Digital Age* (pp. 224–245). Westminster: Palgrave Macmillan.

Graham, M., Hjorth, I., & Lehdonvirta, V. (2017). Digital Labour and Development: Impacts of Global Digital Labour Platforms and the Gig Economy on Worker Livelihoods. *European Review of Labour and Research, 23*(2), 135–162.

Hearn, A. (2010). Structuring Feeling: Web 2.0, Online Ranking and Rating, and the Digital "Reputation Economy". *Ephemera: Theory & Politics in Organization, 10*(3/4), 421–438.

Huws, U. (2013). *The Making of a Cybertariat: Virtual Work in a Real World*. New York: Monthly Review Press.

Huws, U. (2014). *Labor in the Global Digital Economy. The Cybertariat Comes of Age*. New York: Monthly review Press.

Huws, U. (2015). *A Review on the Future of Work: Online Labour Exchanges, or 'Crowdsourcing': Implications for Occupational Safety and Health*. Bilbao: European Agency for Safety and Health at Work, Discussion Paper.

Huws, U. (2016). Working Online, Living Offline: Labour in the Internet Age. *Work Organisation, Labour & Globalisation, 7*(1), 1–11.

Irani, L. (2015). Difference and Dependence Among Digital Workers: The Case of Amazon Mechanical Turk. *South Atlantic Quarterly, 114*(1), 225–234.

Kosnik, A. (2013). Fandom as Free Labor. In T. Sholz (Ed.), *The Internet as Playground and Factory* (pp. 125–144). New York: Routledge.

McKenzie, W. (2013). Considerations on a Hacker Manifesto. In T. Sholz (Ed.), *The Internet as Playground and Factory* (pp. 91–99). New York: Routledge.

Meil, P., & Kirov, V. (2017). *Policy Implications of Virtual Work*. London: Palgrave Macmillan.

Michailidou, M., & Kostala, E. (2016). Young Entrepreneurs and Creative Collectives: Greek New Media Workers in Constant Crisis. In J. Webster & K. Randle (Eds.), *Virtual Workers and the Global Labour Market* (pp. 57–76). London: Palgrave Macmillan.

Morini, C., & Fumagalli, A. (2010). Life Put to Work: Towards a Life Theory of Value. *Ephemera: Theory & Politics in Organization, 10*(3/4), 234–252.

Nixon, B. (2015). The Exploitation of Audience Labour: A Missing Perspective on Communication and Capital in the Digital Era. In E. Fisher & C. Fuchs (Eds.), *Reconsidering Value and Labour in the Digital Age* (pp. 99–114). Westminster: Palgrave Macmillan.

Olivier, F., & O'Neil, M. (2015). *Digital Labour and Prosumer Capitalism. The US Matrix.* London: Palgrave Macmillan.

Ritzer, G., & Jurgenson, N. (2010). Production, Consumption, Presumption. *Journal of Consumer Culture, 10*(1), 13–36.

Scribano, A. (2017). *Normalization, Enjoyment and Bodies/Emotions: Argentine Sensibilities.* New York: Nova Science.

Smythe, D. W. (1977). Communications: Blindspot of Western Marxism. *Canadian Journal of Political and Social Theory, 1*(3), 1–27.

Terranova, T. (2013). Free Labor. In T. Scholz (Ed.), *Digital Labor. The Internet as Playground and Factory* (pp. 46–78). New York: Routledge.

Toffler, A. (1980). *The Third Wave.* New York: Bantam.

Vercellone, C. (Ed.). (2006). *Capitalismo Cognitivo.* Rome: Manifestolibri.

CHAPTER 4

Location and Data Visualisation Culture in Chile

Francisco Osorio

INTRODUCTION

As Wilken and Goggin (2015) argued in the book *Locative Media*, we are witnessing different practices, uses, meanings, emotions, and possibilities (among other aspects of social life) because people are using location technology, mainly through mobile phones. They define locative media as the use of information, data, sounds, and images about location (although they say the definition is challenged by the complexity of real-life experiences). Why is this important? Because, as they say, it is the emergent media of our time.

The anthropological question is how this technology is being used in different cultural settings. The literature review is very short as well as the case studies. In this text we address the question by focusing on Chile because it is a country in the global South where technology is increasingly used intensively in people's daily life.

Yet, there is little research dedicated to understanding location technology in Latin America. There is a 2015 study in Mexico (Goggin and

F. Osorio (✉)
University of Chile, Santiago, Chile
e-mail: fosorio@uchile.cl

© The Author(s) 2019
A. Scribano, P. Lisdero (eds.), *Digital Labour, Society and the Politics of Sensibilities*, https://doi.org/10.1007/978-3-030-12306-2_4

Albarran-Torres 2015), on the *Geolocalization Law* of 2011 that gave more power to law enforcement to access mobile phone data (not only calls but also location). Brazil has attracted many studies on augmented reality, location services and urban space, as well as locative mobile media. For instance, Lemos (2011) has argued that previous forms of use of communication technology were independent of context (place) but today augmented reality examples in urban spaces have merged together technology and place for different objectives. Nevertheless, it is hard to find studies in Latin America.

One obvious stumbling block is the lack of a common word in the dominant languages used in Latin America to signify location. If we take the English word *location* and make a rough translation into 'locación' (just changing a *t* for a *c* plus the accent on the last vowel), the meaning would be different for our purposes. According to the Spanish Royal Academy of Language, the Spanish word 'locación' comes from the Latin *locatio* and it is a legal term for lending a property (but this meaning is no longer in use in common Spanish). Today 'locación' means place as, for example, a film production crew looking for a place to shoot a scene (same idea of the famous expression 'location, location, location'). Therefore, the rough translation of media location as 'medios de locación' makes no sense in Spanish.

We propose that the Spanish translation of media location is 'medios de localización'. If we make the same exercise but from Spanish to English, the word 'localización' means localise. According to the *Merriam-Webster* dictionary, there are two meanings for localise. The first refers to keep something within a limited area (which is not the case in Spanish). The second is to find or identify the location of something. This is exactly the Spanish meaning of 'localización'. Perhaps that is the reason why mobile phone operative systems in Spanish activate this function using the word 'localización'. English operative systems use location.

If we consider another language, for example, that of the Mapuche people from Chile, in their language the word 'pen' refers to see or find. So, to talk about location, they say: I saw it, I found it (pefiñ). The concept of location, we could argue, is a personal or direct action by the speaker in their language.

Both the English and Spanish languages also relate to this discussion of the concept of the local. In a literature review in Spanish academic databases (such as scielo.org and redalyc.org) the concepts 'locación' and 'localización' refer mainly to the debate about globalisation, the local being the opposite of the global or, as some academics say, something in between such as 'glocal' (both global and local). It is possible to expect in years to come Spanish research articles using 'medios de localización' in the sense of media location.

But language moves fast. In the middle of the 2000s, a new concept started to be used by news agencies, the government, and universities: data visualisation. The concept is very clear to the public because graphics that represent data has a long history in the media. In that context, what is the new is the strong Internet culture of Chileans that allows them to visit a governmental site (such as the Ministry of Education), locate a school (in the search box), and have a map and statistics of the school to interact with using a web page. Data is not only available but shown interactively on a website.

As location technology and the mobile phone have merged with smartphones, the history is so short that almost all the reporting in here is only a couple of years old. For writing this text, raw data was hard to obtain, so the main source of information used were public sources and direct observation. From 2014 to 2017 Chilean national newspapers were read daily to find information. A Google alert was also created about location services in Chile and the keyword was used on social networks to find out some more information. Governmental websites were also used and the author was always trying to find new information and examples, even by word of mouth. The result of that process forms the empirical data for this text.

LEGAL CONTEXT IN CHILE

The first time Chilean law used the concept of location (in the sense of this text) was in 1997. It was the general law No. 19,521 (http://bcn.cl/1oz7m) for fishing and agriculture, establishing as mandatory the use of an automatic geographical positioning system with satellite support for all fishing and research boats. The purpose of the Chilean Fishing Office was to track down information for the monitoring, control, and surveillance of offshore ships to make decisions about administration and management of biological resources. If a licensed fishing boat did not transmit location information within six hours, it was requested by authorities by radio.

It is interesting that the first use of the concept refers to boats' location, so the fishing industry is the one connecting information and public policies about natural resources in the current trends—data is transformed into information to make decisions. It also makes sense in Chile because the fishing industry is key to the economy and a source of conflict about the use of the sea with neighbouring countries and the wider Pacific region.

The second object Chilean legislation was interested to locate was vehicles. In 2002 the Office of Transport and Telecommunications issued the regulation No. 677 (http://bcn.cl/1u0sa) making mandatory for all public transport in Santiago to use a location device and established the Vehicle Automatic Location Service. The location of every bus is sent to a control centre using the mobile phone network or radiofrequency. The centre is run by a private company that can only pass information to the Public Transport Division inside the Office of Transport and Telecommunications.

With that data, the Chilean government transformed Santiago's public transport in 2007, creating the first use of a contactless smart card for an integrated bus system run by private companies, called *Transantiago*. Although still in use, it falls short of promises, such as an efficient distribution of frequencies between buses (even when the control centre can map their location and inform drivers). Other failed promises were bus shelter monitors informing how far away a bus was. What it is possible to use and work well (data from 2015 to 2017) are mobile phone apps informing the bus location in relation to the user, if the phone is connected to the Internet. An SMS service is also provided if the user texts the bus shelter code to the Transantiago control centre.

In 2002 Chilean law used for the time the word GPS in the context of the mining industry referring to the Global Positioning System technology. It is a technical document (regulation No. 3576) created by the Mining and Geological Office (part of the Ministry of Mining) setting up the standards for the whole industry. That legislation was updated in 2013 (regulation No. 3576) and among the jargon the text says that technological advances are moving fast so that the legislation needs to be in line to allow government offices to process data to better serve the country in all aspects related to mining.

In 2005 the word GPS was also used to regulate bus services in the second major city of the country, called Concepcion, making it mandatory to 'use a Global Positioning System (GPS) to capture, process, register and transmit information related to the operation of the public transport' (regulation No. 2246).

That word fixed in the minds of Chileans, making GPS a noun commonly used in colloquial language referring to location technologies. Interestingly, the first time the term 'mobile phone' was used in Chilean law was in 1982 within the General Law No. 18,168 that regulated all aspects of telecommunications (http://bcn.cl/1lyp6). That awarded the first public service licence in 1988 for mobile phone operations to the Chilean Telephone Company (which no longer exists) by the regulation No. 189 (http://bcn.cl/1twqw). So today Chileans say that their mobile phones have GPS features.

LOCATION EXPERIENCES

In this section we describe how location technologies have entered into Chile, both in the public and private sectors, with some references to university experiences and other sectors.

Public Sector

In 2014 the government published the document 'Chilean Policy on Geospatial Information: Decision making with landscape information' (IDE 2014). During the early 2000s, the Office of National Assets came up with the diagnostic that more than 80% of public decisions were based on location data, but there were no centralised ways to access that information for decision making. If the Chilean government wanted to use more efficiently its scare resources, some coordination was needed between all the parties involved. That led to the creation in March 2006 of the Chilean Coordination System of Territorial Information by the presidential decree No. 28. The executive order also introduces some interesting ideas. It argues that information about public goods are public and, therefore, it should be transparent to citizens. It also highlights the importance of information and communication technology and proposes to use the concept of 'electronic government' (that idea did not succeed in the long run). Therefore, location information should be available on the Internet, freely. By 2013 that system transformed into IDE-Chile, the unit of Spatial Data Infrastructure, under the Office of National Assets. On its website (www.ide.cl) it is possible to access information about agriculture, transport, health, weather, water, energy, earthquakes, and city planning, among other kind of location data.

Although the information is updated and all government units must comply, still the website is not widely used or known to the wider public (and sometimes the information is hard to get). They declare that the Chilean policy on geospatial information tries to address those issues based on the principles of relevance, opportunity, quality, independence, collaboration, transparency, and availability, among others. Nevertheless, their efforts remain widely unknown.

In 2015 this unit conducted the international seminar 'Territorial information for public management and citizen access' (IDE 2015). Among the speakers were Abbas Rajabifard and Ged Griffin (Melbourne University), Stuart Frye (NASA), Alex Barth (Open Street Map), Rolando Ocampo, and Antonio Arozarena (United Nations Initiative on Global Geospatial Information Management or GGIM).

The IDE Director, Alvaro Monett, argued that it is possible to have more diverse and higher quality information, accessible and usable for the government and citizens, to make informed decisions at the national and local level. The model is to have IDE units inside every high-level office and regional or local government. In 2015 the central IDE unit managed to have 800 layers of information on everything one can imagine, such as car accidents, justice programmes for the youth or places to visit on holidays. By 2016 they created 23 ISO standards.

In that seminar, United Nations speakers mentioned that in August 2013 the American chapter of the GGIM was created (meaning all the countries in the continent, not just the USA). The first meeting was held in Mexico in September 2014. The objective is to share statistical and geographical information, research climate change, create standards, and give assistance on spatial data infrastructure to country members. The University of Melbourne and NASA speakers addressed management of global and natural disasters. Open Street speakers addressed the collaboration between citizens and the government. There were also university researchers, regional level officers and local NGOs speaking on different subjects ranging from smart cities to weather information.

By 2011, the Ministry of Education posted on its website the location of all the schools in a downloaded file (no longer available) to use with Google Earth. It was interesting that some information was also available as metadata, such as ownership (private, public, or semi-public in the Chilean case) and some basic school characteristics. By 2016 it had evolved to a dedicated website (www.mime.mineduc.cl) where all schools are on Google Maps with metadata, such as fees (some schools are free but others have monthly fees), if the school have been sanctioned, and the average score for the last three years in the math and language national test. The map also shows the location of nearby schools with the score pinned to them, so it is very easy to spot how well a given school is performing in comparison to others in the same area. Because it is a Google Map, you can see other information, such as traffic, public transport stops, and even the Street View option (if available).

The Ministry of Justice in 2014 used for the first time a GPS tracking bracelet for 5000 inmates in a partnership with the company SecureAlert. Those were the cases in which a sentence could be served in a house or restricted facility. That system continues to be used.

The Chilean National Bank (Banco del Estado) in 2015 made available on its mobile phone app all location information about ATMs, branches, offices, and other services related to this financial organisation. It was part of the campaign 'mobile bank' led by the institution.

The Chilean Police Force (www.carabineros.cl) in 2015 updated its own crime location system called 'System of Analysis of Territorial Information' (SAIT, originally created in 2010) where every report is mapped alongside some metadata: type, time, victim characteristics, and modus operandi, among others. The SAIT website is not available to the public but their reports are communicated by news organisations.

Also, in 2015, three institutions using police information created the website Crime Map (no longer available). Those are the Association of City Councils, the Observatory of City Council Security and the private company InstaGIS. It worked by entering a postal address and the site gave back crime statistics related to that place on a Google map. For example, if a serious crime was committed a week before, the area is flashed red while surrounding places are colour coded showing different crime frequencies by weeks, months, or years.

In 2016 the government started to discuss a new constitution with different levels of citizen participation. The most widely known by the media and the public were called 'local encounters'. It consisted in a gathering of 10–30 people, self-selected, residents on a local council that inscribed their meeting on a dedicated governmental website and followed a protocol (unaconstitucionparachile.cl). Among the information the group gave was the address where the meeting took place. Other information included some basic members' information, of course the content of what they discussed, and even a picture as a testimony of the event. The information is available through the government website datos.gob.cl.

Because every group informed the address, the Center for Semantic Web Research (ciws.cl) of the University of Chile, created a web application to explore concepts used in those local encounters. For example, in the search box you entered 'political parties' to see where in the country that concept was used. It could be zoomed to the local council level. All the information was displayed on an Open Street Map. The purpose was to 'map' the discussion to see where in the country some idea is considered for a new constitution, which allowed interesting comparisons at the regional and local level.

Private Sector

A study by Google and the company TNS in 2015 about what they call micro moments (Hernandez 2015) shows that 70% of Chileans use mobile phone apps to find an address and 25% use them daily for that purpose. This is higher than Argentina, Colombia, Mexico, and Peru (where the survey was also conducted). This is possible, according to Ana Gomez, Google Chile Marketing CEO, because 3G and 4G networks are pervasive and smartphones are the norm, rather than feature phones. Data from 2015 (published on 2016 by the Chilean government at subtel.gob.cl) shows that Internet access reached 13 million (in a country where the whole population is 17 million) and that 80% of those connections where made on smartphones.

The study defines micro moments as the action to pause a conversation or activity and search on the mobile phone for the following questions: I want to know (what time is the next bus), I want to buy (where is the nearest shop), I want to do (how to make a meal), and I want to go (the fastest route to the shopping mall). In Gomez' words, because information for Chileans is easy to access, they do not plan but rather move by impulse or ask questions on the fly over the Internet, so shopping become hazardous. That behaviour should only increase because in late 2015 Google maps allowed offline navigation in Chile for all mobile devices using the application, so even in the absence of a phone data contract or even Wi-Fi, users can navigate through the cities.

In this context, Uber is increasingly capturing interest in the capital city (as well as Cabify). In 2015 the city of London sanctioned that Uber was legal after lawsuits against the company. Sao Paulo in Brazil, Buenos Aires in Argentina, and Santiago in Chile also had protests by established taxi drivers, and some Chilean governmental officials have been quoted in the press arguing against Uber, but so far, Uber continues as usual despite all that. The relationship between mobile phone users and taxi drivers has existed since 2012 with Easy Taxi (a start-up of Rio de Janeiro), but they work with traditional black and yellow cabs. The company Safer Taxi also arrived in 2012, with the same business model. Uber is the third player in Santiago (arriving in 2014). By 2016 they were reaching five more cities. Uber claims that 10% of their drivers are women (partners they call them), six in ten partners own the car and they can make up to four times the Chilean minimum wage (in 2016 it was USD 390).

Location technologies for commercial vehicles have a longer history in the Chilean industrial sector. Because of the importance of mining industries, most vehicles have location devices on them. The public transport system also uses the same technology. As the prices go down, medium and small companies are also using location hardware and software to control and optimise their own vehicles and delivery services.

Some Santiago motorways are privately operated, so to use them, vehicles must have an electronic tag (the free flow system) that communicates the position to the company running that motorway in order to send the bill later for using a particular section of the road. It started in 2005. This is another example of how location technology became part of drivers' daily life and it is almost invisible to users' experience.

In 1999, a Chilean private company (Tastets System) registered the Internet domain www.gps.cl. It shows how GPS technology started to get the attention of local entrepreneurs. In 200 the company worked with the local telecommunication company Entel to track vehicles, but it was only in 2006 that they created the first mobile application to monitor commercial vehicles. They claim that in 2015 almost a quarter of local vehicles used their technology.

In 2011 only two car companies in Chile (Renault and Subaru) had navigation systems in some high-end models. For most regular car drivers, it was very expensive and useless because maps were inaccurate and satnavs were expensive. By 2013 it was another story. According to local car sellers, almost 40,000 were sold that year. By 2016 it was normal, a standard.

As average national income increased in the 2000s, high earning people use the technology in private cars in case of theft. Very expensive cars entered into the market and, alongside that, more car robberies, either to facilitate further crimes or to sell those vehicles in foreign countries. If before an alarm was a standard issue on cars (old and new), today location technology for car tracking is becoming the norm.

By 2016 car navigation hardware (satnavs) became less frequent as the mobile phone provides today's mapping and turn-by-turn services. Also, as display monitors were integrated into cars, drivers connected their smart phones by Bluetooth for navigation while listening to music. The most popular apps are Waze and Google Maps. Drivers have different reasons to prefer one or another and sometimes they used them indistinctly.

Universities and Other Local Experiences

The University Diego Portales is developing the System of Accessible Geolocation Information (www.sigachile.cl), a website and an app for people with mobile disabilities around the city of Santiago. Displayed on a Google map, it shows using colours how accessible a place is or the facilities it includes for people with special needs.

The Centre for Social Conflict and Cohesion Studies (www.coes.cl) published in 2015 the first Chilean survey on conflict, inequality, and location. The multidisciplinary team made several reports on their findings, such as luck of trust in institutions and the growing feeling of intense anger and violence among Chilean nationals. For our purpose, interestingly the survey also recorded the geographical coordinates of those interviewed. Nevertheless, the team did not know exactly what to do with the information. Previous surveys could narrow down the analysis to cities but never to this level of accuracy. So, the researchers where trying to correlate the main variables (such as violence, income, education, and many others) with location data. In the words of the Centre's Director, Luis Valenzuela, this is like opening the door of a room you never used before, so you do not know what is in there.

SOCIAL IMAGINARY OF DATA

From a comparative perspective, some trends described in Chile are almost the same as in other countries, where location technology moves in stages from novelty to integration. For example, Uber has shown the same pattern in other countries, where at the beginning very few people used the system (mainly in affluent parts of Santiago), but when transformed into something bigger, local owners of licensed cars fought against Uber. Later, both systems continue to run and the general public are using them indistinctly. Another example are satnavs, a novelty at first but today replaced by smartphones and the use of Google maps or Waze navigation, almost a normal routine of the driving experience.

What is different could be found elsewhere. We propose that the Chilean case exemplifies the situation where government data visualisation and location is open but underused by citizens. That could be explained because the relationship between citizens and the state is different, in this regard, from some developed countries.

Personal data is given by Chilean citizens to the government as a Facebook user does. Chileans are more willing to give personal data to governmental agencies, the police, local authorities, and private companies because Chileans use the number of their national identity card as a username when they relate to an organisation (public or private). For example, a person goes to a pharmacy to buy some pills for a headache. The counter staff will show the options, make the sale and before accepting the money will ask: what is your national identity card number? The customer will give it right away and the sales person will do basically two things after entering the number on the computer terminal: look if the username has some benefits (mostly discounts) and store the information on the company server (so they know that such username purchased those products).

That idea is related to a loyalty card, such as Tesco (the UK supermarket), where the customer has a small plastic card on his key rings and passes it to the sales point before paying. The difference in Chile is that the private and the public sectors do not need any card because the whole country uses one identity number for all purposes (and people are willing to provide it). The citizen in most cases does not show a physical ID (the national card itself, a passport, or driver licence) but says out loud the number. Only in official matters do people show the ID (if it is requested by the police or customs and immigration), but in everyday life, the number is spoken out.

Over the years, the amount of data on Chilean citizens has allowed the government to avoid asking some questions because it already has it. For example, if you happened to fill a tax return form (such as the American IRS or the British HMRC), the government will do it for you. Only foreigners react (sometimes badly) when asked for an identity number. For Chileans it is part of their daily lives. If you are visiting a friend in a building, the staff will give a parking space asking for your car licence plate and your identity number. Examples go on and on. No one seems to be upset about it.

But things are changing. In late 2015, the Telecommunications Office modified the phone dialling system so that land lines and mobile phones had all nine digits. To help citizens, the agency asked a private company (Cursor Inc.) to create an App (for Google Play and Apple Store) to update the user's phonebook. It was widely used (a million downloads) until someone on Twitter noticed that the application not only accessed the contact list but the phone location. That led to the Member of Parliament Juan Antonio Coloma to present a motion about why a private company was accessing more information than it needed. The private company and the government reacted saying that the only purpose was to have statistical information about the campaign and application use among citizens, and that data was treated anonymously.

The examples above show how citizens allow the government to access personal data. The interesting point is that the government, through the unit of Spatial Data Infrastructure (www.ide.cl), feeds this information back to citizens on an open platform (datos.gob.cl). More interestingly, citizens are mostly unaware of this service and hardly use it.

Therefore, location data and metadata related to it are available but Chileans mostly do not see it. More importantly, citizens are giving data every time. One argument is that people willingly give information about themselves (in fact, they are not forced to do it and they can always say no). Another argument is that they give data because it is not perceived as control over them, but as a benefit. For example, retail companies give discounts, so people perceive handing over the national identity number as a way to obtain lower prices in shopping products. It is very easy to argue that what people perceived as benefits are in fact strategic decisions to capture data to increase sales. Nevertheless, Chileans do not perceive it as control over them, most of the time.

So, people give data in exchange for something: a discount or security. For example, by tracking the owner's vehicle people value security over privacy. Some people track family members by apps on their smartphones. Uber uses the same principle because the driver's identity is known, the customer's identity is known to the driver (and both can rate each other), the journey is mapped from start to finish, and the company has all this information in exchange for discounts and security (the cost being the lack of privacy).

The Cultural, Social, and Political Implications of Locative Media in Chile

Wilken and Goggin (2015) say that locative media are the harbinger of the emergent media of our time, from Big Data to drones, from the Internet of Things to logistics, all with their urgent cultural, social, and political implications. Therefore, the specific question is what could be those implications in Chile.

Saker and Evans (2016), based on research in the UK and USA, argue that some people use Foursquare to construct their own identities. Following this insight, we can ask if this is also the case in Chile. As Saker and Evans describe, Foursquare is a location-based social network (LBSN). This technology originally was a standalone phone application and it was used as such in Chile. But as in the UK, Facebook integrated the check-in function into its interface, so Chileans started to use Facebook instead to fulfil the same idea: here I am (mainly a restaurant, an event, or the airport). Google places is also used in this regard. As Saker and Evans describe, people do not check-in at home, work, or a doctor's appointment but at venues of interest to others. For some people, it is a way to say they are fun and they like to have a good time. The same happens in Chile; for example, professionals that need to travel very often will check-in in airports around the country, showing that they work hard but also have an interesting job.

Licoppe and Inada (2016), based on research on Japan and France, propose the concept of timid encounters to explain the behaviour of mobile gaming players using location technology. They argue that those players experience a tension while playing. In one sense, they are easy to spot and recognised but also, they what to keep a distance and hardly interact when playing the same game in the same location (metres away of each other). In Chile that was the case with Pokémon Go. Released in Chile in August 3, 2016 (in Japan it was July 2016), people were aware of the game before hitting the country. On the day of its release, hundreds of players met at parks and shopping malls to play the game. It was a national event. Some days later very few people were interested. For some Chileans, the game used data so heavily that their monthly mobile plan was struggling to cope. For others, there were no interactions between players, just sharing the same place while playing. Nevertheless, some people liked the game and sometimes they played while on public transport, so they could find Pokémons along the route.

Heolzl and Marie, thinking about the new forms of cities with a focus on Hong Kong, argue that 'with ubiquitous mobile connectivity the city is becoming an 'extended spatial network' [...] where physical and digital data, and the relations between them are being agglomerated into networked databases of merchandising, surveillance and control' (2016: 382). That is also the case of Chile, the difference being that Chileans do not care that much about the networked databases.

This is our main proposal. Because of a previous culture of sharing data with the government and the private sectors through a standardised ID number, Chileans have less problems trusting the government, the police, or the retail business with location data about themselves. Data is available, is open but hardly used by citizens to make decisions in the public context. The private world is closed (social networks, retail), but in that case citizens give their location and metadata in exchange for services or discounts. All in all, location media is invisible, part of daily life and the changes it is producing in people are just beginning to be documented.

CONCLUSION: TO SHARE OR NOT TO SHARE MY LOCATION

Location technologies and work are becoming intertwined in Chile. In the beginning of the twenty-first century, the government changed from the left to the right and, strange as it may sound, back to the left and then back to the right. Between 2014 and 2018, during the Bachelet presidency (from the left), the economy stagnated and unemployment rose. Among the strategies to find work, many people entered Uber to earn income. By 2018 about 70,000 drivers were working for Uber. By 2019 the company projected 100,000 drivers.

The importance is that a new form of work is possible because of location technologies, something not available in the century before. Chileans joined the new form of self-employment by driving their own cars and using location to find clients through a mobile phone application.

Using Fuchs and Sandoval's distinctions (2014), there is a relationship between physical work and digital work. In our case, driving as public transport is an example of physical work. What is new is that, on top of that, the layer of digital information is added to the physical work, allowing location driving to exist. In the old system, a normal taxi driver scouted the city for clients. A taxi driver needed to guess where the clients were, missing many opportunities to find them. By using digital information, the current driver does not have to guess, because the client shares location data with the driver in real time.

In this example, work implies a physical dimension as well as a digital one. The new layer is metadata on top of a material object. Take for example a physical map. We used to drive using maps but today the layer of real-time information on top of maps allow us to avoid traffics jams or find clients.

But this relationship between work and location technologies is just beginning. Using Fuchs & Sandoval's proposal (2014), we have subjects (S) using technology (T) on objects of labour (O) that creates a product (P). Therefore, we do not know yet what form this relationship may have in the future.

For example, an Uber driver transports people until they come out with a new service: to transport food. In this case, a person needs some food from a restaurant and uses a mobile phone application to ask for delivery. But consider another possibility. Suppose you are about to get married and the photographer does not show up. You panic until you grab your mobile phone, open the wedding app and locate photographers near the event. Then, you ask them which one could work for you because the wedding is about to start. This application does not exist in Chile, as far as I know, but it is possible to imagine such a service, and many more to come. Another example comes from online shopping. It used to be the case that if you bought something by phone, there was no information about the parcel between placing the order and the arrival to your house or postal office. Today many Chileans buy in China through AliExpress. It is always possible to track the product in space. You know where it is, the company also knows, so you can complain if it never arrives. Those experiences are new and are perceived as useful because of location technologies.

Sharing your location allows work to happen. The problem is to share or not to share our location. After the Facebook and Cambridge Analytica scandal, the balance between information and privacy is hard to find. Many called to stop using social networks and block applications from giving location data, nevertheless Chileans continued to use Facebook and Uber. Location technology is part of daily life it seems.

The consequences are unfolding and social scientists need to pay careful attention to new forms of work allowed by location technologies. If the Internet of Things happens to be part of daily life, location will be pervasive. In that moment, metadata will travel through space and time, alongside objects and people.

REFERENCES

Fuchs, C., & Sandoval, M. (2014). Digital Workers of the World Unite! A Framework for Critically Theorising and Analysing Digital Labour. *tripleC*, *12*(2), 486–563.

Goggin, G., & Albarran-Torres, C. (2015). Locative Media, Privacy, and State Surveillance in Mexico: The Case of the Geolocalization Law. In R. Wilken & G. Goggin (Eds.), *Locative Media* (pp. 148–161). New York: Routledge.

Heolzl, I., & Marie, R. (2016). Brave New City: The Image in the Urban Data-Space. *Visual Communication, 15*(3), 371–391. https://doi.org/10.1177/1470357216642638.

Hernandez, M. (2015). *Micro-momentos: pequeños grandes momentos que llenan la vida de valor.* Google Blog Post: https://www.thinkwithgoogle.com/intl/es-419/articles/micro-momentos-llenan-vida-valor.html

IDE. (2014). *Política nacional de información geoespacial: información del territorio para la toma de decisiones.* Santiago: Gobierno de Chile ediciones.

IDE. (2015, September 8–9). *Proceedings of the First International Seminar 'Información territorial para la gestión pública y el acceso ciudadano'.* Santiago de Chile. http://www.ide.cl/descarga/presentaciones-de-seminarios.html

Lemos, A. (2011). Realidade aumentada. Narrativa e midias de geolozalizacao. In A. Sanchez (Ed.), *Mobile: Reflexión y experimentación en torno a los medios locativos en el arte contemporáneo en México* (pp. 85–103). México: Cenart.

Licoppe, C., & Inada, Y. (2016). Mobility and Sociality in Proximity-Sensitive Digital Urban Ecologies: 'Timid Encounters' and 'Seam-Sensitive Walks'. *Mobilities, 11*(2), 264–283. https://doi.org/10.1080/17450101.2014.988530.

Saker, M., & Evans, L. (2016). Locative Media and Identity. Accumulative Technologies of the Self. *SAGE Open, 6*(3). https://doi.org/10.1177/2158244016662692.

Wilken, R., & Goggin, G. (2015). *Locative Media.* New York: Routledge.

CHAPTER 5

Borders and Archives Under the New Conditions of Digital Visuality

Sergio Martínez Luna

Introduction

Since identity is always a borderland, borders are places for the construction of identities. The contradictions inherent in globalisation processes, currently accentuated by neo-protectionist policies, range from multicultural tolerance to an obsession with security. These become apparent in borders, both as control and surveillance scenarios, and as cultural counter-hegemonic practices for the construction of otherness. Border policies are today linked to contemporary visuality, the circulation of images and ways of seeing and being seen. This visuality is a digital visuality, a specific but dominant form of communication. It is in the management of the policies of otherness and difference that the power associated with visuality shows where it is aimed, and its influence on the distribution of abilities, rights and obligations. The transformations generated by the processes of digitalisation are articulated in social change, not in a deterministic, technological sense, but as trends on which values, identities and knowledge are modelled. The massive circulation of images implies a profound change in the conditions of their reception and use, and of their production and

S. Martínez Luna (✉)
Universidad Carlos III de Madrid, Madrid, Spain
e-mail: sermarti@hum.uc3m.es

© The Author(s) 2019
A. Scribano, P. Lisdero (eds.), *Digital Labour, Society and the Politics of Sensibilities*, https://doi.org/10.1007/978-3-030-12306-2_5

reproduction. If an image's representative scope loses weight in favour of operativity and performativity, the question about the truthfulness and reality of the image becomes articulated within the question of to what extent an image is capable of participating in the reality of the world, of whether an image is effective, yields benefits or generates affective bonds.

IDENTITY, OTHERNESS AND VISUAL CULTURE

Digital visuality has an ambiguous nature in terms of both the emancipatory potential of instantaneous connectivity and of new forms of social control and repression. The fiction of the contemporary is that of global transnationalism ruled by capital, self-proclaimed as the only instance capable of projecting the utopia of a cross-border interconnectivity (Osborne 2011). However, the very logic of capital disregards and postpones the formation of a global political and knowledge community. The supposed free movement of people, goods and images is a contemporary delusion through which capital constructs the scenario of an unlimited world system, with no conceivable exteriority. The imperatives of mobility and flexibility are allied with dematerialisation processes. Rather than overcoming the body and materiality, they seek to displace exploited bodies to an invisible global economic periphery (Vindel Gamonal 2014). These processes are not so much implemented in the sphere of production but in the spheres related to the consumption and circulation of goods; therefore, the latter cannot be identified directly as autonomous spaces for criticism. However, displacement and border crossing, diaspora and migration are bodily experiences that question the allegedly immaterial fluidity of the globalised world.

Like the repeatedly promised political community disassembled by capital according to the logic of the market, the transnational, cross-border community of knowledge, abstracted beneath fetish words such as the knowledge society, innovation or excellence, is suspended in a liminality, always still to be achieved. It could even be said that this phase of capitalism leads us to a liminal state that leaves us suspended between a modernity that has not just finished saying goodbye—although its principles are exhausted, they maintain an imperative force—and a future that is unknown. Globalisation entails the possibility of building a global and politicised common sphere. Such a possibility can only be addressed by recognising that globalisation depends on a specific ideological, economic and cultural model of the world. Recent discourses on a supposed tendency towards de-globalisation dialogue with globalisation itself. As a complex process globalisation cannot be simply undone. Once a process reaches a certain level of complexity, it goes beyond a point of no return that makes reversing impossible. Globalisation can still be an opportunity to overcome the old dichotomies and dual modes of thought and action organised around the logics of the centre and the periphery. However, that opportunity is not evident; it is not simply given.

In this regard, it can be said that the issue of the comparison between what is local and what is global resurfaces through the processes of globalisation. Production, circulation and consumption of collective images and imaginaries shape the dialectic between the local and the global. If an imaginary is a certain repertoire of images that shape processes of identification and socialisation through their imposition, acceptance, appropriation or rejection, the very notion of ideology can be understood as built upon some of those repertoires. Inserted into the dialectics between the global and the local, images acquire a geopolitical dimension and an active role in the construction of knowledge and cultural divide and difference. Today the issue of the border is linked to visuality. The dialectic between seeing and being seen and the criteria of legitimisation of some images above others are part of border politics as the exercise of power with effects on real bodies.[1] There are parallelisms between the movement of images and people. According to W.J.T. Mitchell (2011) border security, law and migration engage the realm of images as the location of both the sensuous and the phantasmatic, both the real and the imaginary. Images precede the immigrants and the phenomenon of global migrant bodies on the move and immigration itself. Media construction of diaspora globally circulates and imbeds in our minds stereotypes and myths, fears and desires, predetermining the conditions of any real encounter with otherness. The politics of images goes along with the politics of border control. Contemporary media viewers and users become a sort of armchair ethnographers—like a reflection of the venerable figure of the early nineteenth-century

---

[1] In his series of panoramic images "Heat Maps" (2016) and the film "Incoming" (2017) photographer Richard Mosse appropriates the capabilities of midwave infrared cameras to record and detect contours in heat (a technology used for military and border surveillance) to show displaced people trapped in borders and refugee camps. His images question the fluidity of global and transnational traffic, a discourse that is often articulated with the idea that digitisation and new media free us from the heavy burden of body and materiality. In these images, the heat dissipated by suffering bodies is an index that migration and displacement are bodily experiences shaped by material forces.

anthropologist—poking into the lives of others, into different ways of life and experiencing the world (Morley and Robins 1995). Of course, the media's way of displaying alterity and otherness contains regressive aspects that legitimise distance, indifference and isolation. The cross-border and transnational community that globalisation continues to promise is frustrated time and again, trapped in a constant flow of disconnected images, where what ultimately matters is the continuity of the media experience, which must never be stopped.

The ubiquitous devices that reproduce images in a multitude of contexts, both public and private, order varied spaces and times around screens and interfaces of different formats and uses. Around them, volatile and spontaneous communities arise, built in the timely convergence of spectators and users (Prada 2012). The modernist perceptual experience, as Walter Benjamin noted, was punctuated by a series of shocks and interruptions, which placed spectators into a dialectical game between integration and estrangement. Today the politics of attention and perception is constructed upon continuous competition between multiple stimuli, images and modalities of reception that serve to consolidate a single discourse— that of capital and its globalised circulation—normatively incapable of giving space and time to what is different, incapable of opening up to the diversity it denies through its aestheticised promotion and exhibition. Despite the contemporary massive visual production, images mean less and less, their ubiquitous presence in all aspects of life neither interferes with nor questions the relationships between power and inequality. On the contrary, images seem to be the most appropriate instrument for maintaining that order of relations, since they are not capable of touching or affecting. They have become part of people's everyday life and existence in terms of indifference and routine. Within contemporary visual culture, the representation and visualisation of violence and suffering are exemplary in this regard. Images of war, terrorist attacks, displaced persons, inserted into global media flows, awaken, at most, fleeting feelings of solidarity and vague consternation that end up diluted in the standardised rhythms of contemporary reception. Nicholas Mirzoeff noted that in the second Gulf War, "more images were created to less effect than at any other period in human history" (Mirzoeff 2005: 67). Despite the massive production and circulation of images of violence the most characteristic feature of that war was the lack of any truly touching and memorable images, precisely because of the intense media saturation.

The shift from a hierarchical nation state to a rhizomatic culture relocated the desire for visualisation as the most appropriate mode for globalisation. In this way, while the body has had to remain linked to a place, a network-based visuality was constructed that allowed an experience of real-time and interconnected global electronic synchronous telepresence (Appadurai 1996). Digital networks are used by political activism to renegotiate the distribution between the global and the local, rehearsing new models of communication and alliance (Sassen 2003). While global dynamics are committed to the formation of new markets and surveillance systems, these activist digital networks are able to configure alternative networks (even though they are interwoven with the prevailing global dynamics). The emergence of the Internet made it possible for local initiatives to be resized in global terms, without losing their anchoring in local realities. Models of political activism emerged across a myriad of digitally connected localities. Spaces, temporalities and depoliticised roles—the home, the school, the neighbourhood, the streets and squares—were reconfigured as political scenarios. Globalisation is above all a massive restructuring of scales. The competition between local and global, driven by the crossing between global digital networks and local contexts, gives presence to those excluded by power and the others. Disempowered subjects become political subjects despite (or precisely because of) their exclusion from the public sphere and public space. Through their presence, the victims of various economic and symbolic forms of violence question issues such as legitimacy, recognition and access to rights. But, according to Nicholas Mirzoeff (2011), while these potentialities remain in force, the emancipatory content of global digital culture has mutated to wholeheartedly sustain the logic of a permanent state of war, based on the convergence between visualisation and exclusion, aestheticisation and social control.

AN INTERFACE IS A BORDER

If critical thought involves thinking of the present against itself, or even thinking of ourselves against ourselves, then thinking of tolerance and hospitality would be the most radical way of deploying critical thinking (Thiebaut 2010). However, neither tolerance nor hospitality can be approached today as if they are detached from the world image that uses them to sustain a consensus that normalises distancing. Such an operation is not effective because the essence of the image or the gaze is inevitably reifying. It is a specific management of visuality that instrumentalises them in this way. It is not only about paying attention to the experience of living with images on a daily basis, but about understanding the terms on which that experience is enacted. Today this experience is distinguished by the fact that the ubiquity of images in a public sphere restructured as an iconosphere is characterised by its tolerated and indifferent day-to-day presence (Cruz Sánchez 2008). Living with ever-present images leads to the annulment of any polemical dimension with respect to the consensual purpose for which they have been put to work.

Digital visuality is stretched thin between the emancipatory content it still retains, and its complicity with discourses and control practices. The digital devices that make this visuality visible serve both the purposes of social control and citizen participation, at a time when every device seems to be restructured as a vehicle for visual (re)production. Surveillance imperatives are weaved into the imperatives of appeal to creativity and networked cooperation, characteristic of contemporary capitalism. The new conditions of visuality rest in the mutations that the capitalist system has experienced in recent decades, by which the logics of profit production become parasites of the fields of symbolism and affective life. Capitalism's insistence on (self)management, availability and performance optimisation forms a subjectivity which is submitted to the imperatives of flexibility and expressiveness, with the entrepreneur as its dominant model (Boltanski and Chiapello 2006; Dardot and Lavat 2013). Images play a main part in this global reorganisation of work and economy, leisure and affectivity (Cánepa 2013).

In accordance with the performativity principle, knowledge and practices are oriented towards the exploitation of their productive potential, according to criteria of efficiency and performance (Cánepa 2013). The system demands performative and participatory public subjects who are precarious and versatile, capable of taking different roles in a variety of changing situations. Submission must be assimilated by each individual, because the devices of power (advertising and innovation, marketing and finance) demand that people construct their own objects of desire, responsibility (and blame) vis-à-vis the varying circumstances of existence. What Adorno called natural coercion is fulfilled when the principle of domination is internalised. In this scenario images prove to be performative. These are images themselves, mobile and hyperconnected as they are that best embody the illusion of an abstract space of free circulation without friction, in which the social position of the participants is obliterated (Žižek 1997).

New metaphors for the screen have also emerged. The screen as a window, frame or mirror (thresholds that enable the viewer to see the world and define a certain reality) gives way to the screen as display. This provides access to information and service repertoires to a viewer-user that must select, intervene and connect a range of data within an ever-moving flow of information (Casetti 2013). It is characteristic of contemporary visuality that this performative force is materialised by technology as action and subjection. Images have an interpellating role and claim an active role in the configuration of socio-affective life. Images provide resources for the reformulation of relationships with reality according to private interests. However, images are not only available for customisation purposes but are also a powerful tool for adjusting frameworks of meaning to the particular concerns of viewers-users.

The proliferation of screens causes texts and images to demand to be clicked on, and constantly reconnected throughout the processes of the visual display of reality. In addition to inter-media convergence, that is, the overlap between different devices for production and distribution of knowledge, there is also a convergence between image, medium and screen. This forms an image interface (Catalá-Domenech 2010) or culture interface, which enables and conditions contact with, exploration and ultimately, colonisation of, reality. Wherever there is an interface, a certain dialectic emerges between control and alienation with encounter and contact. Contemporary images (understood as interface images) have a transitional and liminal function that synchronically separates and connects heterogeneous times and spaces. Images present a border dimension to the extent that the processes of meaning that they produce and embody distance themselves from any linear logic be it semiotic, rhetorical or informational.

Digitisation, virtual reality and cyberspace seem to dissolve the consistency of reality, bodies and eventually the human subject itself. Human perception seems to have become obsolete in a post-media state of affairs; the flow of data no longer needs to adapt to human perceptual capacities, in the face of a post-human horizon where such capacities are automated and superseded by technology. Subjects become mere spectators of the processes which construct their own identity narratives. Utopian hopes linked to the endless enhancement of that which is human are projected onto technology, and this involves overcoming the important conditioning factors of the body. Faced with this, it seems appropriate to approach convergences and divergences, the multiple folds between the physical and the technological in the digital world, as features of contemporary culture and politics. But it is in the fluid boundaries between the embodied human perception and the gaze of technological artefacts where contemporary visual and material culture is redefined. The genealogy of digital culture must be separated from the binary logics that ultimately reduce the debate to the defence or the rejection of a mind and a disembodied gaze as characteristics of digitalisation (Munster 2006). Rather, this process would require exploring the ways in which perception, the body and the senses interact with machines within specific times and places.

These encounters are made possible and conditioned by the mobile, interconnected ubiquity of media interfaces. These hover in a tense balance between a potential immediate connection between the self and the others, and the idea of the interface as an interested mediator of communication and the public sphere. But it is possible to understand the interface as an autonomous area of aesthetic and political activity in which both tendencies are found (Galloway 2012). If the performative capacity of interfaces is recognised, they become not so much objects as processes. An interface is not something, it does something (Verhoeff 2016). The interface is both link and separation, simultaneously encouraging the illusion of a total understanding of complexity and the possibility of imagining other forms of reciprocity capable of remapping global flows. For German scientist Otto Rössler, an interface enables a contact and an experience of the world in terms of unconditional friendship. It is a transactional space that assumes egalitarian starting positions (Marzo 2015). But an interface can also be an instrument for the rejection, exclusion and reaffirmation of dominant roles in contact areas blighted by conflict and coercion. Hence, interface screens today take on the dimension of a border, as multiplied seats of such contradictions. Interface screens are instruments of colonisation, because through interpellation and the imperative of participation, they articulate surveillance and tracking strategies, extend the established imaginaries and naturalise normative meanings and identities.

An area to be explored at this stage is the ambivalence that places these devices as pillars for the construction of participatory citizenship and interactions in the public sphere and space, on the one hand, and as instruments for control and aestheticisation, on the other. An example are the urban screens that reconfigure urban surfaces as non-static elements that interact with the environment. The possibilities of the digital visualisation of data, images and texts on the surface of buildings not only change their surface and structure but also expand the potential for the production of city, citizenship and public space (Haeusler et al. 2013; Pop and Stalder 2012). But the purpose of fitting buildings with interactive screens frequently results in the depletion of such possibilities when the relationship between building, exterior appearance and urban space is alienated. The media façade alienates the surface of the structure of the building on which the device is inserted, and the urban context onto which the screen is projected is reduced to a scenario of economic competition, as it attracts the attention of citizens, or even monitors their physiological characteristics, behaviour and preferences (as is the case with biometric recognition systems and gladvertising technologies). This example illustrates that interfaces can be instruments to control access to the public sphere and space, and to colonise imaginaries; and they can also project lines of flight for multiplicity and transformation, as opposed to the territorialisation of reference fields and codes assigned between borderlands.

The construction of identities is thus intensely mediated by discourses, practices and visual devices. Images and imaginaries act as transparent mediators that condition transitions and transactions between cultural groups, institutions, spectators, users and consumers. The much-vaunted abolition of walls in the globalised world was part of a process intended to perfect and aestheticise forms of separation. The aerial images of refugees taken by a drone on the Hungarian border in 2015 showed the contradiction between globalised visuality and the material reality of human catastrophe, which was depicted at a tolerable and vertical distance.[2] Multicultural tolerance was never separable from the anxieties linked to economic recession, terrorism, race and religion. These contradictions, repressed through the iron-clad alliance between consumption and fear, cause times and spaces, cultures and lifestyles to be disconnected and depoliticised.[3] Security and control are the two conditions for keeping

[2] On the cultural and historical significance of aerial visuality, see Mark Dorrian and Frédéric Pousin (2013).

[3] The works of artists such as Guillermo Calzadilla, Jennifer Allora, Marcos Ramírez 'ERRE', Guillermo Gómez Peña, Electronic Disturbance Theater, Antoni Muntadas, Javier Téllez, Joana Moll, to name a few, show a concern for the border both as a context for the exercise of political power and as a site to elaborate alternative mappings, as well as others forms of encounter, subjectivity and identification. Maybe the most outstanding example of a cultural initiative of this kind is *inSite*, which has commissioned and curated artistic interventions by international contemporary artists in the San Diego-Tijuana border since 1992. *InSite* promotes artistic practices committed to explore the complexity and diversity of the border as a site for negotiation and resistance, translation and activism. See http://insite.org.mx/wp/en/insite/. On the other hand, it is worth noting that, as Raul Gschrey (2011)

others out, while reinforcing and distorting feelings of harmony and free-dom (Pires do Rio Caldeira 2000). These drifts towards isolation are not only a protection strategy against the threat of violence. They are also part of the creation of sophisticated spaces of segregation that block the possibility of an unregulated encounter with others. In the current globally networked world the increasing polarity between those inside and those outside is still part of a politics of material space. In his study on the architecture of guard houses in luxury housing developments in Mexico City, Mauricio Guillén (2006) notes that these buildings operate as both a symbol of order and safety and a symbol of status that is exhibited to the outside of these enclosures. The standard of taste becomes a spatial and geographical criterion that demarcates what lies beyond guard-gated residential communities, but which also changes everything inside these complexes into a closed and aesthetised image of themselves.

An Interface Is a Border (on Borders and Archives)

A border is a limit that separates and connects people, practices, gazes, times and spaces.[4] It signals a moment of crisis that highlights the limits of cultural domains, leading them to face that which is different from them. A border has much of what Michel Foucault (1997) called heterotopia. The spaces of life are traversed by relations that define locations which are transitive, juxtaposed and irreducible among themselves. In every culture there are real places outlined within the social institution that constitute counter-locations, in which the other real locations of that culture are represented, inverted and answered. They are places that make up both a system of opening and closing (and a particular temporality, a heterochrony), revealing the limits of the naturalised fiction in which the real spaces

argues, "while Border Art in the North American context has been produced and discussed for decades, larger bodies of artistic and academic work on Europe's borderlands are only beginning to emerge in the new millennium". According to Gschrey, this is because of the developing supranational structure of the EU and the establishing of supranational regimes of policing EU external borders, which is related to an intense reconfiguration of European identities.

[4] The usual approach to migration and border control is analysis through a spatial lens. However, "by hiding the temporal aspects of their spatially-dressed border and migration control strategies states and international law reveal that they are not yet ready to abandon the comfortable terrain of calculable and predictable absolute view of the space" (Yahyaoui Krivenko 2016: 340).

are strengthened. Thus, friction emerges between two incompatible regimes of existence, from the very interior of the one that has declared itself to be hegemonic, in order to allegorically show its limits. When taking into account the conceptual complexity of the term 'border' (meaning geographic and historical separation or the distribution of categories of gender, race, class or ethnicity), it reveals that the liminality created by borders configures the classification of differences, and the regulation of economic and cultural displacements.

Therefore, in order to understand this interfacial dimension, it is useful to explore the articulation between border and archive, with which the former shares the ability to exclude and include, discard or give visibility to some other bodies, practices and discourses. Both for Derrida (1998) and for Foucault (2002 [1969]), archives, rather than being merely intended to record, produce an event and reality. The archive manages memory, history and knowledge; it is a microphysics that shapes policies and subjectivities. Power needs to control both archives and borders in order to distribute capabilities and bodies, access rights and exclusions. Foucault elaborated the term archive not as the sum of all historical documentation produced by a culture, or as the specific institution where all those texts and objects are storage. The Foucauldian archive is rather the law of what can be said (and seen). That is to say, the archive is the system that governs the appearance of statements as unique events. Although such a definition is detached from the practice of archiving, it can nonetheless be fruitful in order to understand the logic of material management and exhibition of documents, artefacts, records and so on. The archive as both a theoretical concept and a physical materialisation is an instrument of power that organises and distributes knowledge and information. The archive, in giving a geopolitical and cultural location to the global processes of constructing and transmitting knowledge and subjectivity, mobility and affection, draws a border and makes it possible to view colonial differences in terms of border thinking.

This relationship between archive and border is traversed by the transformations of contemporary visuality in two senses. Firstly, the image was linked to the modern project of classificatory objectification of the world, and thus to the institution of the archive. As the performative dimension of the image becomes intensified, it offers repertoires that invite an intervention in the world according to participatory mandates (Cánepa 2013). Memory in contemporary culture is a process turned towards the interconnected production of data. More concerned with synchronous processing, this interconnected memory questions the role of the archive as a stable location for collection and preservation (Brea 2007). If this erodes the dependencies of the archive from power and origin (Derrida 1998), a possibility arises to imagine other archives removed from any obligations to wholeness and exhaustive classification, as well as to the preservation of the past as a fetishised accumulation of time (Bordons 2009). The new forms of electronic synchrony and relationality change the conditions of production and access to knowledge and memory. It is thus possible to articulate these transformations of the archive with the concept of border. In the archive, methods of inclusion and exclusion that manage otherness and hospitality—for example, multicultural forms of normative tolerance which lead the other to invisibility and silencing—are attempted. The archive thus demands a concept of limit that recognises border mechanisms of exclusion and inclusion, conditions of access to knowledge, as well as the contradictory laws of hospitality and hostility.[5] As a consequence, it is "not the limit of the border and the subjects who inhabit borderlands, but the limit that is the bo(a)rder" (Michaelsen and Johnson 1997: 33), that is, the limit that is at the border and in its implicit boarder. The boarder embodies and often suffers the unsolvable tensions of hospitality as both subject and object of the law of the border and the archive. If borders are enacted practices that do not stop at the territorial borders but they shape the national and even global space and operate within them they are located on the body: "bodies carry borders on them" (Brah 2016: 4).

Accordingly, when addressing the conceptual complexity of the term border—from geographical and historical separation to the distribution of categories related to gender, social class, immigration and ethnicity—it can be noted that in the realm of liminality outlined there, differences are classified and reordered, and the migratory paths of identities are regulated. In short, borders make archives. The demarcation of borders is a process more mobile than it intends to be when it is defined as the point of arrival of a series of arranged operations of separation and distribution. The border only makes sense in reference to the contexts in which it is

---

[5] Jacques Derrida argued that the concept of hospitality is aporetic. According to him, absolute hospitality before others is not a possible scenario as such. There is an internal and insoluble contradiction in the notion of hospitality since to be hospitable, it is necessary that one must be the master of the house, nation or country. Hospitality requires that one have the power to host by exerting control over the others who are being hosted. Multicultural tolerance is simply unable to recognise and rework this tension. See Jacques Derrida and Anne Dufourmantelle (2000).

applied, and its establishment is linked to the variability and historicity of those contexts. As a consequence, the distribution of identities, spaces, times and sensitivities that borders establish is an invitation to question their own unstable criteria for demarcation, the contexts that dictate objectification and the internal separations that they cause. The archive creates a border and the border creates an archive. Border and archive pose a question about cultural knowledge and its limits.

But, secondly, contemporary visuality combines the mandate of participation and effectiveness with that of security and surveillance. For spectators-users, participating and performing mean adding data to the archive of their life paths, preferences and contacts. This mandate needs to be internalised also in terms of participation in the project of global control and surveillance. Today, according to Foucault, the destiny that awaited the panopticon (i.e., its expansion as a generalised function of the disciplinary apparatus throughout the social body) has been fulfilled. Driven by new technologies and democratised access to surveillance apparatuses, the panopticon acquires a decentred and consensual character, and is disseminated as an all-encompassing gaze that regulates the lifestyles and the habitable reality for individuals (Hier 2003; Whitaker 1999).

Surveillance technologies manage identity, borders and otherness according to the logic of total visualisation. Facial and biometric recognition, electronic passports, CCTV devices, radars and infrared and motion detectors are combined with walls, fences and barbed wire. Border policies are visual policies involved in a biopolitical and post-human turn of territorial management. They are determined to manage the complexity of borders in terms of visual control driven by new technologies of visual surveillance (Polgovsky 2016). However, there are other ways of being and being seen; other visual experiences not associated with access control or the inquisitive gaze. Visual experiences also have to do with vulnerability, with the material density of bodies that set a limit and expose blind spots, opposed to transparency and calculability. Derrida (1999) said that tears see.[6] They are a specific visual and bodily experience that cannot be reconciled with spectacle, classification, exclusion and surveillance. Tears expose the inviolability of a secret, setting a limit to the processes of total recognition and understanding. The experience of secrets leads less to a levelling of discrepancies and differences that appear at the border than to

[6]On the significance of tears as a visual experience in Derrida, see Martin Jay (1993: 522–523).

a problematisation of the concepts that are at stake there—bodies, identities, differences, transgression and translation—and a recognition of the limits of theorising about the border as a cultural index, a tool of analysis or a scenario of cultural production.[7] The archive and the border segregate and secrete (Michaelsen and Johnson 1997). Contemporary images lie between the fluidity and transparency of a world that aspires to reduce reality to its total visibility, and that exposed limit that demands reflection about material bodies, borders, (de)territorialisation and illegibility.

CONCLUSIONS

Contemporary visuality hovers in a tense balance between the aspiration to full visibility and pervasive limits and exclusions. This demands a reflection on borders and the encounter with otherness. A pragmatics of visuality opposed to the obsession with transparency, the control of bodies and knowledge, the fantasy of a total classification and categorisation of the other, has to do with the exercise of imagination (as the human ability to transform images and create new ones) committed to democracy and solidarity. It is through imagination that borders and interfaces and areas of cultural contact are reconfigured and repositioned in terms of a political and controversial openness to modes of knowledge and community that cannot be reduced to the identification of the real with that which is given to see. It is necessary to make and display images of the separations and borders that the global order naturalises, in order to reposition the gazes, the voices and the rejected bodies.[8]

According to the thinker Jose Medina (2012), imagination is a process of social production of images, collective imaginaries and narratives that might, through practices of resistance and disagreement, mediate, rework and question social perceptions and interactions. This pragmatics is based

---

[7] In the *arché*, in the archive and its law, the etymology of the arcane and of the secret also reverberates: the archive not only saves but also codifies, encloses and encrypts. On the relations between secret and archive, see Roberto González Echevarría (2000).

[8] A prominent example of critical visual practice in this sense is the work of Spanish artist Rogelio López Cuenca. In the context of the Straits of Gibraltar, López Cuenca has developed several artistic projects (*El Paraíso es de los extraños* (2001), *Al Yazira Al Ándalus* (2001), Dem Wunde®land Entgegen (2003), *Walls* (2006), *Le Partage* (2008)) on the border of Spain and Morocco as an identity conflict zone where imaginaries and bodies, fears and hopes, violence and border control systems, continually meet and collide. See Rogelio López Cuenca (2008).

on a radical conception of democracy, sociability and solidarity. It is through this conception that borders, memories and subaltern bodies are reshaped and positioned, in terms of a political and controversial opening, to ways of knowing and being together that are normatively rejected by the prevailing logic that insists on reducing what is real to what is disclosed for viewing. It is necessary to picture the separations, the borders, the exclusions that globalisation assumes are permanent and ontological in order to approach ways of border crossing capable of repositioning rejected bodies, gazes and voices. If the global flows and networks of information and affectivity are exploited by economic rationality, it is appropriate to explore how connectivity and relationality could be transformed into social capital for a variety of actors in situations of inequality and oppression, in other words, how to intensify the conditions for debate and conversation under the sign of cosmopolitan democracy and diversity (García Canclini 2004). Nomadism has been caught up in the logic of multicultural tolerance and fantasies about overcoming the issues of the body and materiality in order to reach a complete and phantasmatic freedom of movement. However, it should be considered that, as Rosi Braidotti (2005) notes, the becoming-nomad means the desire for change and flow, the right of every individual to reinvent themselves within processes of transformation opposed to the statism of the unitarian subject. Criticism and political practice are no longer recognised in the task of revealing a hidden meaning which denounces ideological disguising, but in the effort to give visibility to what, through its very exhibition, remains ignored and excluded by assimilation, to learn to look where it is repeated to us that there is nothing to see. According to Nicholas Mirzoeff (2011) the main imperative in the contemporary hegemonic visuality is precisely "Move on, there's nothing to see here". Thinking borders and border crossings can be ways of putting into question that hegemonic authority by claiming autonomy to contest the hegemonic order that establishes what is (not) visible and to whom. Both archives and borders are one of those places we must to learn to look at again.

REFERENCES

Appadurai, A. (1996). *Modernity at Large. Cultural Dimensions of Globalization.* Minneapolis: University of Minnesota Press.

Boltanski, L., & Chiapello, E. (2006). *The New Spirit of Capitalism.* London: Verso.

Bordons, T. (2009). Archivos posibles. *Estudios Visuales, 6*, 82–91.

Brah, A. (2016). Border Crossings. In C. Benjamin (Ed.), *Policing Borders, Boundaries and Bodies* (pp. 3–6). London: SOAS, Centre for Migration & Diaspora Studies.

Braidotti, R. (2005). *Metamorfosis. Hacia una teoría del devenir.* Madrid: Akal.

Brea, J. L. (2007). *Cultura_Ram.* Barcelona: Gedisa.

Cánepa, G. (2013). Imágenes del mundo, imágenes en el mundo: del archivo a los repertorios visuales. *Poliantea, IX*(16), 179–207.

Casetti, F. (2013). What Is a Screen Nowadays? In C. Berry, J. Harbord, & R. Moore (Eds.), *Public Space, Media Space* (pp. 16–40). London: Palgrave Macmillan.

Catalá Domenech, J. M. (2010). *La imagen-interfaz. Representación audiovisual y conocimiento en la era de la complejidad.* País Vasco: Universidad del País Vasco.

Cruz Sánchez, P. A. (2008). *Ob-Scenas. La redefinición política de la imagen.* Murcia: Nausícaä.

Dardot, P., & Lavat, C. (2013). *The New Way of the World.* London: Verso.

Derrida, J. (1998). *Archive Fever: A Freudian Impression.* Chicago: Chicago University Press.

Derrida, J. (1999). *Mémoires d'aveugle. L'autoportrait et autres ruines.* Paris: Musées Nationaux.

Derrida, J., & Dufoumantelle, A. (2000). *Of Hospitality.* Stanford: Stanford University Press.

Dorrian, M., & Pousin, F. (Eds.). (2013). *Seeing from Above. The Aerial View in Visual Culture.* London: I.B. Tauris.

Foucault, M. (1997). Of Other Spaces: Utopias and Heterotopias. In N. Leach (Ed.), *Rethinking Architecture: A Reader in Cultural Theory* (pp. 330–336). London/New York: Routledge.

Foucault, M. (2002 [1969]). *The Archeology of Knowledge.* London/New York: Routledge.

Galloway, A. (2012). *The Interface Effect.* Cambridge: Polity Press.

García Canclini, N. (2004). *Diferentes, desiguales y desconectados. Mapas de la interculturalidad.* Barcelona: Gedisa.

González Echevarría, R. (2000). *Mito y Archivo. Una teoría de la narrativa latinoamericana.* México D.F.: Fondo de Cultura Económica.

Gschrey, R. (2011). Borderlines: Surveillance, Identification and Artistic Explorations Along European Borders. *Surveillance & Society, 9*(1), 185–202.

Guillén, M. (2006). Island Hopping. Politics of Visuality in Contemporary Mexico. In M. Miessen & S. Basar (Eds.), *Did Someone Say Participate? An Atlas of Spatial Practice* (pp. 234–240). Cambridge, MA: MIT Press.

Haeusler, M. H., Tomitsch, M., & Tscherteu, G. (Eds.). (2013). *New Media Facades. A Global Survey.* Stuttgart: Avedition.

Hier, S. P. (2003). Probing the Surveillant Assemblage: On the Dialectics of Surveillance Practices as Processes of Social Control. *Surveillance & Society, 1*(3), 399–411.

Jay, M. (1993). *Downcast Eyes. The Denigration of Vision in Twentieth-Century French Thought*. Berkeley: University of California Press.

López Cuenca, R. (2008). *Hojas de ruta*. Valladolid: Patio Herreriano, Museo de Arte Contemporáneo Español.

Marzo, J. L. (2015). La genealogía líquida de la interfaz. *Artnodes, 16*, 5–16.

Medina, J. (2012). *The Epistemology of Resistance*. Oxford: Oxford University Press.

Michaelsen, S., & Johnson, D. E. (1997). Borders Secrets: An Introduction. In S. Michaelsen & D. E. Johnson (Eds.), *Border Theory: The Limits of Cultural Politics* (pp. 1–40). Minneapolis: Minneapolis University Press.

Mirzoeff, N. (2005). *Watching Babylon. The War in Iraq and Global Visual Culture*. New York/London: Routledge.

Mirzoeff, N. (2011). *The Right to Look*. Durham: Duke University Press.

Mitchell, W. J. T. (2011). Migration, Law, and the Image: Beyond the Veil of Ignorance. In S. Mathur (Ed.), *The Migrant's Time. Rethinking Art History and Diaspora* (pp. 59–77). Williamstown: The Sterling and Francine Clark Institute.

Morley, D., & Robins, K. (1995). *Spaces of Identity: Global Media, Electronic Landscapes and Cultural Boundaries*. London/New York: Routledge.

Munster, A. (2006). *Materializing New Media: Embodiment in Information Aesthetics*. Hannover: Dartmouth College Press.

Osborne, P. (2011). The Fiction of the Contemporary: Speculative Collectivity and Transnationalism in The Atlas Group. In A. Avanessian & L. Skrebows (Eds.), *Aesthetics and Contemporary Art* (pp. 101–123). Berlin: Sternberg Press.

Pires do Rio Caldeira, T. (2000). *City of Walls. Crime, Segregation, and Citizenship in Sao Paulo*. Berkeley: University of California Press.

Polgovsky, M. (2016). Move and Get Shot: La política post-humana de la imagen. *Campo de relámpagos*. http://campoderelampagos.org/critica-y-reviews/ 17/12/2016. Accessed Aug 2017.

Pop, S., & Stalder, U. (Eds.). (2012). *Urban Media Cultures*. Stuttgart: Avedition.

Prada, J. M. (2012). *Otro tiempo para el arte. Cuestiones y comentarios sobre el arte actual*. Valencia: Sendemá.

Sassen, S. (2003). *Contra-geografías de la globalización*. Madrid: Traficantes de Sueños.

Thiebaut, C. (2010). Tolerancia y hospitalidad. Una reflexión moral ante la inmigración. *Arbor, 744*, 543–554.

Verhoeff, N. (2016). Urban Interfaces: The Cartographies of Screen-Based Installations. *Journal of Television & New Media, 18*(4), 305–319.

Vindel Gamonal, J. (2014). La imagen de las cosas: Cuerpo y objeto ante la crisis del consumo. In A. Fernández Polanco (Ed.), *Pensar la imagen/Pensar con las imágenes* (pp. 53–92). Salamanca: Delirio.

Whitaker, R. (1999). *The End of Privacy: How Total Surveillance is Becoming a Reality.* New York: The New Press.

Yahyaoui Krivenko, E. (2016). Considering Time and Migration and Border Control Practices. *International Journal of Migration and Border Studies, 2*(4), 329–344.

Žižek, S. (1997). *The Plague of Fantasies.* London: Verso.

CHAPTER 6

The Society 4.0, Internet, Tourism and the War on Terror

Maximiliano E. Korstanje

INTRODUCTION

Since the attacks to the World Trade Center (WTC) on September 11 of 2001 (a tragic event baptized as 9/11) the world was radically altered, paving the way for the rise of new international relations while the current global stability that marks the geopolitical relations was at the least reconsidered (Pyszczynski et al. 2003). Political analysts proclaim a quest for sustainable security in view of the stock and market crisis that whipped the US and Europe in 2008 (Suri and Valentino 2016). To put this bluntly in other terms, the needs to rethink national security strategy, in which the Bush administration coined the term "the war on terror", doubtless marked the epicentre of a political crisis in the US and its allies (Kirshner 2016; Inboden 2016; Hall 2016). As Suri and Valentino put it, the global financial crisis, which recently occurred, not only placed the US into a paradoxical situation, simply because the struggle against terrorism demands a great deal of financial resources, but undermined the possibilities for weaving alliances with different autonomous nations. No matter

M. E. Korstanje (✉)
University of Palermo, Buenos Aires, Argentina
e-mail: mkorst@palermo.edu

© The Author(s) 2019   95
A. Scribano, P. Lisdero (eds.), *Digital Labour, Society and the Politics of Sensibilities*, https://doi.org/10.1007/978-3-030-12306-2_6

the ideology of the administration, it is remarkable that the mediocrity of American strategic leadership jeopardizes the political stability of the government due to the excessive cost accumulation, adjoined to the decline of the US as an economic power (Suri and Valentino 2016). Meanwhile, some neo-pragmatic voices call attention to the dangers of the US retreat from its leading position as a watchdog in view of the radicalization of modern terrorism and the advance of Islamic State in Iraq and Syria (ISIS; Cronin 2015; Khader 2016). Still further, the digital technologies, which today connect the world, provide a fertile ground for the radicalized cells to instil their message of panic and extortion. As Mahmoud Eid (2014) brilliantly observed, a strange symbiosis between the media, which looks to cover terrorism-containing news to gain further investors, maximizing its profits, and the terrorist groups, which benefit from making their crimes public, converges. In the culture of witnessing, Luke Howie (2015) adds, any news is covered, packaged and disseminated to any geographical point in hours engaging a remote audience with the facts as never before. This begs some interesting questions that deserve to be discussed—through this chapter—such as, is technology a path to create a culture of fear? Or simply an alternative aimed at fighting against terrorism? Why has terrorism transformed in a sort of popular entertainment? What are the connections between terrorism and mobilities? And lastly, what are the direct effects of terrorism on the organization of labour in tourism fields?

All these above-mentioned questions illustrate part of the doubts cast by international analysts in the specialized literature, but unfortunately, to date, they remain open. The first section discusses the nature of digital technology from a critical perspective while it lays the foundations towards a new encompassing model for understanding Society 4.0. In this respect, the second section alludes to how terrorism manipulates the cultural background of the West, or to be more exact, the cultural basis of the spectacle in its favour. Third, part of the reflection presented earlier leads us to rethink Slavoj Žižek's insights, eloquently discussed in his book *The Universal Exception* (2014). Per his viewpoint, 9/11—as a founding event—and terrorism, in particular, not only woke Occident from the slumber, it was but interrogated on the alienatory nature of digital technology. As he notes, in *The Matrix Saga*, Morpheus said Neo, "Welcome to the Dessert of the Real", to symbolize the passage of a comfortable but unreal life (which may very well be provided by digital technology) and an always hostile reality. Most certainly, Žižek insists polemically that the virtual world, far from serving as an emancipatory platform, puts mankind into an illusory dream. Last but not least, we highlight the changes accelerated in organizational culture—firstly in tourism and hospitality industries—after 9/11. Islamophobia, which is part of a new type of racism, surfaced and involved different facets and stages of societal order. Tourism, which is based on the host-and-guest encounter, exhibits a fertile ground for the manipulations of long-dormant stereotypes forged in the colonial system. Though technology would create a more open society, terrorism inversely closes the borders to strangers, affecting one of the mainstream values of Western civilization: hospitality (Korstanje 2017).

TECHNOLOGY AND THE DIGITAL SOCIETY

One of the most critical voices in discussions of digital society was Jacques Ellul. Unlike other colleagues, he energetically adopted a negative connotation on technology. Though technology should be originally oriented to accelerate—if not optimize—the productive processes, no less true is that it undermines critical thinking, commoditizing citizens and transforming them into consumers. To put this in slightly other terms, the technological order instrumentalizes human activity, using machines to achieve the technocratic goals posed by capitalist society (Ellul 1962, 1992). For Ellul, technology is not the servant of humans, but an "artificial system", that commoditizes the human will. In the quest of efficiency, capitalist society uses technology to create an active force which is oriented to production, and of course consumption (Ellul 1964). An authoritative voice in Ellul's studies, Carl Mitcham holds that technology not only expands the efficiency towards new horizons, but also generates new unseen effects on the environment. Ellul struggled to introduce an ethical approach into the anthropocentric perspective that capitalism developed (Mitcham 1997). Based on a similarly minded argumentation which coincides partially with Marx's legacy, which held that technology prepares society towards the class struggle indicating the course of history, Ellul focused on "the technique", "not the capital", as the driving force that looks for total efficacy. Marx's world has gone, as Ellul noted, while "capital is no longer the dominant force it was in nineteen century; instead it is technology, which he defines as the totality of methods rationally arrived at an absolute efficiency" (Mitcham 2013: 21). To cut a long story short, like Marx, Ellul understood that economy and technology were inextricably intertwined. Rationality is not limited to certain fields of production, it escapes to the productive system involving various spheres of social life. In medicine, education and the entertainment industry, the cost-benefit analysis pivots on the quest for achieving results. Most probably, the reluctance of the first Christian theologists in the US found in Ellul a good resource for forging a critical perspective revolving around the depersonalization brought by capitalism. Ellul's works, hence, was more important in the US than in France, as Mitcham masterfully clarifies (Mitcham 2013). In this way, George Ritzer (2013) reviews the concept of technological society to validate his previous assumptions on McDonaldization. In consonance with Ellul, Ritzer acknowledges that the rational technique moulds the protocols, practices, behaviour and bodies oriented to work, but what is more important, the ruling technique defines "the rules of the games". Underpinned in the proposition that McDonaldization is an advanced stage of global capitalism, he toys with the belief that the nature of technology can be framed in four clear-cut dimensions. Firstly, the principles of McDonaldization rests on efficiency, which means the correct selection of means to achieve ends, while secondly, predictability signals the need to foresee the consequences of previous decision-making processes. Thirdly, as Ritzer recognizes, calculability measures quantity rather than quality, reminding us of the importance of statistics and mathematical models in our contemporary world. Lastly, the notion of control allows the standardization of procedures, which inevitably leads towards a process of dehumanization (Ritzer 2013). The possibilities that humans would be replaced, at a later decade, by machines were one of the concerns of Ellul in his texts. While in other centuries, man was the centre of the universe, in capitalism he transforms into a mere commodity (Bauman 2005).

As with the previous argument presented, Andrew Feenberg—echoing Marcuse's contributions—alerts to the use of technology to control the workforce. Technology, per his viewpoint, not only domesticates the rank-and-file workers but it modifies nature through the capitalist wage system. One might not dissociate technology from rationality since both are two sides of the same coin. While the former is used to make our world safer, the latter ideologically legitimates the domination of ruling elite (Feenberg 1995). In 1965, Robert Boguslaw pinpointed the rise of a new class prone to technology. These aficionados to high-tech enthusiastically embrace the probability as a guiding cultural value of society. The idea of alienation, as it was studied by Marxists, sets the place for a new form of powerlessness which is derived from the individual rejection of critical thinking (Boguslaw 1965). More oriented to enhance profits than in promoting ethics, the future scientists shall devote their time to con-structing fictional landscapes to manage personnel and workers, than in understanding facts as they are. With the benefits of hindsight, the current theories in organizational management reveal two important assumptions. On the one hand, there is an undeniable tendency to re-educate workers through the repression and symbolization of emotions. In the current working conditions, a bunch of experts and management—many of them trained and skilled in psychology—learn how positive emotions may be conveniently expressed while negative ones should be avoided or covered. This point creates a one-sided discourse, where discontent, discrepancy and conflictivity are certainly demonized. In this way, workers unable to express their discontent should accept passively what the managers suggest (Illouz 2008; Scribano and Korstanje 2017; Scribano 2017; Korstanje 2018), in what Hochschild dubbed as "the managed heart" (Hochschild 2015). On the other hand, as Paul Virilio foretold, the role of modern science is not given in offering solutions to protect people or saving lives, but, rather in developing predictive models to avoid the risks that may place the status quo in jeopardy. With a focus on climate change, Virilio presents a radical criticism of modern scientists, who serve to the yoke of capital, looking for further investment and profit maximization while the current habits of hyperconsumerism and the technological background which today compromise the planet are not dismantled (Virilio 2010).

Last but not least, Virilio's insight narrows to the much deeper discussion left by Jean Baudrillard, where technology and the creation of pseudo-events occupy a central position. For Baudrillard, technology plays a leading role in creating utopian scenarios, which are enrooted in the future. He cites the plot of Spielberg's film, *Minority Report*, where Police helped by Precogs curbed crime to zero rates. These Precogs are psychics whose skills are amplified by high-tech, permitting them to predict crimes before they happen. This confronts Roman jurisprudence, in which case penalties can be only applied to real crimes. Besides, as Baudrillard warns, the climate of paranoia in *Minority Report* is not markedly different from the US war on terror, where the information is dully manipulated to forecast risks, which never take place in reality. This leads Baudrillard to sustain that events have set the pace to "pseudo-events" forging what he named as "the spectacle of disaster" (Baudrillard 2006).

TERRORISM AND THE CULTURE OF SPECTACLE

Over recent years, terrorism has posed as a serious challenge or threat for the Occident. Officials declared the urgency of coordinating efforts in defeating terrorism. The obscene cruelty directed against non-combatants and civilian targets outraged public opinion in the main consolidated democracies. The rise of ISIS and the public decapitation cemented a philosophical debate respecting the ethical roots of terrorism (Primoratz 2004). Equally important, classic terrorism targeted important celebrities, governors, politicians and police chiefs, while now, they prefer to kill innocent travellers, tourists, journalists or contractors (Korstanje 2017). The fact is that terrorism not only amply showed (and humiliated the West) how four civil aeroplanes may be weaponized against the world's most important military and economic power, the US, but suggested the serious inability of government to protect their citizens (Sandler and Enders 2004). The industries of mobilities and tourism, which were the pride of the West to date, were used by terrorists to perform the cruellest terrorist attack the US suffered in its history. To wit, David Lyon and Zygmunt Bauman (2013) argue convincingly though 9/11 did not create the background for the adoption of "high tech" surveillance, such an event accelerated the conditions for its reproduction. The authors allude to the term *adiaphorization* as the division between rationality and ethics. Modern wars are not fought face-to-face any longer; instead, now drones target objectives while military personnel monitor the campaign from a desk. Lyon and Bauman said that they are not blamed for the actions at the same time, their effects are framed as "collateral damages". The concept of adiaphorization reminds that their decisions are dissociated from the resulting aftermath. Originally, technology was created to find rapidly and eradicate those dangers that may jeopardize society, but over years, the situation opened the doors for a paradoxical situation where the counter-terrorist violence was controlled by machines, while the digital technologies allowed governments to control and spy upon their own citizens. The culture of liquid surveillance reveals that technology can be used to protect the home, whereas it can be an object of fetishism which marks the difference between those who can pay for further security from the hapless others who are disposed from the basic human rights (Lyon and Bauman 2013). In consonance with this, David Altheide (2014) discusses critically Snowden's case as a triumph of fear over democracy. Snowden was labelled and castigated by the government as a traitor, but in so doing, less is said respecting the role of government intruding in the citizens' private lives. Under the auspices of security, the American government constructed a tight system of surveillance, which justifies the violation of individual rights. As Geoffrey Skoll (2014) writes, one thing is for sure, the scandal revolving around the NSA (the US National Security Agency) displays how technology—in the culture of hypersurveillance—aims to control populations. Fear mongering, far from inculcating commonly shared practices to enhance homeland security, engenders a climate of fear to provide the nation state the complete and partisan monopoly of force, undermining civic dissidence in different ways.

In his classic and seminal book, updated after Donald Trump gained the presidency, David Altheide (2017) brings into reflection to what extent the current climate of fear that Americans have experienced, stems from the needs of consuming terrorism as a spectacle. The last presidential debate between Clinton and Trump pitted the fear of tyranny, which was historically expressed by the founding parents of Republic, against the fear of strangers. Trump won, Clinton lost, but the fact is that the psychological fear moved the elections and campaign in both sides. Altheide (2017) acknowledges that media operationalized the effects of terrorism, which heavily resonated in American public opinion, to nourish a long-dormant culture of popular entertainment. As he suggests,

This edition of Terrorism and The Politics of Fear illustrates how symbolic meaning about safety, danger, and fear can lead to major institutional changes and even war. (Altheide 2017: x)

He starts from the premise that Donald Trump reached the presidency by taking advantage of the climate of distrust, and fabricated fear, packaged and disseminated by the media to obtain further investors. Fear has its biological roots, as Altheide recognizes, but in the US, it is historically situated as a preferable commodity ready to be consumed. The fear of alterity acts as a conduit to revitalize not only daily frustrations, but also gives the owners of capital a privileged position for dissuading the dissident workers. This is aggravated by the fact that today events happening in remote geographical points can be framed and presented as nearer to the TV viewers. The spectatorship is often bombarded with news decontextualized from their real background, in which case, what happens in one corner of the global impacts in the other. As Altheide puts it, one of the ethical matters consists in presenting information to citizens they are really unable to grasp, which is associated with an uncanny interplay between fear and profits. As a result of this, fear is often manipulated and used by politicians to impose political or economic policies that otherwise would be widely rejected. The climate of fear instilled by government paves the ways for the rise of dangerous populisms which daily threaten the check and balance institutions (Altheide 2017). It is important not to lose sight of the fact that terrorism is often catalogued as a criminal act, while media is a positive phenomenon. However, Mahmoud Eid has put this into question. The mediatization of terrorism corresponds to a lower-cost strategy to gain further profits on the side of the media, while terrorists need publicity for their acts. This symbiosis led Eid to coin the term *Terroredia*, which is formed by terror and media. In his terms,

> Meanwhile, in order for both to survive, terrorists seek to garner public attention and the media seek to find stories to sell. In a sense, both parties target wide-ranging audiences (although for different purposes); hence, they interact in a highly toxic relationship that involves a process of exchange necessary for their survival. Acts of terrorism provide media stories that result in more broadcasts, press texts, and digital data bytes, while the media coverage brings public attention to terrorists—the oxygen necessary for their existent. (Eid 2014: 24)

The attacks on the World Trade Center on 11th September 2001 brought substantial changes not only in the way the US conceived its homeland security, but also other peripheral nations, which stayed on the sidelines of the previous conflict between Bin Laden and George Bush senior, faced a securitization process accompanied with an unparalleled hysteria. To a major or minor degree, it is safe to say henceforth terrorism unveiled a long-dormant fascination and obsession in American spectatorship for gazing upon death, a new emerging phenomenon theorized by Tumarkin (2005) as "traumascape". As Luke Howie (2012) puts it, terrorists do not want a lot of people dead, they like a lot of people watching! This suggests that one of the chief goals of terrorists is not strictly associated with violence as the specialized literature suggests, but prefers a vicarious sentiment of fear amplified precisely in those who do not stand at the centre of the picture. With some hindsight, Howie found a correlation between physical distance and fear mongering. Precisely, as Howie maintains, those societies situated in the global Southern periphery underwent higher levels of anxiety that often led towards an atmosphere of mistrust and terror than hapless New Yorkers. In this context, Fragopoulos and Naydan (2016) object to the already-established literature, which places terrorism as the main threat for the Occident. Rather, they toy with the belief terrorism inaugurated a novel artistic cult which is used to thematize the trauma of 9/11. Such a cultural movement includes movies, novels and visual arts, as other commoditized forms of consumption. Even if terrorism ignited a debate around the limitations in the way security is conceived in the Western tradition, no less true is that a new "aesthetics of 9/11" replicates the background of trauma sublimating towards reified forms of dark consumption. Most certainly, the art objects displayed to modern tourists transmit a symbolic discourse oriented to explain the attacks on the WTC. Authors appeal to the paradoxes of 9/11, which can be synthesized in the following way: *at the time we desperately try to forget the phantom of terrorism, we involuntarily invoke it as the centrepiece of our lifestyle.* The souvenirs of 9/11 are sold to visitors and tourists who are interested in knowing further just what there happened, but paradoxically the fictional theatre orchestrated around the Ground Zero in NY impedes a genuine understanding of the reasons terrorists were moved to attack the US.

> Despite near-immediate controversy because its crass commercialism on a literarily sacred site… the father of a 9/11 victim, the gift shop continues to market its (m)ugs, T-shirt, scarves and other souvenirs to visitors willing to pay the price – be it an monetary one, an ethical one, or some combination. The gift shop emerges because 9/11 happened but emerges to capitalize on 9/11 as though 9/11 as an emotional event never happened. (Fragopoulos and Naydan 2016: 6)

Fragopoulos and Naydan's main thesis is that art consumption aims to commercialize disasters and traumatic events in order to help people to deal with suffering, encrypting memory into a dark unconsciousness that remains in the past, insofar as a partial (repressed and invented story) is imposed upon the next generations. This happens because dark sites of consumption—like Ground Zero—never describe facts as they really occurred.

Ultimately, recent studies move to a critical perspective that denounces terrorism and inscribes it into a complex cultural platform, which is created not only to entertain lay citizens but displaces the causality of events towards a fictional landscape, externally fabricated and imposed to prevent social change. Like celebrities, terrorists are embedded with a culture of gazing (witnessing) that makes from the tragedy a criterion of attraction, if not pleasure maximization (Howie 2009, 2012; Howie and Campbell 2017; Korstanje 2016; Tzanelli 2016).

SLAVOJ ŽIŽEK AND THE DESSERT OF THE REAL

Although it is not possible to lump together all Žižek's works in this section, we rather shall delve into *The Universal Exception*. Preliminarily, he starts from the premise that the bipolar world, where the US conducted a symbolic war with the Soviet Union, was finished. This caused a melancholia for left-wing scholars, who not only embraced a conservative view but developed a cynical attitude, which overtly criticizes what in effects it validates. These scholars proclaim on the negative effects of capitalism in the day to day life, but they did not make the minimum effort to change the situation. This evinces a clear dissociation between *the subject of the enunciated and the subject of the enunciation*. In other words, postmodern politics coincides with the terrorist's message, which reminds that I want you not only to do what I want, but I want you to do it as if you really want to do it! Žižek argues convincingly how people remain subject to an "extreme civility", which intends expanding the belief democratic citizens are free to decide, when really they are strictly determined by "the Big Other". Needless to say, this "Big Other", which is opposed to little Other, is not a physical entity, nor does it relate to "the Big Brother" as many scholars assumed. It represents the syntactical, grammatical, implicit norms, social conventions that daily mould the individual and collective behaviours. Whether the relations between capital owners and workers are part of the little other, the underlying conditions of labour exploitation signals to the Big Other. As Žižek puts it,

> The role of civility in modern societies to the rise of autonomous free individual – not only in the sense that civility is the practice of treating others as equal, free and autonomous subjects, but, in a much more refined way, the fragile web of civility is the social substance of free independent individuals. (Žižek 2015: xv)

As cited above, the extreme civility symbolically exhibits the opposite; oddly the act of feigning people is free when really it is not. We live, undoubtedly, under the hegemony of totalitarian regimes, which are camouflaged in liberal democracies. One of the aspects that defines the dictators is that they are prone to pose *criminal law so severe that* if followed literarily all we are guilty of something. In what, at least for this reviewer, is the best chapter of the book ("Heiner Muller out of Joint"), he discusses the essence of liberal democracy from an innovative angle. He posits a more than pertinent question, namely what would happen if a political party which is next to win an election, refuses the founding values of democracy? Is this emerging party punished or pressed to operate in clandestine life?

As Žižek questioned, liberal democracy should be esteemed as a formal legality, disposed to resolve some adversarial positions in the game.

> Democracy... concerns above all, formal legality: its minimal definition is the unconditional adherence to a certain set of formal rules which guarantee that antagonisms are fully absorbed not the agonistic game. Democracy means that whatever electoral manipulation takes place, every political agent will unconditionally respect the results. (Žižek 2015: 59)

After all, Žižek's debate enlivens the dichotomies between the formal "written law", and what he dubs as "the obscene superego", which exemplifies the hidden law. Žižek echoes the example of the Klu Klux Klan (KKK) in Southern America. The former prohibited extreme punishments against hapless blacks, whereas the KKK deployed different disciplinary mechanisms to legitimate their monopoly of force outside the law. Any member of KKK was a renowned member of his community, but he might be very well exiled while rejecting a direct order of a superior to lynch a black. In that way, Žižek adds, the system conserves a light and dark side to keep a narrower scrutiny of its members.

In this perspective, Žižek attempts to discuss multiculturalism in different ways. Leo Strauss imagined an aristocratic society where some secrets should be kept from lay persons, veiled by their ignorance. Most probably, Žižek's thesis can be synthesized with Socrates' trial. He was *guilty as charged "because philosophy is a threat to society"* (p. 62). To put this bluntly, the current crisis of democracy suggests that just after revealing the necessary lie, the ruling elite remains naked. In factual terms, though the revolution was orchestrated by the relegated peasant and working classes, the Communist party ideologically subverted the sense of reality to impose a fabricated story that explains for the workforce the reasons behind their difficult conditions of life. Let us clarify readers that the term *exploitation* was elaborated according to the interest of the party and its leaders. Under the authority of Stalin, the Communist party worked as a mediator between the workers, who needed to be cultivated and educated according to Marx's manifesto, and the reality. Once the Soviet Union fell, a new unimagined reality surfaced. Nonetheless, the same happened in the Western societies once 9/11 woke Americans from their slumber. Žižek adamantly insists that the notion of leisure was discursively drawn to fit with the class struggle in the Soviet Union, which explains a (distorted) answer to the state of exaltation to which workers are daily subject. This raises the question, to what extent can leisure be conceived as a distortion of reality?

In the *Matrix Saga*, Morpheus tells Neo "welcome to the desert of the real" to symbolize the passage of the virtual world to the real. In consequence, 9/11 and modern terrorism not only confronted us with the belief that we move in a wonderland, a tradition which is inaugurated in the plot of *The Truman Show*, but also interrogated the ontological essence of the West. In the plot, Neo is disconnected from the Matrix while Morpheus explains his entire life was a virtual dream. The dessert of the real seems to be the toughness Neo should face from that moment on. What is more relevant, the West has developed (through the introduction of leisure and media consumption) a virtual landscape, where the risks of life are eradicated. He mentions the example of the new products placed at the disposal of consumers in the market, such as coffee without caffeine, beers without alcohol and so forth, to describe a fabricated existence deprived of all threats of real life. In this virtual world there are no looming dangers that may place the system in jeopardy; at least there were not, until the rise of 9/11. The shock that invaded the US is not different to Neo's surprise to realize his life was a complete fake. Žižek, in this vein, confirms that modern leisure placates the critical thinking of workers into an emotionless virtuality (Žižek, 205). Unless otherwise resolved, terrorism wakes up the West from its slumber while interrogating the ethical dilemma of Society 4.0.

Terrorism, Tourism and Labour

Although much has been debated regarding the effects of terrorism in legal jurisprudence, that is, in human rights (Gearty 2007; Ranstorp and Wilkinson 2013), migration (Nassar 2009; Bosswell 2007) and crime policies (Simon 2007; Calveiro 2012), among others, less has been said on how the culture of terror domesticates daily worker unions, fixing not only the economic agenda but moulding working conditions and interclass relations (Skoll 2016; Howie 2012). In this vein, Professor Skoll carefully reviews the different discourses orchestrated around the idea the hat the workforce should be entertained by cultural consumption or intimidated, in case of conflict or discontent, by the imposition of fear. From its inception American governments appealed to fear (against communism, against terrorism or anything else) as a disciplinary mechanism of control, articulating liberal economic policies that otherwise would be never accepted (Skoll 2016). In view of this, Canadian journalist Naomi Klein, in her book *The Shock Doctrine*, stipulates that neoliberalism, which in an expanding force, needs from fear to disarticulate the institutions of checks and balances present in democratic culture. There is a new capitalism of disaster, which not only organizes a new territory of fear, but introduces concrete measures oriented to legitimate the idea of creative destruction (Klein 2007). Richard Sennett, in the same way, theorized on the radical changes the labour market suffered over recent decades. As a co-manager of its own risks, the worker is bereft between changing of jobs to affirm the status quo, and accepts labour instability as a challenge for a proper career. In this respect, as Sennett insists, capitalism not only disorganizes the social relations around the productive system, but also educates workers to accept the uncertainty and job insecurity as the preconditions of a successful professional career. Creative destruction, which is the symbolic touchstone of capitalism, was a notion formulated by J. Schumpeter. His connotation was given to the social forces, which are certainly disposed to renovate the source of production, in order to innovate production from within. The need of innovation is inevitably to destroy while creating (Sennett 2011). David Harvey calls attention to the relations between creative destruction and neoliberalism. In consonance with other critical voices, he argues that any system that proclaims itself a hegemonic requires the orchestration of ideological but concrete concepts. Capitalism has historically built a conceptual framework with the focus on the liberalization of relations, production and fostering values such as freedom and democracy. To some extent, some external forces as fascism or communism have threatened these ideals, but what is more important, after the 1960s neoliberalism failed to give answers to citizens in respect of job security, economic prosperity and upward social mobility. The Oil embargo, accelerated by the Arab-Israeli war, not only placed the economic matrix of the Occident between the wall and the deep blue sea, but also urged the consolidated capitalist economies to change their sources of energies. In the middle of this mayhem, the idea of a creative destruction played a leading role in narcotizing an ever-angry mass of low paid workers (Harvey 2007).

As with the preceding argument, Luke Howie conducted a more than an interesting investigation to explain how terrorism and the war on terror are gradually transforming the current forms of production, as well as the labour market in Australia. He unravels a strange paradox in the capitalist system. While private security guards are essential links in the securitization process, they are low paid, deprived of a permanent contract or subject to an ongoing precaritization, which leads to poverty, alcoholism and drug abuse. Howie argues convincingly that tourism and hospitality industries echo on the importance of security and safety, but at the same time, the role of private security guards is trivialized or hired by organizations that daily make vulnerable their working conditions and of course, their rights as workers (Howie 2014). In this respect, though terrorism has no direct implications for peripheral nations like Australia, no less true is that it intervenes in a climate of increasing occupational stress, adjoined to a changing organizational culture. The attacks perpetrated in New York, Madrid and London remind us that the victims were working people. Terrorism, henceforth, for Americans and Europeans was a real threat, but in Australia—though some tourists have been killed in Bali—terrorism sounds a phantom character. What happens in Australia, following Howie, signals to the fear of terrorism without terrorism!

Here two assumptions should be made. On the one hand, 9/11 and the derived events in London or Madrid were symbolically monopolized by the government glossing over other similar events that occurred in other nations. On the other, Australians only understand terrorism through the lens of mass media or journalism. This recreates the background towards an atmosphere of extreme anxiety, where the message of what terrorism is, seems to follow conventional etiquette and is stereotyped by the ruling elite (Howie 2005, 2007). As he found, September 11 ignited a new type of cultural racism, which was camouflaged under the guise of Islamophobia, and crystalized in a real discrimination for Arabs and Muslims. Many of the interviewees in Howie's research showed not only their fear of being in contact with Muslims, but an irrational racism oriented to isolate these ethnic groups—in the name of security—(Howie 2007). In tourism, hospitality and other service industries, this reality is particularly true, above all in the staff which is oriented to deal and interact with foreign (Muslim) tourists. Another additional problem, besides discrimination, consists in the distress workers feel while meeting with Muslim visitors. Howie emphasizes the dichotomies of counterterrorism, which says overtly that people do not cede to fear, while at the bottom, in concrete practices, some discriminatory practices against Islam and Muslims prevail. Islamophobia represents today a vivid sentiment of discrimination, which operates through a floating signifier. Islamophobia reminds us of a much deeper anti-Arab sentiment manipulated and replicated for the elite to conserve its privileges (Poole 2002). Though prejudices are inherent to the human mind, helping the individuals to sort through reality, Islamophobia depicts a radically different setting. As Saeed (2005, 2007) puts it, for some reason white social scientists overlook the problem of Islamophobia as an excessive reaction to the fear caused by terrorism. The discursivity of Islamophobia rests not only in western colonial constructions with respect to the East, as a known place that deserved to be domesticated, but 9/11 and the discourse behind securitization also give the best excuse to subordinate Muslim culture to the European Matrix. Around Islam, the media portrays an image, which associates their ancient culture as hostile to Christianity. After all, Islamophobia hides a great trauma in the post 9/11 era, reaching to vast audiences across the globe. The aftershocks generated by terrorism and the attacks on the WTC not only structured internally the politics of the US, but also its international relations policies (Awan 2010).

Conclusion

This chapter brings the problem of terrorism, Society 4.0 and the cultural organization in tourism into the foreground. In consonance with Corey Robin, we must accept that fear plays a double role. On the one hand, fear paralyses the citizens—who in the name of further security—sacrifice their autonomy and basic rights. On the other, it allows the invention of an external enemy oriented to enhance social cohesion (Robin 2004). Doubtless, 9/11 quickened changes, associated with the neoliberal agenda, that were conducive to labour precaritization worldwide (Skoll 2016; Altheide 2017). Additionally, in tourism and hospitality industries particularly, the front desk staff experienced anti-Arab sentiment, which was fostered by the fear of terrorism. As discussed in this chapter, terrorism not only shocked but woke the Occident from its slumber. Žižek suggests that 9/11 marks the beginning of an epoch, where the free citizens are enslaved by the culture of consumerism and virtual reality. The same technology aimed at making from urban cities safer (exemplary) centres were weaponized against the most important targets, the Pentagon and the WTC. To put this bluntly, terrorism interrogates and encroaches in the fictionality created by a mediated society, where events are commoditized and sold as pseudo-events. Paradoxically, in contemporary society terrorism is conceived as a danger, which triggers the surface of the most recalcitrant racism, and as a "show", made to keep the workers under control (Korstanje 2016; Tzanelli 2016). Last but not least, Islamophobia as a tactic of domination imagined by the ruling elite, plays a crucial role introducing "the enemy", similar to the metaphor of the Trojan Horse. The witch-hunts initiated in the US against the Muslim community reveal not only the impossibilities of workers and unions to confront the owners of capital, but also how the discourse of security is functional to policies intended to increase the precariousness of work.

REFERENCES

Altheide, D. L. (2014). The Triumph of Fear: Connecting the Dots About Whistleblowers and Surveillance. Special Issue, M. Korstanje (Ed.). *International Journal of Cyber Warfare and Terrorism (IJCWT)*, *4*(1), 1–7.

Altheide, D. (2017). *Terrorism and the Politics of Fear*. New York: Rowman & Littlefield.

Awan, S. M. (2010). Global Terror and the Rise of Xenophobia/Islamophobia: An Analysis of American Cultural Production Since September 11. *Islamic Studies, 29*(4), 521–537.

Baudrillard, J. (2006). Virtuality and Events: The Hell of Power. *Baudrillard Studies, 3*(2), 1–9.

Bauman, Z. (2005). *Liquid Life*. Cambridge: Polity Press.

Bauman, Z. (2013). *Consuming Life*. Cambridge: Polity Press.

Boguslaw, R. (1965). *The New Utopians: A Study of System Design and Social Change*. Englewood Cliffs: Prentice-Hall.

Bosswell, C. (2007). Migration Control in Europe After 9/11: Explaining the Absence of Securitization. *JCMS: Journal of Common Market Studies, 45*(3), 589–610.

Calveiro, P. (2012). *Violencias de Estado: la guerra antiterrorista y la guerra contra el crimen como medios de control global*. Buenos Aires: Siglo veintiuno editores.

Cronin, A. K. (2015). ISIS Is Not a Terrorist Group: Why Counterterrorism Won't Stop the Latest Jihadist Threat. *Foreign Affairs, 94*, 87.

Eid, M. (Ed.). (2014). *Exchanging Terrorism Oxygen for Media Airwaves: The Age of Terroredia*. Hershey: IGI Global.

Ellul, J. (1962). The Technological Order. *Technology and Culture, 3*(4), 394–421.

Ellul, J. (1964). *The Technological Society*. New York: Vintage Books.

Ellul, J. (1992). Technology and Democracy. In *Democracy in a Technological Society* (pp. 35–50). Dordrecht: Springer.

Feenberg, A. (1995). Subversive Rationalization: Technology, Power and Democracy. In A. Feenberg & A. Hannay (Eds.), *Technology and the Politics of Knowledge* (pp. 301–322). Bloomington: Indiana University Press.

Fragopoulos, G., & Naydan, L. M. (Eds.). (2016). *Terror in Global Narrative: Representations of 9/11 in the Age of Late-late Capitalism*. New York: Springer.

Gearty, C. (2007). Terrorism and Human Rights. *Government and Opposition, 42*(3), 340–362.

Hall, J. W. (2016). To Starve an Army: How Great Power Armies Respond to Austerity. In J. Suri & B. Valentino (Eds.), *Sustainable Security: Rethinking American National Security Strategy* (pp. 166–197). Oxford: Oxford University Press.

Harvey, D. (2007). Neoliberalism as Creative Destruction. *The Annals of the American Academy of Political and Social Science, 610*(1), 21–44.

Hochschild, A. R. (2015). The Managed Heart. In A. R. Hochschild (Ed.), *Working in America* (pp. 47–54). Abingdon: Routledge.

Howie, L. (2005, October 28). There Is Nothing to Fear But Fear Itself (and Terrorists): Public Perception, Terrorism and the Workplace. In: Social Change in the 21st Century Conference, Centre for Change Research, Queensland University of Technology.

Howie, L. (2007). The Terrorism Threat and Managing Workplaces. *Disaster Prevention and Management: An International Journal, 16*(1), 70–78.

Howie, L. (2009). A Role for Business in the War on Terror. *Disaster Prevention and Management: An International Journal, 18*(2), 100–107.

Howie, L. (2012). *Witnesses to Terror: Understanding the Meanings and Consequences of Terrorism*. New York: Springer.

Howie, L. (2014). Security Guards and Counter-Terrorism: Tourism and Gaps in Terrorism Prevention. *International Journal of Religious Tourism and Pilgrimage, 2*(1), 7.

Howie, L. (2015). Witnessing Terrorism. *Journal of Sociology, 51*(3), 507–521.

Howie, L., & Campbell, P. (2017). *Crisis and Terror in the Age of Anxiety: 9/11, the Global Financial Crisis and ISIS*. New York: Springer.

Illouz, E. (2008). *Saving the Modern Soul: Therapy, Emotions, and the Culture of Self-help*. Chicago: University of California Press.

Inboden, W. (2016). Reforming American Power: Civilian National Security Institutions in the Early Cold War and Beyond. In J. Suri & B. Valentino (Eds.),

Sustainable Security: Rethinking American National Security Strategy (pp. 136–165). Oxford: Oxford University Press.

Khader, M. (Ed.). (2016). *Combating Violent Extremism and Radicalization in the Digital Era.* Hershey: IGI Global.

Kirshner, K. (2016). Dollar Diminution and New Macroeconomic Constraints on American Power. In J. Suri & B. Valentino (Eds.), *Sustainable Security: Rethinking American National Security Strategy* (pp. 1–21). Oxford: Oxford University Press.

Klein, N. (2007). *The Shock Doctrine: The Rise of Disaster Capitalism.* New York: Macmillan.

Korstanje, M. E. (2016). *The Rise of Thana-Capitalism and Tourism.* Abingdon: Routledge.

Korstanje, M. E. (2017). *Terrorism, Tourism and the End of Hospitality in the West.* New York: Springer Nature.

Korstanje, M. E. (2018). *Tracing Spikes of Fear and Narcissism in Western Democracies Since 9/11.* Oxford: Peter Lang.

Lyon, D., & Bauman, Z. (2013). *Liquid Surveillance: A Conversation.* Cambridge: Polity Press.

Mitcham, C. (1997). *Thinking Ethics in Technology: Hennebach Lectures and Papers, 1995–1996.* Boulder: Division of Liberal Arts and International Studies.

Mitcham, C. (2013). How the Technological Society Became More Important in the United States than in France. In H. Jeronimo, J. L. Garcia, & C. Mitcham (Eds.), *Jacques Ellul and the Technological Society in the 21st Century* (pp. 17–34). London: Springer.

Nassar, J. R. (2009). *Globalization and Terrorism: The Migration of Dreams and Nightmares.* New York: Rowman & Littlefield Publishers.

Poole, E. (2002). *Reporting Islam: Media Representations and British Muslims.* London: IB Tauris.

Primoratz, I. (2004). State Terrorism and Counter-terrorism. In I. Primoratz (Ed.), *Terrorism* (pp. 113–127). London: Palgrave Macmillan.

Pyszczynski, T., Solomon, S., & Greenberg, J. (2003). *In the Wake of 9/11: Rising Above the Terror.* Washington, DC: American Psychological Association.

Ranstorp, M., & Wilkinson, P. (Eds.). (2013). *Terrorism and Human Rights.* Abingdon: Routledge.

Ritzer, G. (2013). The Technological Society: Social Theory, McDonaldization and the Prosumer. In H. Jeronimo, J. L. Garcia, & C. Mitcham (Eds.), *Jacques Ellul and the Technological Society in the 21st Century* (pp. 35–48). London: Springer.

Robin, C. (2004). *Fear: The History of a Political Idea.* Oxford: Oxford University Press.

Saeed, A. (2005). Racism and Islamophobia: A Personal Perspective. *Identity Papers: A Journal of British and Irish Studies, 1*(1), 15–31.

Saeed, A. (2007). Media, Racism and Islamophobia: The Representation of Islam and Muslims in the Media. *Sociology Compass, 1*(2), 443–462.

Sandler, T., & Enders, W. (2004). An Economic Perspective on Transnational Terrorism. *European Journal of Political Economy, 20*(2), 301–316.

Scribano, A. (2017). *Normalization, Enjoyment and Bodies/Emotions: Argentine Sensibilities.* New York: Nova Science.

Scribano, A., & Korstanje, M. E. (2017). Emotions and Epistemology: A Path for Reconsideration in the 21st Century. *International Journal of Human Rights and Constitutional Studies, 5*(2), 111–129.

Sennett, R. (2011). *The Corrosion of Character: The Personal Consequences of Work in the New Capitalism.* New York: WW Norton & Company.

Simon, J. (2007). *Governing Through Crime: How the War on Crime Transformed American Democracy and Created a Culture of Fear.* Oxford: Oxford University Press.

Skoll, G. R. (2014). Stealing Consciousness: Using Cybernetics for Controlling Populations. Special Issue Edited by M. Korstanje. *International Journal of Cyber Warfare and Terrorism (IJCWT), 4*(1), 27–35.

Skoll, G. R. (2016). *Globalization of American Fear Culture: The Empire in the Twenty-First Century.* New York: Springer.

Suri, J., & Valentino, B. (2016). *Sustainable Security: Rethinking American National Security Strategy.* Oxford: Oxford University Press.

Tumarkin, M. M. (2005). *Traumascapes: The Power and Fate of Places Transformed by Tragedy.* Melbourne: Melbourne University Publishing.

Tzanelli, R. (2016). *Thanatourism and Cinematic Representations of Risk: Screening the End of Tourism.* Abingdon: Routledge.

Virilio, P. (2010). *University of Disaster.* Cambridge: Polity Press.

Žižek, S. (2015). *The Universal Exception.* London: Bloomsbury Publishing.

PART II

Politics of Sensibilities
and Digital Labour

Labour, Body, and Social Conflict: The "Digital Smile" and Emotional Work in Call Centres

Pedro Lisdero

One of the characteristic features of the global transformations of the "world of work" is related to the reconfiguration of a set of flexible processes aimed at the expropriation and commodification of the cognitive and affective corporal energies of workers (Scribano et al. 2015; Lisdero 2013). This seems to be a transversal phenomenon, which not only affects the "old" and new "occupations" but also constitutes a central element of the structuring processes of social relations (even beyond the borders of the workplace). The forms from which Western modernity was accustomed to commodify the vital forces seem to find a new point of redefinition, as Society 4.0 expands quantitatively and qualitatively.

In this sense, the aim of this chapter is to look into some of the contributions of the sociology of bodies/emotions in order to understand the manifestations of social conflict linked to new labour scenarios, as a starting point from which to understand the processes of social structuration (Giddens 2003). Specifically, the purpose here is to explore a few of the meaningful dimensions of conflicts associated with the Call Centres (CCs) sector.

P. Lisdero (✉)
CONICET, Córdoba, Argentina

© The Author(s) 2019
A. Scribano, P. Lisdero (eds.), *Digital Labour, Society and the Politics of Sensibilities*, https://doi.org/10.1007/978-3-030-12306-2_7

The activities of this sector have become a paradigmatic[1] *locus* from which the "emotions" in the naturalization of "working conditions" in emerging digital labour contexts can be analysed.

Based on this objective, the following argumentative strategy is proposed. Firstly, several general theoretical considerations underpinning the analysis will be made. Secondly, the processes of work insecurity observed in the sector from the emergence of precarious bodies will be described. Thirdly, the "potentiality for collective action" of the bodies-that-work will be especially problematized, emphasizing the issue of "emotional work" (Hochschild 1983), as a privileged standpoint for its interpretation. The lines of analysis presented will be based upon quotes from interviews with workers from CCs, who participated in protests in the city of Córdoba, Argentina, during the period 2006–2013; on data gathered through observation of public protests; and parts of data from an online ethnographic research project based on blogs, Facebook profiles, and other social networks and sites used by the organizations organizing these protests.[2]

In the conclusions, we will recast the phrase "slavery of the souls" (Colectivo Situaciones 2006) in order to problematize, from the perspective of the actors, the meaning of the social mechanisms previously linked

---

[1] For a different perspective, but starting from the same premise assumed here about the possibilities of an analytic perspective on CCs, see Braga (2009): "Precisely because we are dealing with a sector which, to an extent, condenses a wide variety of capitalist productive re-structuration inherent tendencies, industrial scale production of information services represents a privileged standpoint for the observation of the contradictions and ambivalences of labour in contemporary society" (p. 66).

[2] The data used in this chapter was gathered as part of a research project funded by CONICET: I have developed a research line that seeks to understand the mechanisms of expropriation of corporal energies among urban workers in the city of Córdoba. In relation to the data presented here, it is worthwhile mentioning that since 2007 we have been engaged in and completed (a) an observation of public conflicts related to the CCs sector in the city of Córdoba, (b) more than 20 interviews with members of organizations linked to the sector, and (c) a virtual ethnographic gathering of data from blogs, Facebook profiles, and Web sites of the work organizations linked to CC. However, in order to emphasize the main argument made here, the data used in this analysis is limited to the 2007–2013 period. During the second decade of the twenty-first century, not only the dynamics of development of the sector are undergoing an inflection—at least in Argentina—but the logic of collective action is also showing distinctive features: the recognition by the *Ministerio del Trabajo de la Nación* of the legal character of the ATCCAC as a work union (Resolution 479/13), and process of nationalization of this organization, which resulted in a rearrangement of actors of the sector, are among the most relevant.

between digital and emotional work. Thus, the "digital smile" as a required disposition for the workers in the sector becomes at the same time the battering ram of an "emotional environment" linked to the new labour scenarios of the power mechanisms imposed by capital in Society 4.0. The instances of manifestation of conflict come at a sensitive time in which to reflect about the limits of these social processes which go beyond "Call Centres" as "specific cases", raising questions about the possibilities of resistance against such mechanisms.

CAPITALISM, EMOTIONS, AND EXPANSION OF COMMODIFICATION PROCESSES

Work has been a central element in understanding the forms of social relationships. As modern capitalist society expands, the daily life of subjects finds in work an organizer of the times, spaces, and areas in which it develops. Consequently, it is not surprising that as the global processes that are associated with what has been called Society 4.0[3] progress not only the "world of work" is put into question but more broadly the connections between "what subjects do" and "the ways in which they are related" (even beyond the productive areas).

Looking back at the transformations of work, a wide variety of studies from diverse disciplines linked to the analyses of the "world of work" in the last decades have revealed a series of transformations that affect the *everyday life* of work relations. Indeed, among the descriptions made about the transformations of the "world of work", we find a variety of perspectives unable to reach a consensus on the characteristics and consequences of these changes, or even on the limits and scope of the analytical units needed to account for them. This could be read as a sign of the high complexity of the phenomenon that goes beyond the different theoretical and epistemic focus of these perspectives (De la Garza 2000). However, a second glance reveals that the reflections about work activities are associated with a variable and heterogeneous set of problematics, most notable: (a) the transformations in the composition of the working class, (b) the technological leap, (c) transformations in the organization of work, or processes of management, (d) transformations in workers' rights, and (e) globalization (Antunes 2005; Del Bono 2002; Novick 2010, Neffa 1999).

---

[3] Some assumptions, characteristics, and implications of Society 4.0 have been developed in Chap. 1: "Introduction: Politics of Sensibilities, Society 4.0 and Digital Labour".

In this sense, the transformations in the "world of work" call for a reconsideration of, among other things, the processes in the sphere of production of commodities in our societies, and particularly in their relation to the constitution of "the-body-of-those-who-work". This latter perspective, and the relationship between these elements (i.e. the constitution of bodies and the processes of production of commodities), is already present in Marx's critique of capitalist society (Haber and Renault 2007; Scribano 2012). The body is thus constituted in tension with the dynamic processes implicating domination and resistance; they are neither matter infinitely malleable by norms, nor simple vessels of social interiorizations. The body becomes relevant for our perspective, as noted by Haber and Renault, not because: "(...) it constitutes the origin or the main locus of resistance but, simply, because it is one of the important factors and a frequent partner in protests actions" (2007: 10).

Looking back at this "indicator" of the state of social relations enables, among other things, a narrative of the recent history of this system as a constant dispute of the bodies against the expropriation of corporal[4] energies initiated by capital (Lisdero 2013). This expropriation process, the origins of which was described by Marx as stemming from the tensions between alienation, expropriation, and dispossession, traces its path in a close connection with the constant impulse to reinvent the modes and resources from which the energy of bodies is transmuted in capitalist social relations. We can therefore say that the history of human work is the history of the expropriation of corporal energies. The political economy of capitalism reinvents itself hand-in-hand with the technological development centred on maximization of the metabolization rates of the corporal energies. Ever more parts of the human are reduced to the reproductive sphere of capitalism: emotions, affections, communicative competences, and so on.

Long gone are the days of the "end of work" ideas fashionable in the 1980s and 1990s; no one today disputes the centrality of work in today's global framework. Thus, the fundamental question today is what are the limits, experiences, possibilities, and contradictions of the new grammar

---

[4] The concept of corporal energy is taken from the work of Scribano, who defines it as "(...) the result of the exchange between physiological systems and the biological processes associated with the durability of the body-individual" (Scribano 2007: 99). Elsewhere I have discussed with more detail the origin of the concept and its wide and polysemic use in the sociology of work (Lisdero 2013b).

generated by the "world of work" in its process of consolidation. The widening scope of the exercise of the accumulation of corporal energies extends to new territories of human and natural being, and redefines in consequence the scenarios and the deployment of processes of struggle and resistance associated with work.

This is the right place to bring to the fore, in relation to the questions raised by these scenarios, the contributions of a sociology of bodies/emotions. In this sense, a quick look at these contributions accounts for a wide and diverse field of study, including the works of Le Breton and Turner, theorists from the second half of the twentieth century such as Erving Goffman (1989) or Norbert Elías (2015), or ideas by Pierre Bourdieu (1999) and Anthony Giddens (2003), among others. As a disciplinary field, some authors place the beginnings of the sociology of bodies and emotions in the work of Brian Turner (Gremilion 2005), others consider Thomas Scheff, Arlie Hochschild, and Theodore Kemper as the real pioneers of the discipline (Bericat Alastuey 2000).

Indeed, from our perspective, the classics of sociology already raised questions about these objects of study, which played a relevant role in their thinking. In this sense, a more or less explicit concern of social theory becomes evident in a problematizing of bodies and emotions in relation to the social processes which constitute the modern social order. The emergence of the state—and a logic of violence as a defence of sovereignty and vigilance as control of difference—"imposes" a research agenda about forms of dominations linked to the corporal. The new geometries of bodies emerging with the new ordering of social relations required a closer look into disrupted and unproductive bodies as threats to order. This is the context for the establishment of certain connections at the time of the birth and reproduction of capitalist social relations, between what has been described as an act of expropriation of bodily energies, and the processes of management of deviant individuals through a scientific intervention upon bodies.

Within the explanations of capitalism, issues of bodies and emotions are recurring problematic concerns for several authors dealing with the analysis of the processes of the emergence and consolidation of a system that produces subjects *for* objects, through the fetishist commodification of life. This is an important point for understanding Marx's analysis, as capitalism is based on making the other into an object of my enjoyment. The subtraction of vitality from bodies is linked to a form of political economy of morality (Scribano 2012) founded on competence, which becomes a moral law regulating practices framed in a set of relations based on the sale of the workforce, under conditions such that the-subjects-who-work (Antunes 2005) are driven to the limits of their corporal reproduction.

However, this way of understanding the processes of capitalist restructuring takes on new forms associated with the development of Society 4.0. The expansion of digital life to the most diverse areas of interaction leads us to rethink what is observed regarding the place of bodies and emotions in labour processes. It is in this direction that the emergence of conflict in the CC sector (of Argentina) allows a condensing of certain significant elements for understanding our societies.

Paradigmatic Conflict: Call Centres in Argentina

From the perspective that we want to present here, the CCs constitute a paradigmatic sector: a field of social relations where there is a meeting between Society 4.0 and digital labour, as new forms of labour commodification of vital energies.

CCs can be understood as "(…) the support developed by some companies to remotely satisfy certain aspects of the relations with their clients; they are telephone platforms which can be directly managed by the company concerned with providing assistance to its clients, or by a providing external company to which the management of the service is outsourced" (Del Bono and Bulloni 2008: 3). Indeed, the expansion of this activity is linked worldwide with the expansion of outsourcing, a trend initially set in play by transnational companies in the 1970s in order to reduce production costs by externalizing processes. It has been estimated that this activity employed, by the first decade of the twenty-first century, close to 750,000 people in Europe (Micheli 2007). In Latin America it employed 675,000 Brazilian (Olivera 2009) and 380,000 Mexican workers (Montarcé 2011).

In Argentina, this "industry" grew exponentially with the devaluation of the currency in 2002, and its corresponding reduction in the cost of work,[5] and a concentration of mainly multinational export service providers. As a result, less than ten companies control the market, and no more six control exports (Del Bono 2010). At that time, it has been estimated that the sector employs around 60,000 workers, located mainly in the

---

[5] CCs were defined, by the Collective Agreement on Labour N.130/75, as a commercial activity, which implied an additional reduction in work costs in comparison to that of the telephone industry.

provinces of Buenos Aires, Rosario, Mendoza, and Córdoba. These cities, according to representatives of the sector, offer a thriving labour market comprised mainly of young professionals and higher education students. Provincial governments have also offered generous fiscal reliefs to the industry, on top of those already granted by the national government. Generally speaking, in Argentina, the development and logic of the CCs' activity seems to have acquired new characteristics as we turn to the second decade of the new century.[6]

Turning our focus to the expansion period of CCs reveals only a few and fragmentary expression of conflict. This is in part due to the fact that outsourcing diluted the traditional political relations of work; worker representation became progressively divided by sectors. At the same time companies, some labour unions, and political power deployed judicial-legal-administrative mechanisms which judicialized potential protests and denied legal status to unions and emerging worker organizations, among other mobilization devices, in the sector. This invisibility of the conflict can also be traced to the more subtle and unseen dimensions of everyday life work relations, for example in the cases of organization technologies and "toxic management" (Braga 2009). In addition, the implementation of "quality standards" in customer assistance services implies the intervention of mechanisms in the constitution of worker's bodies that impact their perceptions of themselves, thus affecting their individual and collective identities.

The disposition required from the subjects, which is taught in "quality manuals" or by the use of euphemisms such as the "telephone smile", expresses the interfering of technology with the body of the worker. Words, feelings, the most "inner" capacities of the subjects, are minutely intervened upon, and the possibility of saying or feeling something different (about-myself or by-myself) in the service dialogue becomes an extremely difficult challenge. In this context, the smile, for example, is incorporated by the subject as a continuous affective state that involves mobilizing intimate energies in order to "get the job done right". This

---

[6] For reasons of space, and given the objectives of this chapter, we will not expand upon the reconfigurations of the sector. However, it is worth clarifying that the successive global crises and their consequences in the local context, the depletion of the replacement niches in the context of a broad rotation of employees, the impact of exchange rate policies on labour costs, and the reconfiguration of the actors' scenario economics intervening in the sector, among other relevant factors, have led to a slight withdrawal and complexity of the activity in our days.

specific relational dimension between bodies/emotions and social conflict reveals the analytical framework of the issue.

The Bodies Behind the Information

An extended image about the type of work linked to the treatment of information is usually that of a relaxed subject, working in a comfortable environment, and receiving good pay for it. It seems that work is separated from the idea of physical "effort". However, CC workers denounce that: "They [businessmen] know they are lying to the people of Córdoba, saying that it's a working school... It's a *meat grinder*: that's what Call Centres are today in Córdoba (...)" (Field notes. Heard during a protest march in April 22, 2009). The voice of the workers themselves leads us to find out what place the body occupies in these production processes.

As part of the analysis of the protests of the CC sector in the city of Córdoba, we observed that (a) the activity of the CCs qualitatively grew from 2002, but initially there was a lack of protests in public spaces; (b) from 2006 on several organizations that carry out visible protest actions have emerged; (c) these actions raise question not only about the sense of timing of visibility but also lead to a rethinking of the apparent lack of conflict during the previous period; (d) and also leads to a reflection about the frames that "make visible" processes staged by actors themselves constituted by the fact of "making themselves heard, making themselves visible", which also raises questions about the theoretical-methodological strategies used to capture the deep meaning of actions (Lisdero 2013b). Thus, between 2006 and 2013, there were "*Cuelgues de Vinchas*" (hanging of headsets), protest marches, *Escraches* (public denunciations), artistic interventions in public spaces, and legal actions, all staged by various organizations, with fragmented identities and organizational structures, but with a limited extent in terms of reach, representativeness of the sector, and mobilization capacity.

However limited, this visibility of conflict does present us with an opportunity to "interpret the messages society sends about its own production and reproduction processes" (Melucci 1996).[7] From this standpoint, and recasting the hermeneutic potentialities of the analysis of

---

[7] We follow here the approach to collective action and social protests first established by Melucci (1994). We also follow the contributions to this approach by Scribano (2005), who conceives a hermeneutics of conflict as the privileged standpoint from which the processes of social structuration are made intelligible.

emerging identities in the processes of collective action, we come to the understanding that the constitution of the actors in protest, in the CCs sector, expresses an unyielding antagonism to political opportunity or to functional adaptation. Instead, the complex meanings of actions which are put into play by the subjects contribute to the redefinition and qualification of the antagonistic dimensions of the relationships between capital and work, and provide clues for rethinking the "transformations" which have taken place in the "world of work" leading up to our time.

The feelings invested by the actors in conflict reveal a strong feature linked to the "body" as a disputed commodity. Thus, when the wall imposed by fear, as a condition of development of the activity, is "breached", and a voice which is non-digestible by the metabolic mechanisms of the "corporate culture" of the companies reveals itself, the image of the "meat grinder" emerges. The metaphoric power of discourse bears its weight directly upon the body-blood of the worker, forcing an adjustment to the literality of the consequences for the bodies that go through the CC's meat grinder:

> "(...) They think we're fools, because we're young, we're the young blood... But no: [we know] that in five years we'll have a social problem in Córdoba, because when you get out of the Call [Centre], you won't be able to find any other job, your hearing, your throat will be all but done for". (Field notes. Heard in a protest march in April 22, 2009)

Although, as mentioned above, the history of social-work relations in the capitalist system can be rewritten as a continuous and dynamic effort of differential expropriation of corporal energies, the redefinitions of the relationships between surplus value and expropriation derived from the experiences studied here show the depredation of bodies "in work" as the expression of a "limit of systematic compatibility" (Melucci 1994).

Depredation in this context takes the dispute about the "potentiality of collective actions" of the bodies-that-work to a level of paroxysm. The heteronomy emerging from the processes of subjectivation involved in these "new labour scenarios" transmutes the relation with the body itself: individually, the subjectivities "affected" by the processes of work in CCs revealed young subjects, "embodiments of rebellion and force", with "burnt-up brains":

> "(...) The word that I retain as the meaning of what the Call [Centre] is, is tiredness. Being fed up (...) (Interview 08: Call Centre Worker)

I, for one, didn't even feel like picking up a book after I left work (...) I would read some other trash, anything except my university readings, but I wanted to get out of there, nullify myself... Not have to think... I didn't want to have any preoccupation, I didn't want anything to do with the university (...)". (Interview 09: Call Centre Worker)

The precarious bodies emerging from these narratives show continuities with at least two events related to CCs in the Córdoba area: the appeal made by an NGO and a group of workers to the Justice Supreme Court to declare the working conditions in the sector as unhealthy[8]; and research done by psychiatrist Dr. Pablo Cólica about the extent of what he termed "the Call Centres stress syndrome" which he defined as a specific manifestation of a "burnout".[9]

It is worthwhile noticing that the effects of these mutilations constitute "body marks" of dependence-heteronomy; these signs are the material manifestations of the impossibility of collective constitution (isolated, depressed, "unhealthy", etc., individuals), or even the shape assumed by the constitution of the individual.

"[The supervisors] call you and tell you: "why are you not picking up calls?" and they call you through your headset, your work tool. You not only get yelled at from one side [by clients], but you're also harassed from this side [by the supervisors], it's not only the client. (...) You feel a terrible invasion of your ears. I'm very sensible with my hearing and for me theses discomforts where the source of a constant suffering...". (Interview 12: Call Centre Worker)

The discomforts, the suffering numbing the senses, are only understood as anchored in the bodies of workers themselves. Thus, CCs become a privileged space for enquiring about the forms of differential appropriation of the vitality of bodies. The corporal sign of exploitation refutes the

[8] In the final months of the year 2008, a group of workers and ex-workers from CCs took their cases to CLIP (a local NGO), denouncing their difficult working conditions. Several legal actions were taken, such as a court order of legal protection for the "Central de Trabajadores de Argentina" ("Central of Workers of Argentina") of Córdoba and a working woman against the ALLUS BPO Center company, the "Aseguradoras de riezgos de trabajo" ("Occupational Hazard Insurers"), and the Provincial Government; a second legal protection appeal against the Federal Government was filed by the CLIP and a homeless woman in Córdoba. For details see: http://clip.org.ar/que-hace-la-clip/casos/calls-centers

[9] See Pablo Cólica (2009) "El síndrome del estrés en los Calls Centers" Editorial Brujas, Córdoba.

"condition of immateriality" as an empty form of describing the experiences in the emergent scenarios of the "world of work".

Just as the digestion processes needs a stomach, the disposition of energies to be expropriated and put in the hands of the surplus value productive apparatus (and the reactivation of the mechanism of expansion of capital) needs bodies (throats, ears, etc.). In spite of the diverse theoretical perspectives that dissolve the body, particularly in relation to the advances and importance of new technologies in the labour processes, productive energy and the powers of expropriation remain the same and base their existence in a biological-organic body in constant redefinition.

Seemingly, the expansion of CCs, and its promises as a "labour model",[10] challenges ideas connecting the material conditions of existence with work, given that their activities are often characterized as effortless tasks for the subjects (not even thinking is required, as conversations are strictly scripted). This creates the fantasy of a worker "emancipated" from the material conditions of his work place. The everyday for these subjects seems exclusively mediatized by information, that is, by digital processes which become a continuous flow of "immaterial energies".

> "These energies are anchored in the chat-product of this job which is subdued by the "quality control" processes of the production line. Thus, workers, constituted as body-information by the digital processes, mobilize data by their activity, generating uniformity in their discourses: "we get paid to read the manuals. If you don't read the manuals, and you give the wrong information, they will deduce money from your salary" (Interview 10: Call Centre Worker)

The erasure of the worker's body is an inherent part of this process of "impossibility" of saying anything beyond "the scripted" and therefore anything about themselves. In this sense, the constitution of identity establishes an appearance of "immaterial task".

However, the demand for productivity itself reveals the material substratum supporting the "chat". In this sense, what the protests in the sector make clear is the break with the idyllic silence marking the erasure of

---

[10] The notion of "model" not only refers to a "management lab" but also to the value dimension deployed by various business and government sectors who claim that CCs are a "successful model" for the public and private management of unemployment. Lisdero and Quattrini (2013).

the-bodies-that-work, as they highlight the redefinition of "materiality" in today's production processes.

Two images: "the harmonious factory without smoke", promoted by business and governments; and "the meat grinders/burner of brains", denounced by collectives in their struggle, focus attention on the relationship between bodies, sensibilities, and social conflict, and alert us to the links between the process of valuation and depredation of the energy of bodies.

If the subject seemed to have liberated himself from the need to "earn his bread with his sweat" and the body was postulated as absent in the production of surplus value, instead traces emerge linked to the process of labour that mark the expropriation of vitality of, and in, the bodies themselves. The absence of bodies in the seeming immateriality of this "digital labour", as in the suggestive "absence of voices against this work model," is an indicator of the redefinition of the materiality these new forms of labour require as a condition for their expansion.

The "Digital Smile"

The body of the workers is not only the source of the vitality that drives the wheel of information, but at the same time it is the territory of a "silent war" (Lisdero 2013) where the subjects fight "against themselves". The possibilities opened by the incorporation of technology in production processes create opportunities to renew the bodily forces, but at the same time it multiplies to unthinkable places the possibilities of surveillance, of control, of intervening and regulating "the most intimate" of bodies: (…) this growing apart from the senses in almost every sense, this distancing from what's human, distancing from everything that's deep, and then you have to answer only what's required every time. And what's required in all aspects they ask you" (Interview 12: Call Centre Worker).

It is particularly important to problematize here the body feelings tensions which can be re-constructed from the analysis of the conflict as a distinctive feature of the ongoing social structuration processes.

We have already mentioned that this analytical axis allows for a broad discussion in the context of social theory. Modernity is founded upon the capacity to regulate/intervene on the sensibility of subjects. We will put in brackets many of these discussions but highlight some of the questions raised by the notion of "emotional work" developed by Hochschild, who defines the term as "(...) the act of trying to change, in a certain degree or quality, an emotional feeling" (1983: 561).

Hochschild explores the emotions that "we want or would want to feel", which means that every individual learns to use a vocabulary of emotions and to follow social rules that cause or hide certain feelings in specific moments (Hochschild 1983). From this author's perspective, emotions are therefore oriented by action and cognition. Firstly, they are conditioned by our previous experiences, and secondly, they act as indicators of the relationship between the environment and the self. From the standpoint of feeling, the self-perspective of the world is unveiled (Hochschild 1979).

The study by Hochschild about crew workers of several airlines, *The Managed Heart: Commercialization of Human Feelings* (1983), follows an axis of reflection connecting feelings to value production processes under certain working conditions. From a perspective linking social structures, rules of feeling, management of emotions, and emotional experience (Hochschild 1979), we see:

> "(...) moves from the logic of the emotional order in the private sphere, to its institutionalization in the socio-economic sphere of labour. (...) This reveals that the worker, especially in certain service sector jobs, does not essentially sell physical force, as was the case during the dawn of industrialization, neither is the worker selling knowledge or rational capacities, as in the higher stages of industrialization, instead he is selling his emotions".
> (Bericat Alastuey 2000: 162)

This peculiarity that affects increasing numbers of workers and produces an ever more common process of self-estrangement in the advanced capitalist system is founded upon a transmutation of the modes of emotional management linked to private life. Thus, the increasing commodification of bodies leads to a transfer of the management of emotions, from the private, to the public sphere, producing a historic discontinuity between "emotional work" and "emotional labour". In the experience of workers, the texture of the relations becomes determined as companies demand something more than a "superficial performance", and instead systematically and coercively require a "deep performance"—albeit softened by gentle day-to-day blows.

Indeed, the "digital smile" sought after from any worker of the CCs' services is defined by the corporate culture:

"The telephonic smile is an important quality if the tele-operators (…) When on the phone, obviously, it is basic, during the first seconds of the conversation it conveys a favourable impression and encourages the caller to listen to what the sales person has to say, and the smile helps the tele-operator relax and feel more comfortable with the call, which also conveys a greater assurance". (Virtual ethnography—Blog TM system)

The definition of the situation, and the work of the subject, blends into a condition that "tends to be natural, relaxed". Thus, the actors in the exchange are but anecdotal dots in a "naturalized" flow structured as a function of time-rhythms of production. This is precisely the sense in which the smile, in the private sphere, is a sign of pleasure of friendship, while in the public sphere it becomes separated from its function of expressing a personal feeling, subservient to the imperative required by the company (Hochschild 1983). This means that workers need to learn to repress or induce personal moods in order to generate kindness or to endure angry costumers. In other words, these workers will have to produce a "digital smile" elicited under a deep performance.

As workers declare:

"You have to put kindness all the time into play, understanding, courtesy. You are required to keep up a "telephonic smile" even under the worst of circumstances. The operator has to be capable of withstanding any insult, but he is not allowed to insult back". (Virtual ethnography—Facebook—Profile "Salta habla Junior"—8-10-11)

Hochschild, in her study about flight crew workers, does not regard smiles as an expression of the opinions of the workers, but of the feelings of the company. Airline companies exhorted flight attendants to smile more, in a "sincere" way, to more passengers. However, she also observed how workers responded to this request not by smiling more, but less: grinning faster, with less than glowing eyes, obscuring the company message. From this insight, the author develops the idea of a "war of smiles" (Hochschild 1983: 128), which opens a promising avenue for thinking about the limits of the strategies for emotional management.

In CCs, this courteous exchange relation is only possible under the conditions of building a commodified and commodifiable account balance, which requires a certain disposition connected to the digital/digitized gesture of the worker. The notion of "digital smile" is here re-signified as mediatized by digital communications. Therefore, the process of "turning into information every energy" operates a deep reconfiguration of the feelings invested by the workers in order to achieve something as contradictory as a "telephonic smile". This raises several questions: what senses do we put into play when we smile digitally? What relations—as functions of feelings and social structures—are implicated in this reconfiguration of the senses? How do perceptions and impressions operate in the definition of the situations that configure the context of the interactions?

In relation to these questions, it is noteworthy that when the definition of the situation comes into contradiction with the productive requirements and threatens, for example, the "flow of the relation", gestures must be re-directed "beyond the intended comfort":

> [Some clients] want to treat you well, you see? "Poor guys, we have to treat them well." But what do people think it is to treat you well?: "Hi, how are you?" And you say to yourself "Oh shit!" When you hear the good vibe coming your way, you say "I shit on the good vibe!" It's one of the worst things that can happen to you on any given day, a client that comes along with a good vibe [Then] (…) with the tone of your voice you cut him short, and you say to yourself "I didn't come here to make any friends" (…) then you just put distance, with the tone, the gesture of your voice, you could say… with a smell of tires,[11] you see? You stop him right there, you put him in the far end of the room. (Interview: Call Centre Worker 2011)

When the conversation threatens to break out of the scripted standardized processes, when comfort crosses productive models, the "digital smile" is displaced by its solidary complement: "the brakes". But in these cases, the digital smile does not express sincere private affection for a friend, nor do "the brakes" refer to an effective interruption of the interrelation situation. What is important in the management of sensibility is that the continuous and scripted flow of the "chat factory" is never interrupted, and that the digital gestures must be connected to the corporal disposition for the maintenance of the relationship.

Thus, the intervention in working subject's sensibility involves the complexity of the sensory apparatus. An isolated activity, in which "listen-

---

[11] The expression *stepping on the brakes* ("la frenada") refers to the smell of burnt rubber left by the tyres of a car when the brakes are stepped on suddenly. Colloquially the expression is used to refer to an abrupt change in the direction of a conversation, by imposition and evidencing a difference in interests or a disagreement.

ing, seeing, talking and typing" is apparently used, is revealed under closer inspection as a set of actions where actors put into play the reconfiguration of the senses: the "smell of burnt tyres" is what defines the re-channelling, "tact"[12] is what is put into play to lead the conversation to a good ending, "listening" is what allows for the detection of sounds that indicate the interruption of the normal flow of the "chatting machine", and so on. The worker is not only involved in his complete corporality, he is also in a process of reconfiguration based on his "adjustment" to the conditions required by the metabolic mechanisms of capital.

In this sense, the social and historical construction of dispositions of an energetic quantum linked to the bodies is associated with the expropriation of a certain operational capacity of the social being (Scribano 2007): for example, in the cases studied here, the possibility of other-chat involving the worker's "own voice" beyond the "manual of answers", or the recognition of himself as a worker, sowing the seed for the emergence of a collective activity beyond the de-identification techniques deployed by "corporate cultures". Therefore, the fragmentation of identities among the few and limited workers' organizations of the sector can be read, from this perspective, as a consequence of the naturalization of the condition associated with "emotional work".

The literature about CCs in Argentina has identified the devices deployed by companies to stress the disposition associated with the incapacity of talking-and-recognizing-yourself, for example: as the tendency to identify and name workers as "kids" (*chicos*). The energy extractive and depredatory features are constituted in the processes related to the coagulation and liquefaction of social action: if the subjects feel like "kids" and not like "workers", it becomes less probable that they will recognize themselves as part of the organized work struggle. These mechanisms, incorporated in the workers themselves, contribute, in adaptive forms in each of the everyday and heterogeneous scenarios of work, to consolidate the absence of "autonomy": workers "are", think, (do not) operate in, and for others, and as we emphasize here, they "feel" in and by others.

The disposition required from the subject instructed by the "quality manuals", such as the euphemism of "telephonic smile", expresses the

---

[12] "Tact" conveys here the meaning of both "touch" and "courtesy". In the same direction, it is interesting to connect this with what we have said about "touching" and "looking" in Chap. 3: "Work and sensibilities. Commodification and processes of expropriation around digital labour".

technological interference in the worker's body itself. Words, sentiments, and the most "intimate" capacities of the subjects are minutely intervened upon. The political economy of morality (Scribano 2012), which reconfigures how to feel, what to feel, and one's mood, is constituted as a defining feature of the social conditions of production, of which the devices deployed by companies are only one cog contributing to sketch the ways of a "possible humanity" of-in these subjects:

> "What is it to do your job well? It's being a robot. (...) Then you get these ideas or turning into, "tum", a robot, "let's be like this, let's do this," and you get there an hour early, and you start looking into all the sales conditions, the contract policies...". (Interview 08: Call Centre Worker)

From the paradigmatic case of the CCs, using corporal expropriation as a key, the complex links between sensibilities and supportability of the conditions of expropriation are revealed. The difficulty in jumping the hurdle of the "digital smile" implies the social fact, as stated in this chapter, that that hurdle is in-corporate. From our perspective, disentangling the workings of these mechanisms contributes to the understanding of the relationship between the metamorphosis in the "world of work" and the processes that define the expansion of Society 4.0, because as noted by Marx: "(...) what differentiates an era from another is not what is done, but how, with what means of work it is done" (Marx 2006: 218).

DIGITAL SLAVERY OF SOULS

The antagonistic character of emerging conflicts in the Society 4.0 offers a privileged space for analysis, and CCs are a paradigmatic case in point, as they offer the possibility of reconstructing the totality of social relations. It is in this sense that exploring the "borders" of conflict relations, where the structures allow for a "slanted view" of everyday interactions, and where mediations between reproductions and "ruptures" are constituted, becomes relevant for sociological analysis. Precisely in the search for mediations which we consider central to our social forms (emotions) we are able to address the need to understand the meaning of "emotional work" in the digital context: a host of energy which occupies a greater part of our lives.

From our perspective, the "digital smile", as an expected and expectable disposition of digital workers, indicates the connections between the "ways of organizing work" and the "naturalized ways of feeling". More to the point, they allow for the connections between a "Politics of bodies" (Scribano 2012) which, as we stated above, features precariousness as a trace of identity, and a regime of sensibility which operates as a condition of possibility of sensorial capacities, naturalizing the precarious conditions of production.

The "slavery of the souls", an expression used by the workers of CCs (Colectivo Situaciones 2006), appears as a mark on bodies pointing to "beyond the spirit of capitalism" in our social formations. This form of being is the "hook" from which the precariousness is sustained and it is the way in which bodies are constituted within the precarious spaces of digital labour. To make these connections explicit also helps to understand the scope and daily transformations involved in the digital revolution of life and labour in our societies.

REFERENCES

Antunes, R. (2005). *Os sentidos do trabalho: ensaio sobre a afirmação e a negação do trabalho*. São Paulo: Boitempo.

Bericat Alastuey, E. (2000). La Sociología de la emoción y la emoción en la Sociología. *Papers, 62*, 145–176.

Bourdieu, P. (1999). *Meditaciones pascalianas*. Barcelona: Anagrama.

Braga, R. (2009). A vigança de Braverman: o infotaylorismo como contratempo. In R. Antunes & R. Braga (Eds.), *Infoproletários. Degradaçao real do trabalho virtual* (pp. 59–88). São Paulo: Boitempo.

Colectivo Situaciones. (2006). *¿Quién Habla? Lucha contra la esclavitud del alma en los call centers*. Buenos Aires: Tinta limón.

Cólica, P. (2009). *El síndrome de estrés en los Call Center*. Córdoba: Brujas.

De la Garza, E. (2000). *Tratado latinoamericano de sociología del trabajo*. México: Fondo de Cultura Económica.

Del Bono, A. (2002). *Telefónica: trabajo degradado en la era de la información*. Madrid/Buenos Aires: Miño y Dávila Editores.

Del Bono, A. (2010). La geografía de los call centers: territorio, trabajo y empleo. In S. Rotiman, P. Lisdero, & L. Marengo (Eds.), *La llamada… El trabajo y los trabajadores de Calls Centers en Córdoba* (pp. 37–66). Córdoba: Universitas.

Del Bono, A., & Bulloni, M. N. (2008). Experiencias laborales juveniles. Los agentes telefónicos de call centers offshore en Argentina. *Trabajo y Sociedad, 10*(9), 1–21.

Elías, N. (2015). *El proceso de civilización*. México: Fondo Económico de Cultura.

Giddens, A. (2003). *La Constitución de la Sociedad*. Buenos Aires: Amorrortu.

Goffman, E. (1989). *La presentación de la persona en la vida cotidiana*. Buenos Aires: Amorrortu.

Gremilion, H. (2005). The Cultural Politics of Body Size. *Annual Review of Anthropology, 34*, 13–32.

Haber, S., & Renault, E. (2007). ¿Un Análisis Marxista de los cuerpos? In J.-M. Lachaud & O. Neveux (Eds.), *Cuerpos dominados, cuerpos en ruptura* (pp. 9–26). Buenos Aires: Nueva Visión.

Hochschild, A. R. (1979). Emotion Work, Feeling Rules, and Social Structure. *The American Journal of Sociology, 85*(3), 551–575.

Hochschild, A. R. (1983). *The Managed Heart: Commercialization of Human Feeling* (2nd ed.). Berkeley: University of California Press.

Lisdero, P. (2013a). La guerra silenciosa en el mundo de los Calls Centers. *Papeles del CEIC, 80*, 1–31.

Lisdero, P. (2013b). Acción Colectiva y Trabajo. Identidad y expropiación en Empresas Recuperadas y organizaciones de trabajadores de Calls Centers en la Ciudad de Córdoba. Doctoral dissertation for submitted for the title of Doctor in Latin American Social Sciences granted by the *Centro de Estudios Avanzado*, Universidad Nacional de Córdoba. *Mimeo*.

Lisdero, P., & Quattrini, D. (2013). Educación, corporalidad y nueva morfología del trabajo. Los Calls Centers ¿escuelas de trabajo? *Intersticios. Revista Sociológica de Pensamiento Crítico, 7*(1), 155–172.

Marx, K. (2006). *El Capital. Tomo I/Vol 1, Libro Primero. El proceso de producción del capital*. Buenos Aires: Siglo XXI Editores.

Melucci, A. (1994). ¿Que hay de nuevo en los nuevos movimientos sociales? In E. Laraña & J. Gusfield (Eds.), *Los nuevos Movimientos Sociales. De la ideología a la identidad* (pp. 119–150). Madrid: Centro de Investigaciones Sociológicas.

Melucci, A. (1996). *Chalenging Codes. Collective Action in the Information Age*. Cambridge: Cambridge University Press, Cultural Social Studies.

Micheli, J. (2007). Los call centers y los nuevos trabajos del siglo XXI. *Revista Confines de relaciones internacionales y ciencia política, 3*(5), 49–58.

Montarcé, I. (2011). Del otro lado del teléfono: identidad y Acción Colectiva. In E. De La Garza (Ed.), *Trabajo no clásico, organización y acción colectiva* (pp. 69–122). México: Plaza y Valdés Editores.

Neffa, J. C. (1999). *El Trabajo Humano. Contribuciones al estudio de una valor que permanece*. Buenos Aires: Lumen Hvmanitas.

Novick, M. (2010). Trabajo y contextos en el desarrollo productivo argentino. In A. Del Bono & G. Quaranta (Eds.), *Convivir con la incertidumbre. Aproximaciones a la flexibilización y precarización del trabajo en la Argentina* (pp. 19–41). Buenos Aires: CICCUS.

Olivera, S. M. (2009). Os trabalhadores das Centrais de teleatividades no Brasil: da ilusão à exploração. In R. Antunes & R. Braga (Eds.), *Infoproletários: degradação real do trabalho virtual* (pp. 113–135). São Paulo: Editorial Boitempo.

Scribano, A. (2005). *Itinerarios de la protesta y del conflicto social.* Córdoba: Copiar.

Scribano, A. (2007). *Policromía corporal. Cuerpos, Grafías y Sociedad.* Córdoba: Sarmiento Editor.

Scribano, A. (2012). Sociología de los cuerpos/emociones. *RELACES-Revista Latinoamericana de Estudios sobre Cuerpos, Emociones y Sociedad, 10,* 93–113.

Scribano, A., Vergara, G., Lisdero, P., & Quattrini, D. (2015). Labor, Emotions and Social Structuration in Argentina. *The IJSSHI, 2*(11), 1679–1688.

OTHER SOURCES

Blog TM System. http://blog.tmsystem.es/

"Sharing Economy, Sharing Emotions" in the Society 4.0: A Study of the Consumption and Sensibilities in the Digital Era in China

Zhang Jingting

INTRODUCTION

From 1978, China entered a new market era thanks to the reform and opening-up policy proposed by Deng Xiaoping.[1] With the rapid growth of the modern industrial economy, technology, science, education, public service, and many other sectors have developed dramatically: the expansion of exports of labour-intensive goods, the big factory of "made in China", rising ratios of GDP (gross domestic product), and so on. So, the path of reform and opening-up has provided the correct direction for the development of the ancient giant. The information age or the digital age

[1] The Chinese economic reform (also called reform and opening-up policy) refers to the program of economic reforms termed "Socialism with Chinese characteristics" in the People's Republic of China (PRC) that was started in December 1978 by reformists within the Communist Party of China, led by Deng Xiaoping who was the paramount leader of the People's Republic of China from 1978 until his retirement in 1989.

Z. Jingting (✉)
Shanghai International Studies University, Shanghai, China

© The Author(s) 2019
A. Scribano, P. Lisdero (eds.), *Digital Labour, Society and the Politics of Sensibilities*, https://doi.org/10.1007/978-3-030-12306-2_8

is a historic period in the twenty-first century characterized by a rapid shift after the era of traditional industry.

Although the digital era began in China from 1980s, while in the developed countries like those of Europe or the United States it started in the 1970s, China has become a leading force in recent years as a major worldwide investor in digital technologies and one of the world's leading adopters of such technologies globally. Since accession to the WTO (World Trade Organization), there has been a rapid growth of foreign investors. However, on the other hand, the large gaps between the rich and the poor and injustice between the capitalism of digital era and the digital labours have expanded. Zhao (2004) expresses the social problems and tensions between the new urban middle classes, who benefit from the digital era, and the contrasting side, the miserable situation of workers and farmers in China.

Therefore, under this analysed situation, according to the McKinsey Global Institute, there are over 670 million Internet users in China,[2] and the "Internet Plus" strategy has been launched as a strategy to encourage hundreds of thousands of people's passions for innovation to build the new engine for economic development.[3] With the development of the Internet and relevant industries, in China millions of new jobs opportunities have been created. For example, the investment in science, technology, engineering, and mathematics—the so-called STEM disciplines—has boosted innovation and economic growth. In this way, the tech-intensive sectors create high-tech STEM jobs and the creation of a single high-tech job generates between 2.5 and 4.4 additional jobs according to the research on the "Future of Work in the Digital Age".[4]

---

[2] McKinsey Global Institute, China's Digital Transformation: The Internet's Impact on Productivity and Growth (July 2014). http://www.mckinsey.com/industries/high-tech/our-insights/chinas-digital-transformation

[3] State Council, China Unveils Internet Plus Action Plan to Fuel Growth (4 July 2015) http://english.gov.cn/policies/latest_releases/2015/07/04/content_281475140165588.htm

[4] https://www.randstad.gr/ugc/wf360/Randstad-Flexibility@work-2016.pdf.   Maarten Goos, Jozef Konings and Emilie Rademakers. *Future of work in the digital age: evidence from OECD countries.*

In that context, the "sharing economy" has quickly expanded in China. Services such as home-sharing, bike rentals, ride-sharing, and car-sharing form a part of people's daily lives. Local and international consumer-to-consumer (C2C) platforms such as Airbnb, Lyft, Uber, Etsy, BlaBlaCar, Didi, Kuaidi, and Alibaba have emerged and developed rapidly. At the international level, according to "Use of sharing economy services by country 2018",[5] we can see that 60% of respondents in China reported that they have used sharing economy services, compared to 47% in the United States and 54% in the United Kingdom. At the national level, the survey of Chinadaily (4 June 2018) shows that China's sharing economy reached 4.9 trillion yuan ($763.5 billion) in 2017, a 47.2% increase from the previous year, and more than 700 million people were involved in the sharing economy last year, an increase of 10 million over 2016. The number of employees hired by shared platforms reached 7.16 million last year, accounting for 9.7% of new urban jobs created that year.[6]

The sharing economy market has provided great convenience for Chinese customers, who are wired and attuned to mobile services. These kinds of sharing services provide solutions to the problems of pollution, overcrowding, and traffic caused by the large population. In this chapter, we not only analyse the situation of digital work and the sharing economy, but the emotions and sensibilities of the Chinese customers when we are "immerged" in the society 4.0 also aroused our attention. How the transformation of consumption affects and guides people's emotions and how to understand the relationship between politics of sensibilities, consumption, digital labour, and so on are some topics that we will discuss in the following part.

A Brief Literature Review

A considerable amount of literature has been generated about the questions related to the digital society in China. Considering this topic, generally we could divide the previous studies into two types: concerns about China and concerns about China in the global world.

---

[5] https://www.statista.com/statistics/881227/use-of-sharing-economy-services-by-country. Share of people who have used or provided sharing economy services worldwide in 2018, by country. Statistics published by the statistics Portal.

[6] Zhu Lingqing. (4 June 2018). "China's sharing economy to grow 30% per year". Chinadaily. http://www.chinadaily.com.cn/a/201806/04/WS5b14d719a31001b82571e031.html

About the first type, more recent attention has focused on digital labour in China. Surveys such as that conducted by Bingqing Xia (2014a) have revealed the miserable working conditions of the workers in the digital industries.

> Based on detailed empirical research in China, I argue that the rapid growth of the Internet industries depends on exploiting these Internet workers, such as the workers in Chinese Internet industries—the new 'sweatshop' of the digital era. Chinese Internet workers have been subsumed in the global capitalist system as the new 'sweatshop workers.' (Xia 2014a: 668)

There is a debate between Terranova (2004) and Barbrook (2005) about Internet users and capitalist production, where the latter lays stress on the contribution of Internet users to the digital economy by analysing the paradoxical relationships between the new form of digital labour and capitalist production, while Terranova considers that he's too optimistic about the autonomy of the gift economy from capitalism. Terranova (2004) emphasizes the absorption of free labour into capitalist production. But Xia (2014b) states that they both fail to capture the ambivalent, complex, and dynamic relationships between labour and capitalism, though the question of "unpaid labour" is an important issue.

Labour in the Chinese Internet Industries, the doctoral dissertation of Bingqing Xia (2014a), also investigates the situation of Internet workers in China which mainly tackled three questions: the work quality of these workers, the social class of Internet workers, and the agency of these workers including their negotiation with, and resistance to, the state and businesses. Although the Internet workers are often highly educated and receive higher pay than peasants and peasant workers, Xia categorized them as a part of the lower middle class in Chinese society.

The Challenge of Labour in China: Strikes and the Changing Labour Regime in Global Factories, the doctoral dissertation of Chris King-Chi Chan (2008), examines the working conditions, labour conflict, and struggles of the workers based on field research about the factories in the city of Shen Zhen, China's first and most flourishing Special Economic Zone (SEZ), in the province of Guang Dong. Chan explained the distinctive forms of class struggle in contemporary China, defined as "class struggle without class organization" by the author. In his opinion, the rapid expansion of global capitalism into China has intensified class struggle in the workplace and beyond, and has given rise to an emerging form of labour protest in the country.

Apart from the dark side of the conditions experienced by Chinese workers, some researchers are also interested in questions concerning rights and protections in the case of Chinese workers (Chan 1998; Dittmer 2001; Gutmann 2004; Mattioli and Sapovadia 2004). Other researchers have paid attention to the progress that the Chinese government has made. Jiang and Xu (2009) interpret the communicative structures of Chinese government websites and their implications for citizen political participation. Through the analysis of 31 Chinese provincial government portals about its web features, Jiang and Xu point that China has made certain progress towards building a transparent, service-oriented, and democratic government administration.

With the development of globalization, a large and growing body of literature has investigated China in the landscape of globalization, as Chinese labour issues have become much more than merely a local matter. In "China, India and the Doubling of the Global Labor Force: Who pays the price of globalization?" Freeman (2005) shows that through the entry of Chinese, Indian, Russian, and other workers into the global economy, there has been a massive increase in the supply of labour, but that this has also caused many problems. "Large numbers of rural workers in China and India could lose from globalization, creating dangers of social unrest, particularly in non- democratic China" (2005: 1).

The issue (July–September, 2017) of *Made in China*,[7] an open access quarterly on Chinese labour, civil society, and rights, analysed Chinese Labour in a Global Perspective. In the introduction, the editors state that "(…) the study of Chinese labour indeed provides a powerful lens—or perhaps a mirror—to further our understanding of the contemporary world and our potential futures" (Franceschini et al. 2017: 6).

In a survey by the Mckinsey Global Institute, Woetzel et al. (2017) investigated China's digital economy at a global level and identified it as "a leading global force". They used "micro-to-macro" methodology to examine microeconomic industrial trends and to understand the macro-economic forces which affect business strategy and public policy in China.

As for the term "sharing economy" in China, more recent attention has focused on the phenomenon, exploring this type of economy's appearance, its expansion, its present situation, and some predictions regarding

---

[7] http://www.chinoiresie.info/PDF/Made-in-China_3_2017.pdf, Vol 2, Issue (3) 2017; Made in china. A Quarterly on Chinese Labour, Civil Society, and Rights. Chinese labour in a global perspective.

its possible future development. In *The sharing economy: The end of employment and the rise of crowd-based capitalism*, Sundararajan (2016) has drawn a panorama about the sharing economy: the definition, digital and socioeconomic foundations, the platforms, the Crowd as the Market Maker, the economic impacts of Crowd-based capitalism, some regulations, and consumer protection. What's more, the author offered some predictions about the future of digital labour. In his statements, China has been taken as a main analysed example, as the apps such as Didi and Kuaidi, have been used widely in order to meet people's mobility needs.

Some studies have focused on particular aspects. For example, Fang et al. (2016) investigated the effects that the sharing economy has on the tourism industry. The case of Airbnb has been analysed.

> The results suggest that the entry of sharing economy benefits the entire tourism industry by generating new job positions as more tourists would come due to the lower accommodation cost. However, since low-end hotels are being shocked and replaced by Airbnb (Zervas et al. 2017), the marginal effect decreases as the size of sharing economy increases. Employees in low-end hotels would lose their jobs, while Airbnb houses do not need to hire any workers. Therefore, the marginal effect of Airbnb decreases along with the replacement of low-end hotels. (Fang et al. 2016: 266)

So, we can see the double-edged nature of the sharing economy. From the above analysed researchers, we can notice that although many studies draw attention to topics related to the digital era, such as digital labour, the sharing economy, and Internet workers, very few authors have been able to draw on any systematic research into the emotions of customers in the process of consumption in the environment of the sharing economy in China. In this regard, we will explore the topic from the three perspectives: (1) why the sharing economy has become so popular in China, from the perspective of traditional Chinese culture; (2) the situation of digital labour and the principal social mass media in China; (3) and finally, the sensibilities of people and their consumption in the digital age.

THE VALUE OF TIAN XIA AND THE SHARING ECONOMY IN CHINA

When we talk about the booming of the sharing economy in China, there are some conceptions that we cannot neglect—"He" (Harmony) and "Tianxia" (All under Heaven). The Word "He" or "Harmony" is coined within a philosophical tradition. Thousands of years ago, Chinese carved the character "He" (和), which means harmony and peace, on tortoise shells. Nowadays the situation has changed, we have entered a more civilized and developed society, with the emergence of the sharing economy. But the core of harmony that is rooted in traditional Chinese culture hasn't changed.

Philosophically, Confucius (551–479 B.C.) illuminated the term "harmony without uniformity", meaning the world is full of differences and contradictions, but the righteous man should balance them and achieve harmony. Other representatives of Confucianism in Ancient China such as Mencius and Xunzi also made an incisive statement about the essence of He (harmony) in human relations, which is regarded as a faculty possessed by human beings that refers to showing love and affection to one's counterparts in social interaction. In addition, Taoism, the other important Chinese ideology, is based on the "Tao" doctrine—which means the way to achieve harmony. The main Taoist postulate is the principle of balance and the relationship of the masculine "yang" and the feminine "yin", and educating people to achieve harmony between "yin" and "yang".

It is worth mentioning that during the Ming Dynasty in China, there was a phenomenon called "Three teachings harmonious as one" (Chinese: San Jiao He Yi, 三教合一), which refers to Confucianism, Taoism, and Buddhism when considered as a harmonious aggregate. In order to understand why this unique case emerged in China, it is essential to understand that harmony is the key concept across Chinese history for the country, the society, and the people. In the one teaching combined by three religions, Confucianism often functioned as a political ideology and a system of values; Taoism has paid more attention to lifestyle and the relationship between humans and nature; and Buddhism offered some techniques and deities enabling one to achieve salvation in the other world.

On the other hand, the notion "Tianxia" (literally "all under heaven") also corresponds to the notion that harmony drives the core of Chinese culture and people's lives. In "The New Tianxia: Rebuilding China's Internal and External Order", Xu Jilin (2015) connoted both an ideal civilizational order and a world spatial imaginary with China's central plains at the core. In the Chinese tradition, people share the value of "Tianxia" instead of Nation or State. Because in the ancient time, when the world and the civilizations distributed in the distinct continents didn't connect, in the values of Chinese people, the word "China" (zhongguo, 中国) refers to the "centre" of the world. In other words, China was Tianxia, the embodiment of the universal.

The other topic that aroused my interest concerns the question of "Civilization and Barbarism". According to Domingo Faustino Sarmiento, it was a concept of dichotomy, where in the context of the Argentine Civil War "civilization" makes reference to the values and ideas of Europe, and "barbarism" to the rejection of them. Unitarians thought that Buenos Aires should impose those values onto the other regions of the country. But considering the value of TianXia, we can notice that the historical relationships between the Han people and the various non-Han "barbarian groups" on China's peripheries are the processes of assimilation, borrowing, and integration. The notions of "Chinese" and "barbarian" were not understood in racial terms but in civilizational terms. For instance, pre-modern Chinese people spoke not just of Tianxia, but also of the difference between barbarians (夷) and Chinese (夏).

However, these notions like barbarism and civilization were completely different from the China/West, Us/Them binary discourse on the lips of today's extreme nationalists. The difference between barbarian and Chinese was determined solely on the basis of whether one had a connection to the values of Tianxia. In Chinese history, The Han people (Chinese) were originally a farming people, while the majority of the Hu people (Barbarians or minority nationality) were a grassland people. In Chinese history, those dynasties such as Liao dynasty (916–1125), Western Xia (Xi Xia) dynasty (1038–1227), Jin dynasty (1115–1234), Yuan dynasty (1271–1368), and the last dynasty Qing (1616–1912) were built by the people of minority nationality in China. These "barbarians" who are in power dominate the "Chinese". Yet during this process, there is a harmonious integration. For example, the blood of the "Chinese" has mixed within its elements of barbarian peoples; from clothing to daily habits, there is not a single area where the people of the central plains have not been influenced by the Hu peoples.

Therefore, from the universal perspective of Tianxia, we could notice the influence of the He (Harmony) as the core value in the Chinese tradition. Historically speaking, Chinese civilization was Tianxia.

After understanding the significance of Tianxia, it's easy to understand the rapid development of the sharing economy in China, because to "share" means we need to offer what we have. The sharing economy presents opportunities for individuals to find extra jobs on the digital platform, generates income, increases reciprocity, enhances social interaction, and provides easy access to the all kinds of resources. So, without the spirit of He (Harmony) and the traditions of Tianxia in the blood of Chinese people, it would have been impossible to create the sharing economy with the rapidity seen over the past few years.

"China's Annual Report on Shared Economic Development (2018)",[8] carried out by the Sharing Economic Work Committee of Association of China Internet,[9] has analysed the situation of the sharing economy in China, and drawn conclusions about its development and progress in 2017:

> In 2017, the transaction volume of China's shared economic market was about 492.05 billion yuan, an increase of 47.2% over the previous year. Among them, the transaction volume in the non-financial sharing sector was 2,094.1 billion yuan, an increase of 66.8% over the previous year. In 2017, the number of employees in China's shared economic platform was about 7.16 million, an increase of 1.31 million over the previous year, accounting for 9.7% of the number of new jobs in urban areas that year, which means that about 10 out of every 100 new employees in the town It is a newly hired employee of a shared economy. In 2017, the number of people participating in the sharing of economic activities in China exceeded 700 million, an increase of about 100 million from the previous year. The number of people involved in providing services is about 70 million, an increase of 10 million over the previous year. (Sharing Economic Work Committee of Association of China Internet[4]: Translated by the author)

From the data, we can see the increase in numbers of Chinese users—including employers and employees in the sharing economy—and the transactions, business, and interests that have been achieved. With such a large population on the platform of the sharing economy, how is people's life configured in the virtual world? What are the main platforms of the sharing economy and the social media in China?

PEOPLE'S LIFE IN THE VIRTUAL WORLD IN CHINA

The report that we have analysed above presented the situation and development in six aspects related to the sharing economy: transportation, housing, finance, knowledge and skills, living services, and production

---

[8] http://www.sic.gov.cn/archiver/SIC/UpFile/Files/Default/20180320144901006637. pdf(中国共享经济发展年度报告2018).

[9] Sharing Economic Work Committee of Association of China Internet is 中国互联网协会分享经济工作委员会 (in Chinese).

capacity. According to this line, we will analyse the daily life of Chinese people reflected in these aspects of Society 4.0.

In the market of transportation, there are three main forms of mobility: Net car (online taxi), shared bicycle, and shared car. Net car includes some platforms like Didi, UBER, Lyft, Grab, Ola, 99, Taxify, and Careem. For example, Didi Chuxing Technology Co., the most important ride-sharing service, an artificial intelligence (AI) and autonomous technology conglomerate in China, provides services such as taxi hailing, private car hailing, social ride-sharing, bike sharing, and food delivery to users in China via a smartphone application (app). On the basis of the statistics, "Shared bicycle" reached its peak in 2017. "The number of shared bicycles exceeded 20 million, and the total financing exceeded 20 billion yuan in China".[10] However, nowadays, with the intensified competition, some shared bicycle brands are facing the difficulties and become "problem platforms". Some enterprises have even closed down and exited the market, while some large enterprises offering "shared bicycle", such as Ofo, Mobike, and Hellobike, have developed their services and merged with other smaller companies.

In the area of shared cars, according to information from the Ministry of Transport of the People's Republic of China, in June 2017, there were more than 40 shared automobile companies in China, and the total number of vehicles exceeded 40,000. Enterprises such as SAIC Gofun, Universal Cars, and car2go have emerged.[11] It is worth mentioning that 95% of the shared cars are made up of the new energy-saving vehicles.

With regard to the area of housing, this has developed steadily. According to the report, the transaction scale reached 14.5 billion yuan, and the financing scale increased by 180% in 2017.[12] The platforms include Xiaozhu, Airbnb, and Tujia. For example, Xiaozhu was officially launched in August 2012 and is a typical representative of housing sharing. It is dedicated to digging out idle housing resources, building an honest and secure online communication and trading platform, and providing users with accommodation options that are different from traditional hotels, being more humanistic, with family atmosphere and more cost-effective.

---

[10] The data is from the "China's Annual Report on Shared Economic Development (2018)".

[11] The information is from CCTV news. http://m.news.cctv.com/2017/06/01/ARTI6BcoBzDbrpAwS5q8oC2P170601.shtml

[12] The data is from the "China's Annual Report on Shared Economic Development (2018)".

For the area of finance sharing, the year 2017 was complicated with adjustments and turmoil. The growth rate of online lending transactions has slowed down from 2016. With the continuous strengthening of the Internet financial rectification work and the implementation of the corresponding regulatory policies, compliance norms have become the main tone of shared financial development. The number of P2P online platforms reached its peak in 2015, with a total of nearly 3500. Afterward, due to some problems, the number of platforms began to decline with the industry's rectification work. In 2016, it dropped to around 2500. In 2017, it dropped further to 1931. However, although the number has declined, the online lending volume still maintains rapid growth. In 2017, the online loan volume reached 280.48 billion yuan, an increase of about 35.9%.[13]

The sharing economy market also provides opportunities for obtaining knowledge and skills. Taking advantage of the network, many applications online have appeared such as Ximalaya FM, a service website that enables users to share audio and personal radio stations where the digital labourers include celebrities, stars, teachers, and experts in various areas. On the other hand, the webcast has reached its boom and entered the content competition stage. But the model of "sharing knowledge" is facing some problems such as those of copyright infringement.

The scale of the shared economic market in China's life service sector continues to expand, and the development of new modes of the sharing economy has profoundly changed people's lifestyles. There are applications of "take out restaurant" (外卖) such as Eleme, Meituan, and Baidu Takeout. Additionally, other services like gymnasia, umbrellas, and KTV could also be shared in some relevant applications.

The area of production capacity is also affected by the sharing economy. China's manufacturing industry is facing an important opportunity for transformation and upgrading. As a new format and new model, the sharing economy provides a new direction for manufacturing industry with the integration of manufacturing and Internet development. With the development of technologies such as cloud computing and the industrial Internet, the penetration rate of the sharing economy into manufacturing industry has gradually increased, and the number of participating companies has also grown. Some traditional manufacturing companies and Internet companies have begun to use capacity for sharing to explore and create a new manufacturing ecosystem.

---

[13] The data is from the "China's Annual Report on Shared Economic Development (2018)".

In this way, after analysing the panorama of the principal aspects of the sharing economy, we can notice that daily life has been changed greatly. On the other side, there is a need to introduce the concept of "social mass media", because on the larger scale, the sharing economy depends on it.

The social mass media has the great influence over the media audience, so it is an ideal channel for advertising and attracting the customers for the sharing economy companies. Due to the limitations on access to the Internet,[14] China has its own social media channels which have similar functions to the likes of Facebook, YouTube, and Twitter. According to a survey by Dragon Social,[15] the ten most popular social media sites in China are WeChat (all-in-on social media in China), Sina Weibo (Twitter of China), Tencent QQ (popular instant messaging app), Toudou Youku (YouTube of China), Baidu Tieba (a search engine forum), Douban (life-style discussion platform), Zhihu (the Quora of China), Meituan—Dianping (the Chinese versions of Yelp), Momo (Tinder of China), and Meipai (Chinese Instagram for video), respectively.

In the last part, we will try to explore the emotions and sensibilities of Chinese people during the process of consumption influenced by the mass social media and the sharing economy.

CONSUMPTION AND EMOTIONS IN THE DIGITAL ERA

As we have highlighted in the literature review, few previous studies have dealt with the problem of people's emotions and sensibilities in Society 4.0 in China with the rapid development of the sharing economy. Scribano and Lisdero (2018) interpreted the relationship between images and digital life. "The expansion of social relationships mediated by ICTs, where the 'images' constitute a central 'tension' in terms of the role and the form of the interactions" (2018: 166. Translated by the author). So, in Society 4.0, the social mass media provide a large number of images, which have affected the sensibilities of people.

Scribano and Lisdero (2018) observed that the transformations referred to imply a complex range of practices that are associated with particular emotional regimes, with policies of sensibilities associated with specific ways of elaborating perceptions, all of which lead to the social production

[14] In China, some applications and websites are not available, such as Google, Facebook, Twitter, and Instagram.
[15] Nha Thai, 10 Most Popular Social Media Sites in China. https://www.dragonsocial.net/blog/social-media-in-china/

of processes for the management of sensations. So, in the transformation of society under the influence of the sharing economy in the digital age, what do Chinese people feel in the practices of consumption? Are they satisfied?

Let's take an example of the consumption of "sharing knowledge". According to the "China's Annual Report on Shared Economic Development (2018)", in 2017, many knowledge-paid products met difficulties in the market, and there are doubts about the "knowledge flooding" and "pseudo-knowledge". According to the survey, 49.7% of consumers paying for knowledge said that they felt "just so", 12.3% said they are not satisfied, the repurchase rate and opening rate of paid products are not ideal, and the average rate of knowledge paid products is only 7%.[16] So we could notice that many customers are not satisfied with the "sharing products" offered by the sharing economy market and they don't have positive emotions.

So, considering the large population of Chinese customers, in order to achieve a better development of the sharing economy, is it possible to guide their sensibilities? We will analyse a successful example. The director Chen Kexin made a short film titled *Three Minutes* for Apple Company using the iPhone X to celebrate Chinese New Year 2018. The film tells the story of a mom who works as a train conductor on one of China's longest routes. Her entire route takes six days to complete and she only gets to spend three minutes with her son and sister at one of the stops. After the film went live, it played more than 13.61 million times on Youku in one day. The number of readers about the relevant article published by Apple's website on the WeChat broke through 100,000+ and won 6800 likes. On social media, we could see countless praises such as "so touching" and "selling well". Because Chen Kexin took the scenery of the difficulties in the spring festival travel, of which the majority of Chinese people have the same experience, it has aroused the collective empathy.

Another typical successful example about consumption and the emotions of customers is "Double 11 Shopping Day (Single Day)" in China. With four characters of "1" which has the significance of Bachelor, November 11th has become a special festival in recent years in China. Taking advantage of the opportunity, in 2009, Alibaba held the first Double Eleven Shopping Festival on Taobao.com, storming online shopping for the very first time. Until now, the shopping carnival has been the most important day to stimulate consumption. The strategies of Alibaba are about guiding the customers to obtain the sensation of "collective pleasure" which lead them to

---

[16] The data is from the "China's Annual Report on Shared Economic Development (2018)".

consumption impulsion. Just as interpreted by Scribano (2015), the complexity of our days could be characterized by the expansion of normalized societies in the immediate enjoyment through consumption.

Therefore, in digital society, with the influence of the sharing economy and social mass media, it seems like the Chinese people's collective emotions and sensibilities could be led and influenced.

CONCLUSION

In the present study, we have discussed the situation and development of digital labour and the Chinese sharing economy. With the comprehension of the values of He (Harmony) and Tianxia (All under Heaven) in the traditional Chinese culture, we can understand why the sharing economy has developed so rapidly in China in the recent years. From some results in "China's Annual Report on Shared Economic Development (2018)", we have analysed six aspects of Chinese people's daily life related to the platforms of the sharing economy: transportation, housing, finance, knowledge and skills, living services, and production capacity. In addition, we paid attention to the popular social mass media in China and their influence. Last but not least, through two examples—the film of *Three Minutes* by Chen Kexin and Double 11 Shopping Day—it is possible to make an assumption that the customers' emotions and sensibilities could be guided in the digital era.

In the digital era, the Internet has become a common way to access the outside world and people are "exposed" in the ocean of information. The new "collectivism" of customers appeared in Society 4.0, related with consumption in the sharing economy, which means that with the impact of social mass media and all types of sharing economy platforms, it is easy to arouse the sensation of empathy, which could cause the collective emotions such as pleasure, sadness, and indignation, and these kinds of feelings would be the motor to stimulate consumption.

REFERENCES

Barbrook, R. (2005). The High-Tech Gift Economy. *First Monday. Special Issue 3: Internet Banking, e-Money, and Internet Gift Economies*. Published in December 2005. Special Issue editor Mark A.

Chan, A. (1998). Labor Standards and Human Rights: The Case of Chinese Workers Under Market Socialism. *Human Rights Quarterly, 20*, 886–904.

Chan, C. K. C. (2008). *The Challenge of Labour in China: Strikes and the Changing Labour Regime in Global Factories.* Doctoral dissertation, University of Warwick.

Dittmer, L. (2001). Chinese Human Rights and American Foreign Policy: A Realist Approach. *The Review of Politics, 63*(3), 421–459.

Fang, B., Ye, Q., & Law, R. (2016). Effect of Sharing Economy on Tourism Industry Employment. *Annals of Tourism Research, 57*(3), 264–267.

Franceschini, I., et al. (2017). Chinese Labour in a Global Perspective. *Made in China, 2*(3), 5.

Freeman, R. (2005). China, India and the Doubling of the Global Labor Force: Who Pays the Price of Globalization? *The Globalist, 3*(6), 1–5.

Gutmann, E. (2004). *Losing the New China.* San Francisco: Encounter Books.

Jiang, M., & Xu, H. (2009). Exploring Online Structures on Chinese Government Portals: Citizen Political Participation and Government Legitimation. *Social Science Computer Review, 27*(2), 174–195.

Jilin, X. (2015). *The New Tianxia: Rebuilding China's Internal and External Order.* Series of Intelectuales (Tomo 13). Shanghai: Shanghai People's Press.

许纪霖. (2015). 新天下主义: 重建中国的内外秩序. 知识分子论丛 (第 13 辑). 上海:上海人民出版社.

Mattioli, M. C., & Sapovadia, V. K. (2004). Laws of Labor. *Harvard International Review, 26*(2), 60–64.

Scribano, A. (2015). Comienzo del Siglo XXI y Ciencias Sociales: Un rompecabezas posible. *Polis,* 41. Available at: http://journals.openedition.org/polis/11005

Scribano, A., & Lisdero, P. (2018). Visual Experience and Social Research: Towards a Critique of the Political Economy of the Digital Gaze. *Religación. Revista de ciencias sociales y humanidades, 3*(9), 165–181.

Sundararajan, A. (2016). *The Sharing Economy: The End of Employment and the Rise of Crowd-Based Capitalism.* Cambridge, MA: MIT Press.

Terranova, T. (2004). *Network Culture: Politics for the Information Age.* London: Pluto Press.

Woetzel, J., Seong, J., Wang, K. W., Manyika, J., Chui, M., & Wong, W. (2017). *China's Digital Economy: A Leading Global Force.* New York: McKinsey Global Institute.

Xia, B. Q. (2014a, June). *Labour in the Chinese Internet Industries.* Leeds: University of Leeds.

Xia, B. Q. (2014b). Digital Labour in Chinese Internet Industries. *Triple C: Communication, Capitalism & Critique. Journal for a Global Sustainable Information Society, 12*(2), 668–693. Doctoral dissertation. Institute of Communications Studies, University of Leeds.

Zervas, G., Proserpio, D., & Byers, J. W. (2017). The Rise of the Sharing Economy: Estimating the Impact of Airbnb on the Hotel Industry. *Journal of Marketing Research, 54*(5), 687–705.

Zhao, Y. (2004). The State, the Market, and Media Control in China. In P. Thomas & Z. Nain (Eds.), *Who Owns the Media? Global Trends and Local Resistances* (pp. 179–212). Penang: Southbound.

CHAPTER 9

The Invisible Face of Digital Labour in Turkey: Working Conditions, Practices and Expectations

Mustafa Berkay Aydın and Çağdaş Ceyhan

INTRODUCTION

The software industry is growing in Turkey. So far, various reports have been published by think tanks, government agencies and employer groups on this issue. On the other hand, the software sector has a very limited number of reports and academic studies on job conditions and the expectations of software workers. Official reports have ignored the labour of software workers. In this study, the labour processes of the software industry workers were examined with regard to the flexibility of the work. In this sense emotional and immaterial labour have also become prominent themes. Lazzarato defines immaterial labour as follows:

> The activities of this kind of immaterial labor force us to question the classic definitions of work and workforce, because they combine the results of

M. B. Aydın (✉)
Uludağ University, Bursa, Turkey

Ç. Ceyhan
Anadolu University, Eskişehir, Turkey

© The Author(s) 2019
A. Scribano, P. Lisdero (eds.), *Digital Labour, Society and the Politics of Sensibilities*, https://doi.org/10.1007/978-3-030-12306-2_9

various different types of work skill: intellectual skills, as regards the cultural-informational content; manual skills for the ability to combine creativity, imagination, and technical and manual labor; and entrepreneurial skills in the management of social relations and the structuring of that social cooperation of which they are a part. (Lazzarato 1996: 136)

In general, the software sector in Turkey is located in three major cities (Ankara, İstanbul and İzmir). The companies in the technology development centres are located in technoparks in Bilkent (Ankara), Middle East Technical University (METU) (Ankara) and İstanbul Technical University (İTU) (İstanbul) campuses. TÜBİTAK-MAM (The Scientific and Technological Research Council of Turkey—Marmara Research Center) data also shows that the software developed in Turkey serves the following fields: production and automation, telecommunication, energy, electrics and electronics, finance, logistics, textile, education, media, defence, health, tourism, construction and public services (Stratejik Düşünce Enstitüsü [Institute of Strategic Thinking] 2012: 12).

The information technology (IT) sector in Turkey has not yet achieved the expected volume, and has not yet arrived where it ought to be. The same can also be said for software and services. According to International Data Corporation (IDC) 2010 data, the size of the informatics market in Turkey is USD 8.549 billion. The hardware market constitutes USD 6.944 billion of it, services market USD 0.909 billion and software market USD 0.696 billion. However, 2017 data shows some changes. According to TÜBİSAD report, IT market reached USD 11.3 billion (2018: 13). According to TÜBİSAD Information and Communications Technologies (ICT) report '...the mix of sector components has been trending closer to that of developed countries since 2013 and the share of value-added activities such as software and services has continued to grow...' (TÜBİSAD 2018: 15). Most importantly, IT market component rankings are on change. For example, by 2017 data, software's market share reached 45% in total IT market, hardware's share was 39% and services was 16%. Only four years ago, by 2013, hardware's market share was 50%, software was 35% and services was 15% (TÜBİSAD 2018: 15).

By 2016, there were approximately 35 large companies operating in the software market in Turkey (Mishra et al. 2016: 929). According to 2012 TÜBİTAK-MAM data, there are 1600 companies which produce software in Turkey. These companies are small- or medium-sized enterprises with weak capital structures. Approximately 35% of these companies are in technology development centres, and 87.2% of them have an Small and

Medium-Sized Enterprises (SME) structure. Fifty-one per cent of them employ less than 10 personnel; 35.7% employ 10–50; 9.8% employ 50–250 and 3% employ more than 250 personnel. Forty-seven per cent of software developers live in İstanbul, and 33% of them in Ankara. The companies in the technology development centres are located in techno-parks in Bilkent, METU and İTU campuses.

According to the 2013 Informatics Sector Report, total export in the ICT sector was TL 1.3 billion, TL 990 million of which was IT and TL 266 million communication technologies. The export figures in the sub-categories of the IT sector were as follows: hardware TL 113 million; software TL 721 million and services TL 156 million (ÇSGB 2013).

Data of 2016 on the ICT Market by TÜBİSAD (Informatics Industry Association of Turkey) is as follows: The TL-based growth of the Informatics Market in Turkey was 14.4%, and it reached a volume of TL 94.3 billion. The TL-based growth of one of the main components of this market, that is, IT, was 11%, with the trading volume of TL 29.6 billion. The TL-based growth of communication technologies reached to 16%, with a trading volume of TL 64.7 million. In IT, hardware sales reached to TL 12.9 billion, software sales to TL 11.9 billion and services sales to TL 4.8 billion. The highest growth rate in IT was that of software sector with a percentage of 16.3. Services sector follows it with 14.4 and hardware sector with 5.1. Communication technologies sector had a trading volume of TL 64.7 billion in 2016; TL 19.3 billion of which were hardware sales and TL 45.4 billion of which were electronic communication sales. In 2016, 86% of the IT services sector, and 60% of software sector, comprised domestic companies. Total export volume increased by 32% and reached TL 3.1 billion; TL 2.041 billion of which came from software sales. Export sales constitute 14% of the total software trade. Fifty-six per cent of exported software was sold to Middle Eastern and African countries, and 20% of it to countries in the European Union. The TL-based growth in the sector, however, was not echoed in the increase in employment rates (http://www.bthaber.com/bilisim-dunyasi/turkiye-bilisim-sektorunun-buyuklugu-95-milyar-tl/1/21636; Accessed 12.03.2018).

The main points stressed in the Strategy and Action Plan for Turkish Software Sector by the Republic of Turkey Ministry of Science, Industry and Technology are as follows: The most remarkable characteristics of the software sector are low investment costs, high employment rates of qualified personnel, and products with high added value. It also contributes to the efficiency and high added value in other sectors. Therefore, the improvements in this sector are so crucial for the entire economy. Improvement and sustainment of the growth in Turkish economy is a shared purpose. So is the improvement and promotion of software sector to have its corner in world market. In this context, it is utmost necessary to support the development of the present companies, and enhance the establishment of new ones for the improvement of the sector and that of Turkish economy. (Sanayi ve Ticaret Bakanlığı [Ministry of Industry and Trade] 2010: 94)

While the employers in IT and the state are so optimistic in their discourse, academic researchers in the sector focusing on the experience of employees depict a different picture. The questionnaire of The Chamber of Electrical Engineers conducted with 438 sector workers shows that the conditions in the sector are far from being hopeful: The questionnaire draws attention to overtime work in the sector, which is a common practice. 37% of the employees overwork so often. 49% of them have to overwork before submission dates. Only 16% of them are paid for their overwork. 75% of the employees work more than 40 hours, and 25% more than 48 hours per week. If we remember demands of the working class on May 1, 1886, i.e. "Eight Hours for Work, Eight Hours for Rest, Eight Hours for What We Will", the workers of technological advance are two centuries behind, in terms of labor rights. (EMO [The Chamber of Electrical Engineers] 2009: 24)

According to Türkmen, the risks the information sector workers face are as follows (Türkmen 2016); insufficient and deficient planning, uncertain goals and requirements, unstable and missing targets, unrealistic time and cost estimates, lack of managerial support, lack of team work and poor communication.

RESEARCH METHOD

The software sector employees were interviewed for this research. In 14 interviews, the three main themes were: (1) their opinions on working conditions in the sector, (2) their position in 'digital labour', and their position in the general labour market and (3) their tendencies to come together and organize. Before the research, the interviewees were approached on the web, and some pre-interviews were held. Then, the researchers conducted in-depth interviews with all the interviewees. The interviews were composed of six semi-structured questions which focused on the above-mentioned three themes. While the researchers were designing and scheduling the interviews, six interviewees insisted on conducting the interviews online. The researchers, however, persuaded them to have face-to-face meetings. We find this case worth noting, since it demonstrated the sample group's web-centred world. Six interviews were held in Ankara, and eight in İstanbul. Our basic data on the in-depth interviews carried out are: three women and five men in İstanbul and two women and four men in Ankara, all of them university graduates.

Half of the interviewees are younger than 30, and the other half are older than 31. Their ages vary from 22 to 42. They can be defined as rather young, as their mean age is 31.9. As Lima and Pires (2017: 779) remark, the workers in this sector are mostly young people all over the world. In Brazil, for example, 51% of the workers in the field defined as digital labour are between 18 and 29 years of age (2017: 779). The data is similar in other countries. The researchers were attentive to include female interviewees in the research, and 30% of the interviews were conducted with female participants, which is the exact share of female workers in the market. A classical study on this field (Badagliacco 1990) remarks that since the very beginning of the computer and digital labour market, female workers have been disadvantaged, and male workers have been luckier than the former. In the 1980s, computers were gradually more widely used in daily life all over the world. This case about gender can be considered as a part of the discussion on 'pioneers'. In the field of digital labour, recent years have been witnessing some improvements in terms of female workers, however, the sector in Turkey is dominated by male workers.

The interviews were carefully conducted as in-depth interviews. The research aims at portraying the 'cognitive mappings' of the workers in terms of the themes mentioned, rather than focusing on a general picture of the realm of digital labour in Turkey.

WORKING CONDITIONS: FLEXIBLE AND INTENSIVE LIFE

As repeatedly claimed in many studies, digital labour is a field where the work hours are flexible and vague (Gill 2009; Huws 2003). However, while the digital workers depict their labour conditions, this fact is expressed as a positive characteristic in many cases. An obvious implication of this condition is *precarization*, but the workers generally like it since they can determine their time management. Gill (2009: 18–19) remarks that this is emphasized mostly by the permanent staff of institutionalized companies. In the present research, permanent staff of corporations who stick to weekly working hours emphasize the flexibility of working hours. Barış (male, 32), for example, has been working in a software company for four years, and states that:

> Working hours are generally so flexible, I can say. I work for 45 hours per week. On some days I try hard and work for 10 hours. I somehow clear it up. ... Our office is so comfortable, I generally prefer to work at the office, and sometimes I work from home.

It is important to note that the opinions of covenanted employees, freelancers and other workers of the companies besides software experts vary. Temporary, project-based labour is a common practice. Regarding the working positions of our interviewees, it is possible to see the follow distribution: Female-Permanent Staff 2, Female-Covenanted Employee 2, Female-Freelancer; and Male-Permanent Staff 3, Male-Covenanted Employee 3 and Male-Freelancer 3 workers.

Flexibility is considered as the nature of the labour by the freelancers. Four participants of the present research are freelancers, three of whom had temporary or permanent positions previously. All the participants are content with freelance working conditions. Some of them state that they might work 80–90 hours in some weeks, but they find independence so important. The only female freelancer among the participants, Bahar (28, female) describes her working conditions as follows:

> I worked in a large company for a short time, and thought I could make it as a freelancer. I was lucky. ... It is not easy though; but I like being independent of any institutions, I suppose. I am worried about future, as everyone is. I believe in myself. ... The difference is that you do not have many colleagues. And I do various things, I do not stay at the same place for a long time. Last summer, for example, I lived somewhere seaside, and worked at the same time. Normally, you cannot do it.

Bahar's account points to a very crucial discussion. The Global Youth Survey 2017—Pathways to Progress conducted by IPSOS on global scale in many countries and cities with 7000 young people between 16 and 24 years of age, showed that 20% of them preferred to work in fields related to 'science and technology', and this percentage is the highest among all others (2017: 6). As a desired work field, technology reflects the tendencies of youth in late capitalism. The same research demonstrated that 69% of the participants want to start their own business (IPSOS 2017: 12). With the exception of three permanent staff in the present research, our participants all expressed similar desires. This, however, should not be considered as a desire to earn more. PricewaterhouseCoopers' (PwC's) research *Workforce of the future The competing forces shaping 2030*, which has been going on since

2007 with accumulated data of 10,000 participants, shows that freelance work will increase and time management will vary (PricewaterhouseCoopers 2018). Standing (2011, 2014) emphasizes the difference between 'work' and 'labour'. The difference of the twenty-first century from the twentieth is the dominance of 'work' and change in the conception of time. Twenty-first century capitalism has been attacking secure and permanent work based on repetition. Capitalism purely focuses on the profits of a very limited number of agents in the world. However, the implications of such interests have an impact on the comprehension of time and work of the regular masses. As studies, including the present, demonstrate, what young digital workers imagine is neither permanent work nor permanent working hours. Therefore, decrease in loyalty, corporate belonging and knowledge does not influence only capital. As Sennett claims, the culture of the new capitalism determines the workers' conception of loyalty (Sennett 2006: 63–64). The superficiality of the culture of the new capitalism, as Sennett describes it, is a problem for its own power (2006: 196–197). Onur (39, male) has an interesting account on this topic:

> I have been working in this company for three years, and it is a long time. I worked for five different companies until now. … My dream is to establish something based on an original software, and make a living out of it till the end of my life. Of course I would go on working, I love computers. But, I do not feel good to be obliged to work. … Why should I be dependent on a company? They prefer contracts, and so do I. You ask about loyalty: Do the companies feel any loyalty to me? Why should I feel loyal towards them, then?

Flexibility is not always considered to be a positive characteristic of digital labour, though. Many participants stated that they work more than what their contracts set forth. Spatial flexibility, they claim, is always used in favour of the employer. As Lima and Pires (2017: 778) remark, the generations Y and Z are so prone to the demand of flexibility from contemporary companies. These companies seem to take advantage of these generations' desire for autonomy and independence. However, as in Lima and Pires' research (2017: 986), the present study also revealed their expectation of a 'stable future'. Companies today make use of the inclinations of younger generations to be 'autonomous', 'independent' and 'flexible' for the maximization of their profit. However, the dreams of young workers in the sector seldom coincide completely with the logic of the system. The problem here is that fair, egalitarian and pro-stable future approaches of the twenty-first century have not been developed yet.

'Constant' and 'solid' formulas of the twentieth century cannot be employed in corresponding institutions. Social justice must transcend the future projections based merely on working hours and conditions, and focus on the civil rights. Otherwise, younger generations would stay indifferent to various calls for the sake of independence, as they are not genuinely fond of regulations and demands of the new capitalism. As Sennett describes, the great transformation which occurred in the period between his books *The Hidden Injuries of Class* and *The Corrosion of Character*, the bureaucracy which used to keep the workers together is replaced by some other mechanisms (Sennett 2006). This process is not the complete form of what is expected from the new capitalism.

In addition to that, flexibility cannot be limited to working conditions. It is also a way of thinking that affects various dimensions of daily life. People think of it as how they live. Such flexibility is a complicated issue with the conclusions of, for example, looking for a new job, choosing to not working and experiencing the legal system. Hatipoğlu-Aydın (2018) emphasized that the working conditions of workers have direct influence on the pursuit of legal rights and has effects on participating in justice processes:

> Precarity is both a working style and a practice of thinking. Justice mechanisms do not allow a tool kit to overcome this flexibility, vulnerability and lack of security. The law comes from behind. For example, some components of the Fordism that can be seen as expansion of the welfare paradigm, became tight with new regulations, decisions and practices in favor of employers. Because this tightening is unilateral, the gap between workers' experiences and regulations that the labor law stipulates is increasing. While the practice is more adaptable to the new period for employers, its and the law's institutional structure is both unreachable for workers and does not exist in their daily lives. (Hatipoğlu-Aydın 2018: 232)

In this manner, the same as non-corresponding institutes of the twentieth century, the legal logic, rights and procedures that reveal the rights become insufficient day by day.

SELF-CONCEPTION OF DIGITAL LABOUR: GOING BEYOND THE CATEGORIES OF THE TWENTIETH CENTURY

Digital workers interviewed in the scope of the present research, not only wage labourers but also the freelancers, have a strong emphasis on 'labour'. Many of them have various opinions on the position of digital/technological labour in the general category of labour. Some of the participants empha-size the originality of their sector. Although digital labour is a rather new field of work, it has a central importance. Fuchs and Sevignani (2013) categorize digital labour into three groups: cognitive digital labour, com-municative digital labour and co-operative digital labour. The participants of the present study are members of cognitive digital labour field. Hakan (35, male) has been working in a corporate company as a system manager for the last six years, and comments on the categories of labour as follows:

> We are a sort of workers, of course. However, our field is so particular. It does not involve any chain of command. It is not repetitive, but creative. ... Sometimes we collaborate in team-projects, however, most of the time we work individually. ... I do not consider our type of work as a classical employer-employee relationship. It has some similar aspects, but it is mostly different than that. ...

On the topic of problems in the sector, participants generally do not refer to the general picture in the sector, but to their individual contracts and individual work relations. In the IT and computer sectors, the limits of individual work and the obligations of team work are often mentioned. One of the basic characteristics of this type of labour is considered to be 'a part of the team', and to contribute in this way (Akturan et al. 2017: 38). However, it is important to note that the self-conceptions of the workers are based on individual processes.

Digital workers find jobs via web sites, such as kariyer.net and LinkedIn. The CVs uploaded on these online platforms are not deleted after one gets a job: as a participant claims, it is always the time to hunt for new positions. Elvan (30, female) did not graduate from a department on informatics, but from the social sciences. She describes her work experience as follows:

> Since I was not educated as an information or software person, I had differ-ent sorts of difficulties. It is so difficult for me to find a job in this sector as I am humanities graduate. However, in our sector, people find jobs with the help of their acquaintances. None of the software developers I know use kariyer.net to find job. If they are good and successful developers, the com-panies find them. Or you can send your CV to some acquaintances, and they forward it to a company. So, it is more difficult for someone like me, from another department; however, if you work hard to improve yourself, learn new technologies, and socialize in conferences or software fairs, you can meet new people from the sector and find job easily.

Most digital workers dream of working independently and establishing their own companies. Digital workers, however, do not consider themselves as workers in the general worker category. Erhan (26, male) is a computer engineer, and a wage-labourer, but he describes his employment as follows:

> In the last analysis, I am a wage-labourer, but our position is distinct, I suppose. You ask about our position in the general labour market. I have been working since I was a student. In the sector, we are more similar to the ones who do their own job. The logic is similar. The company provides you with the job, and you can do it anywhere you want. I mean, spatially. Workers do not have such opportunities and conditions, I suppose.

Among the problems in the sectors, besides the disadvantages of flexible work hours, the digital workers often emphasize the difficulties of reality based on personal development. Özgür (23, male), a young software engineer, works in a company and lists the problems of the sector as follows:

> Qualifications of the people is a problem in the sector. There are not many people equipped with up-to-date knowledge and open to self-development. The main problem is that they either do not realize, or not accept their deficiencies. Many do not follow latest developments, new studies, new tools. The ones who follow them just read about it, and they cannot produce new products using those tools. My analogy for this is as follows: Imagine someone who watches all Formula 1 races, and know all the names of crews, from the drivers to technical teams, and who won which year's race, which car has better speed, who can corner better, and all other details.

Most of the participants have never been organized in a syndicate, society or party. Two exceptional participants were related to some circles due to their political ideas while they were at university. They both consider it as an important 'experience', however, without any implications in their lives and actions today. Mustafa (34, male) was once related to leftist circles, and interprets the workers of his sector as follows:

> The workers of this sector are so individualistic. You have to adapt yourself to the same thinking, there is no other way. I have the same political concerns as I did before, but people around me are so different. We are workers, we are wage-labourers. However, this field is one of its kind. Being a worker in this sector is totally different.

Some other interviewees state that they feel themselves privileged as the sector is privileged. Şeref (31, male), a computer engineer, prefers to use the concept 'professional' while defining himself. A professional, to him, is an educated person who has independent skills. Wage labour is not a comprehensive frame to include everyone. He describes the sector in Turkey by referring to his experience abroad:

> To tell the truth, the software sector is one of the most privileged sectors in Turkey. The state supports the sector with tax incentives and support programs. They do not do in US, believe me. However, in our society, we do not have the entrepreneurial spirit. And, we are a Mediterranean society. Accept it or not, we are lazier than many countries.

Digital workers are concerned about social inequality and injustice, although these concerns are not centred around their companies. Although they do not mostly define themselves as workers, unequal distribution of social resources makes them emphasize labour in general terms. In terms of exhaustion and cynicism, the participants are not pessimistic. Cynicism is defined as the idea that all individuals are basically self-seeking; and the one who has this pessimistic idea is called a cynic (Alan and Fidanboy 2013: 166). While the participants make comments on individualism, however, a general pessimism towards others is not relevant. In another study on the information sector in Turkey, this was related to work satisfaction (Alan and Fidanboy 2013).

On the other hand, the concerns about *precarity* are highly common. Although they foresee the future of the sector in Turkey as vague and precarious, they have the hope to find new jobs. It should be noted that their income is decreasing compared to the past. Relatively more experienced, older interviewees emphasize this fact.

COLLECTIVITY: VALUES AND DEMANDS

Today, the state of distribution of social resources and equality is considered to be highly worrisome for billions of people on Earth. Neoliberal policies have triggered similar developments in all parts of the world. Not only do billions of people have to struggle with absolute poverty, but also poverty becomes a common feeling in the age of consumption. Turkey has the highest 'inequality' scores among European countries (TÜİK 2016). Despite such a state of affairs, strong and persistent social/political movements have not been established over the last two years, compared to the past, except as bits and pieces in some countries. The existence and impact of classical worker organizations are decreasing. Especially in third world countries in the process of industrialization, a revival in social movement syndicalism can be witnessed. These movements gather labour movements with various dynamics together, and attempt to comprehend the social realm outside the workspace (Fairbrother 2008; Scipes 2011). It is obvious that it will take a long time to construct a decided alternative against precarity and mass poverty on a global scale, however there are some searches for more immediate solutions for the suffering of large sections of society. As the world revolves around consumption today, social policies of the future are expected to include discussions on support mechanisms, and even basic income. An interesting study on *Conditional Cash Transfer Programs* in Latin America emphasizes the following issues:

> The links between sociability, life experiences and sensibility that occur in the relationship between massive social policies and policies of emotions have been adapted and upscaled to a world of consumption; a fact that, in short, implies the triumph of capital reproduction at a global level. (Scribano et al. 2015: 16–17)

Only one of the interviewees emphasized the need and the opportunity to a workspace-based workers' union, a syndical action and collectivity. This emphasis can well be related to the participant's political background back in their university years. The participants are all somehow aware of social, political, cultural and economic processes. Some of the interviewees share their experiences in and interpretations of the Gezi Protests, which occurred in 2013 in Turkey. This is interesting and crucial: the participants are mindful about current social movements, environment, daily life, social rights and freedoms. Their participation level in petitions on web-based platforms such as Change.org and the like is high. These people seek and find jobs via LinkedIn, socialize through Facebook and Instagram, and get up to date on Twitter. Since they can speak English, they are also well aware of global problems. In terms of classical concepts and scales of the twentieth century, they might be considered apolitical, however they clearly have a tendency to get informed about the agenda. For example, the mask in the movie *V for Vendetta*, which later became the political symbol of *Los Indignados* of Spain, and of other riot movements in other countries (see Gerbaudo 2017) is also an important symbol for Oktay (29, male). Oktay's comments on collectivity and social struggle are as follows:

> I experienced Gezi, here in İstanbul. I had never participated any demonstrations before. There was a distinct dynamism there. I could not believe my eyes when I saw lots of people wearing the mask of my favourite movie's protagonist. I felt I was not alone, there were many like me. ... The world must be more fair. I know about USA. It is the same there. There are enough source in the world, but many are excluded from the opportunity to reach it. And, we need to live how we wish.

Ayça (31, female) claims that she also participated Gezi protests, and has been participating in March 8th demonstrations since then. Ayça's account on politics and collectivity is as follows:

> I do not like politics. I never liked it. It is not for me. Gezi, in my opinion, was a response against politics. Struggle, working class, syndicate are concepts that I feel distant. I want to be free. That's what I know. I want to be let alone, because I feel like drowning sometimes. ... Politics will not be able to alter such things.

The politics Ayça positions herself within is distant from the established order we all experience with an entire set of institutions today. As a female digital worker, she is so conscious of all social processes. As many participants unconsciously revealed their problems with working conditions, they also revealed their political tendencies, although they claim that they are apolitical. This case would remind us of Negri and Hardt's concept of 'multitude' and its political implications (Hardt and Negri 2004). The participants demonstrated a critical stance towards the system based on consumption, with its exhausted institutions and emotionless logic. This may become visible in various ways in particular cases. Additionally, digital labourers contemplate on 'network' and their way of working, and attempt to define the political realm in terms of such a conception. Therefore, their political approach tends to distance them from the bureaucratic and rigid political forms of the past. This does not show, however, that they support ultra-liberal and individualistic theses. The positions they take seem to be the precursor of coming collectivity and new social movements.

CONCLUSION

The software industry has a key role in the future planning of the Turkish economy. The size of the sector and its competitiveness gradually increases. The number of young, educated workers employed in this sector is also increasing rapidly. This new generation of employees sees flexibility as an advantage to their own interests. However, this situation also involves contradictions and dualities in itself. On the one hand, flexible working conditions and loyalty to the workplace are reduced; the labour process, on the other hand, is emotionally challenging employees. Some relatively advantageous situations, such as working from home, results in the feeling of loneliness and leads to an increase in the time spent at work. Pressures based on ongoing professional self-development strategies and learning software programmes seem to be related to the nature of the work, but after a while they can be turned into an advantage for the employer. This new type of work culture can be characterized as a 'new youth culture' whose members are less loyal to employers, feeling privileged but this can be easily transformed into another work culture. The increase in the number of employees in this sector can turn this emerging workers' culture into a dangerous class position as a precariat. Particularly young white-collar workers, who were not emotionally satisfied during the Gezi uprising in 2013 and were at risk of becoming unemployed, played a pioneering role. All these possibilities will be determined by class composition on the global, regional and national scale, where immaterial labour is central. For the time being, even if organizational anxiety is held back, employees of older working age can claim for more institutional identity from their employer. Finally, class divisions, expansion of the precariat army and occupation of life entirely through biopolitics will lead to the crystallization of these young employees' sense of flexibility.

REFERENCES

Akturan, A., Günsel, A., & Becerikli, M. (2017). Duygusal Emek Kavramı ve Duygusal Emeğin TakımBaşarısı Üzerindeki Etkileri: Bilişim Sektörü Çalışanları Üzerinde Bir Uygulama. *Uluslararası Turizm, Ekonomi ve İşletme Bilimleri Dergisi, 1*, 34–47.

Alan, H., & Fidanboy, C. Ö. (2013). Sinizm, Tükenmişlik ve Kişilik Arasındaki İlişkiler: Bilişim Sektörü Çalışanları Kapsamında Bir İnceleme. *Süleyman Demirel Üniversitesi Sosyal Bilimler Enstitüsü Dergisi, 1*(Büro Yönetimi Özel Sayısı): 165–175.

Badagliacco, J. M. (1990). Gender and Race Differences in Computing Attitudes and Experience. *Social Science Computer Review, 8*(1), 42–63.

ÇSGB (Ministry of Labour and Social Security). (2013). *Ulusal İstihdam Stratejisi 2013 (Strategy of National Employment).* http://www.uis.gov.tr/media/1198/uis_izleme_degerlendirme_raporu138-150.pdf; http://www.uis.gov.tr/media/1198/uis_izleme_degerlendirme_raporu138-150.pdf. Accessed 3 Dec 2018.

EMO (The Chamber of Electrical Engineers). (2009). EMO Bilişim Çalışanları Anket Sonuçları (EMO Software Sector Survey). http://www.emo.org.tr/ekler/68cab8427ff385d_ek.pdf?dergi=. Accessed 20 Nov 2017.

Fairbrother, P. (2008). Social Movement Unionism or Trade Unions as Social Movements. *Employee Responsibilities and Rights Journal, 20*(3), 213–220.

Fuchs, C., & Sevignani, S. (2013). What Is Digital Labour? What Is Digital Work? What's Their Difference? And Why Do These Questions Matter for Understanding Social Media? *TripleC, 11*(2), 237–293.

Gerbaudo, P. (2017). *The Mask and The Flag: Populism, Citizenism and Global Protest.* London: Hurst.

Gill, R. (2009). *Technobohemians or the New Cybertariat?* Amsterdam: Institute of Network Cultures.

Hardt, M., & Negri, A. (2004). *Multitude: War and Democracy in the Age of Empire.* New York/London: Penguin.

Hatipoğlu-Aydın, D. (2018). *Güvencesiz Adalet: İşçilerin Hukuk Deneyimi Üzerine Bir Temellendirilmiş Kuram Çalışması.* İstanbul: On İki Levha Yayıncılık.

Huws, U. (2003). *The Making of a Cybertariat.* London: Merlin Press.

IPSOS. (2017, June). *IPSOS Global Youth Survey 2017: Pathways to Progress.* https://www.citigroup.com/citi/foundation/data/p2p_global_youth_survey_full_data.pdf. Accessed 15 Feb 2018.

Lazzarato, M. (1996). Immaterial Labor. In P. Virno & M. Hardt (Eds.), *Radical Thought in Italy: A Potential Politics* (pp. 133–148). Minneapolis: University of Minnesota Press.

Lima, J. C., & Pires, A. S. (2017). Youth and the New Culture of Work: Considerations Drawn from Digital Work. *Sociologia & Antropologia, 7*(3), 773–799.

Ministry of Industry and Trade. (2010). *Turkish Industrial Strategy Document 2011–2014.* https://www.ab.gov.tr/files/haberler/2011/turkish_industrial_strategy.pdf. Accessed 1 Dec 2018.

Mishra, A., Azıcı, A., & Çetin, S. (2016). Software Evolution in Turkey. *Tecnicki Vjesnik, 23*(3), 929–935.

PricewaterhouseCoopers. (2018). Workforce of the Future: The Competing Forces Shaping 2030, *pwc.com,* 2017. https://www.pwc.com/gx/en/services/people-organisation/workforce-of-the-future/workforce-of-the-future-the-competing-forces-shaping-2030-pwc.pdf. Accessed 2 Mar 2018.

Scipes, K. (2011). Understanding the New Labor Movements in the "Third World": The Emergence of Social Movement Unionism, a New Type of Trade Unionism. *Critical Sociology, 19*(2), 81–101. (First Published Jul 1, 1992).

Scribano, A., De Sena, A., & Cena, B. R. (2015). Social Policies and Emotions in Latin America: A Theoretical Approach to Their Analysis. *Corvinus Journal of Sociology and Social Policy, 6*(2), 3–19.

Sennett, R. (2006). *The Culture of the New Capitalism*. New Haven/London: Yale University Press.

Standing, G. (2011). *The Precariat: The New Dangerous Class*. London/New York: Bloomsbury.

Standing, G. (2014). *A Precariat Charter: From Denizens to Citizens*. London/ New York: Bloomsbury.

Stratejik Düşünce Enstitüsü (Institute of Strategic Thinking). (2012). *Türkiye'de Yazılım Sektörü (Sofware Sector in Turkey)*, SDE Analyze Report, Ankara.

TÜBİSAD (Turkey Informatics Industry Association). (2018). Information and Communications Technologies (ICT) 2017 Market Data Report. http://www.tubisad.org.tr/en//images/pdf/tubisad_2018_ict_market_data_en.pdf. Accessed 3 Dec 2018.

TÜİK (Turkish Statistical Institute). (2016). Gini Katsayısı AB'de 0.310 oldu (Gini Coefficient 0.310 in EU). http://www.tuik.gov.tr/basinOdasi/haberler/2016_109_20161020.pdf. Accessed 1 Feb 2018.

Türkmen, M. (2016). *Bilişim Sektöründe Çalışanların Psikososyal Risklerinin Değerlendirilmesi ve E-Devlet Proje Çalışanları Üzerine Bir Uygulama (Evaluation of Worker's Psychosocial Risk Factors in ICT Sector and An Application for E-Government Project Workers)*, Ministry of Labour and Social Security, Directorate General of Occupational Health and Safety, Unpublished Thesis for Occupational Health and Safety Expertise, Ankara.

CHAPTER 10

An Approach to Creative Work in the Global Economy of Risk and Uncertainty

Juan A. Roche Cárcel

Introduction

Westerners have actually not had too favourable an opinion about work. Quite the opposite, work has represented—throughout our history and nearly always—an obligation, if not a torture. Nevertheless, today, when work is undergoing a deep crisis—as highlighted by the economic and sociological literature—it comes as a surprise to check that, even so, we are incapable of revaluing it, of managing to understand its true meaning for the life of humans, of individuals and of societies.

Indeed, work is in crisis; it has become a scarce asset of the past which not everybody can access on an equal footing, to which must be added that the different models set in motion with the aim of activating it at best end up generating a number of patches which do not succeed in solving the root problem. As a result of this, a considerable number of workers above the age of 45 have been unemployed for a long time and will

---

English translation by Víctor Pina, Senior Lecturer, University of Alicante, Spain.

J. A. Roche Cárcel (✉)
University of Alicante, Alicante, Spain
e-mail: ja.roche@ua.es

© The Author(s) 2019
A. Scribano, P. Lisdero (eds.), *Digital Labour, Society and the Politics of Sensibilities*, https://doi.org/10.1007/978-3-030-12306-2_10

probably never return to the labour market in sufficiently good conditions to maintain their families; women have greater difficulty in finding jobs than their male counterparts, and when they do find those jobs, their salaries are significantly lower than those of men, thus reinforcing the historical gender inequality; and young people find it really hard to access their first occupation, which clearly seems to suggest that their hopes of leading a comfortable life, similar to—or better than—their parents are further and further away.

The enthronement of creativity as an emerging force in the field of social sciences, its empowerment as a nearly absolute energy, might lead us to think that it would constitute a useful response to overcome the work crisis, and even to endow this activity with prestige and take it to the place where it should really belong. The aim sought with this chapter therefore consists in confirming whether or not creative work has achieved such aims; whether it has actually pursued them; whether or not, in addition to generating fast and large profits for the creators and firms that have hired them, it has become a powerful force both regarding social cohesion and the globalisation of economy, of society and of democracy and its values.

Seeking to develop the aforementioned aims, and following the instructions of Adrian Scribano and Pedro Lisdero, editors of *Politics of Sensibilities, Society 4.0 and Digital Labour* particularly in its second part, Politics of Sensibilities and Digital Labour, where this work fits, this chapter has been divided into four sections. The first one, meant as a general introduction, is followed by the section 'The Crisis of Work in Late Modern Society', where I will try to define work, to frame it within the negative perception that the West has traditionally had about it, additionally synthesising the two models by means of which our civilisation strives to provide employment, and finally summarising the characteristics of work at present. As for the section 'Creative Work in the New Global Economy', it focuses on creative work in the context of the global economy and, inside it, I will place the emphasis on defining what creativity and the global economy are, on describing the most essential features of cities and creative industries, and how the latter are causing new inequalities. Lastly, the section 'Final Reflections' will offer some final reflections aimed at analysing the main traits currently assumed by creative work.

THE CRISIS OF WORK IN LATE MODERN SOCIETY

Work or Free Time

Work has been poorly regarded throughout Western history (Tezanos 2001: 11–2), but the nascent capitalism made a positive assessment of work and its 'orderly' life, the same as monastic and military existence; or expressed differently, factory whistles will soon joyfully sound after the bells of monasteries and the trumpets of military camps and barracks (Naredo 2002: 39–40).

This revaluation of work continues at the dawn of economic science, as exemplified by William Petty, the nineteenth-century economist and statesman, when he argues that 'Earth was the mother and Work the father of wealth.' This idea gradually took shape with Adam Smith—according to the position he defends, a nation's wealth derives from its work (Smith 2007: 13)—Ricardo and Marx, since Father-Work stopped collaborating in Mother Earth's productive activities to become the most important wealth production component, and even the only one, since those thinkers perceived that the earth itself could be replaced by work. The subsequent step in this change process took place in the nineteenth century when capital, which had initially been a collaborating instrument of earth and work in productive tasks, began to replace them both (Naredo 2002: 42).

This long historical process ultimately resulted in the 'political economy'—as it was still called by Adam Smith (Smith 2007: 13)—and the social forces which took physical and social care of individuals—the family, the tribe or the city—falling into decline or undergoing a deep transformation. Then the productivist rationale of work collapsed to such an extent that work was conceived as an individual and social goal and as a means both to socialise and to achieve promotion in the professional, economic and social fields. Work consequently turned—as Max Weber used to say (1997: 51)— into the main factor of an 'intramundane asceticism' regime, as a response to man's feeling of loneliness and isolation (Naredo 2002: 43–4). We thus find ourselves before the highest peak of work appreciation.

This does not mean, though, that modern individualism succeeded in eliminating the attack upon ordinary work, or that it freed human beings from the ancient dominations and dependences. What it did do was to rationalise the old hierarchy system and to preserve it by means of renovated forms, as pointed out by Veblen when he speaks about the 'idle class' and about the contempt for the ordinary-life jobs which were typical of the previous hierarchical societies (Veblen 2000: 39; Figueras and Moreno 2013: 169). It is true that the classical Greco-Roman and Christian contemptuous vision of work will remain valid until the nineteenth century, and highly active while aristocracy survived, since this social segment masters society's general worldview and rejects work as being unworthy of their noble condition, and even economic activity and the money that it brings, even if that activity allows them to lead an ostentatious and luxurious life (Sombart 2009: 70).

It suffices to recall in this sense that a number of important authors have highlighted the negative impact that the world of industrial labour has on social relations. For instance, Adam Smith claims that, despite creating order, industrial routine appeases human character and represses solidarity, to which must be added that he criticises the fact that society progresses in material terms but not morally. Furthermore, specialist workers in factories need little or no effort as far as reasoning or judgement are concerned (Sennett 2000: 38–40), they lose autonomy (Gratton 2012: 21) and they become reified—Max Weber writes about the impersonal nature of modern work, about its senselessness and about its scarce joy (Thaa 2008: 13)—and alienated (Marx).

Karl Marx himself fails to enhance the dignity of work when he inserts it into two concepts: alienation and commoditisation. The former is present in *Los Manuscritos económico-filosóficos* (The Economic-Philosophical Manuscripts), where work appears as an essential factor in the development of the materialistic and historical conception, insofar as it constitutes the activity mediating between nature and the human being. What is more, it expresses the efforts made by human beings to regulate their relationships with nature, the transformation of which allows them to become a part of nature themselves. Marx additionally stresses in the same work that he understands alienation at work, because productive activity in capitalism is lived as a crushing burden which causes not only suffering and tiredness but also mental and physical discomfort. As has traditionally been done in the Western world, Marx also opposes work and leisure, the latter being the only thing which allows human beings to enjoy themselves and to lead a more comfortable life, whereas in the former nobody expects to be able to make the best of their skills and talents, to develop their creative potential or to experience pleasure. Instead, work constitutes a sacrifice which humans are obliged to 'offer' if they want to survive or exist more comfortably (Fraiman 2015: 236–7).

As for work commoditisation, it is analysed by Marx in *El Capital* (Capital) and within the context of goods fetishisation. It should thus come as no surprise to check that he exclusively views it as a commodity similar to sugar with which workers can cover their living expenses, and accordingly survive (Marx 1985: 9). It thus follows from the Marxian vision that life and work have drifted apart, since treating the latter as a value of change rather than one of use implies undervaluing work once again. Life may be a gift, but the conditions which make that life possible are not given to us as a present.

The nearly 30 years from 1945 to 1973 witnessed a situation of overall economic progress on the planet as a whole, and particularly in the Western universe. Indeed, a true 'golden age' of economy seemed to be enjoyed after World War II, thanks to which hunger and poverty had decreased, all the countries in the world—including the least developed ones—increased their gross domestic product, and inequalities were reduced (Hobsbawm 2001: 29 ff.). A social-order-based Society of Work was likewise established during those decades which fought poverty and relinked the individual to society. Adding to this that full standardised employment is achieved, together with mass consumption and an economy based upon security, on certainty and on the boundaries defined between work, capital and the democratic state (Beck 2007: 24, 99), it becomes easy to understand why this was a period during which democracies enjoyed a progressive stability (Held 1993: 273). Who remembered then that work alienated the worker in the capitalist production system—as Marx said—if everybody could afford to buy a fridge, a car or a dwelling, or to take their children to school, or had a basic healthcare system, an unemployment insurance and a decent pension guaranteed for the time when the age of rest and retirement came?

We cannot fool ourselves, though; the illusion that work leads to progress, that working dignifies human beings and allows them to lead a good life, only lasted a few decades. The oil crisis, together with an essential instability of the economy, which enters a real 'Age of Uncertainty' which does not permit the discernment of sustained growth in the future, but rather a series of almost permanent and structural crises (Galbraith 1984), immerses work in a deep recession without its positive valuation having managed to become fully rooted in the collective imagery. Therefore, work fails to transcend us as human beings, to build us as highly civilised beings able to enjoy the post-materialistic democracies announced by Inglehart (1991) in which happiness was proposed to us as society's highest value. The unfair and uneven distribution of work—at best—or its lack—at worst—has made work become a truly desired asset, though never surrounded by the 'aura' of important and significant things in life. This explains why we need to work to build the material conditions of life, but not so much the spiritual ones. It could not have been otherwise because late capitalist society strongly links work to anxiety, contingency, risk and uncertainty; indeed, work currently constitutes an 'anxiolytic, precarious, instable and high-risk activity which causes deep physical and psychological wounds, increasingly enormous social inequalities and a corrosive deterioration in the meaning-value of life' (Roche Cárcel 2013: 3).

In short, work has not had good press in the history of Western civilisation; working has been assimilated with a curse or torture and has not been related to a noble and virtuous activity which builds us as free human beings, but to the compelling needs of society's lowest and most menial segments or classes. How do we conceptualise work today, when it seems to be scarcer than ever and is not equitably distributed? Work thus finds itself before a crossroads fraught with uncertainty which society seems to have few chances to come out of successfully, since it is contextualised between two irreconcilable extremes. On the one hand, unemployment and compulsive work, competitiveness, lack of solidarity and social segmentation increase jointly, and paradoxically. It all refers us back to a society that wishes to be democratic and therefore based on an egalitarian trend, but which seems to be trapped in a highly mythicised way of understanding work, while simultaneously proving unable to solve the negative consequences that it provokes and to place limits on the social risks that it generates. On the other hand, a desire exists—or rather utopia, I would say—to consciously reduce the overwhelming prevalence of commercial production and paid work so that other freer, more creative and more cooperative types of activities can be possible (Naredo 2002: 47).

The Two Western Labour Models of Work

This society otherwise questions the prosperity of economies and the democratic social liberal state (Held 1993: 276) and a situation of total collapse arises where work has also fallen into a deep and perhaps irreparable crisis (Tezanos 2001: 70). And most worryingly, this is a serious, structural crisis because it has resulted from a complex interrelation of five forces of change which seem to be unstoppable and which, together with positive aspects, bring undesired effects too: technology, globalisation, demography and longevity, natural resources and society (Gratton 2012: 25). Furthermore, the crisis of work is caused by—and generates—significant structural changes with respect to the traditional industrial society. After all, it entails the decline of a specific society and civilisation model in which work plays an essential role, that of its pattern as employment, that of its connection with wage-based relationships and that of its conception as a social activity (Tezanos 2001: 28–232).

As an illustration of this deep mutation, the two traditional Western work models (Sennett 2000: 54) inevitably seem to lead us to a dead end. On one side, we can find the 'Rhenish' model typical of the Netherlands, Germany, France, Israel, Italy, Japan and the Scandinavian countries. The nations where this model is applied do not have full employment, but there seems to be a sort of correcting factor facilitated by the Welfare State which has reached an agreement with trade unions and companies to achieve this aim, and which provides economic aid to the unemployed, thanks to which their dramatic situation can be alleviated. Nevertheless, one cannot prevent such negative aspects as the gradual disappearance of industrial jobs, the numerous cases of early retirement and the difficult access to employment for youngsters and women. To which must be added that, either pushed by the circumstances or consciously, the countries under this model are making socio-labour regulations more flexible in favour of the business community (Tezanos 2001: 50–1) and reducing the state's competences, thus breaking the old pact between work and capital, between capitalism, the 'Care-Giving' or Welfare State and Democracy (Beck 2007: 14, 99; Requejo 1990: 125). This results in a weakening of the safety cushion that it represented for workers in general and especially for the most underprivileged ones; as a consequence, those excluded from the alliance put the blame on democracy, which consequently loses part of its legitimacy (Beck 2007: 155).

The second paradigm of work, the 'Anglo-American' one, is basically implemented in the United States and the United Kingdom. It is characterised by having an almost absolute faith in free-market capitalism and by its conception of state bureaucracy as being subordinated to economy. In turn, the labour market implies a small cost, which is linked to the insecure, sporadic and low-paid jobs that it offers (Tezanos 2001: 50–1). Greater and deeper inequalities consequently arise in this model—between those who have a good, well-paid job and those who do not have one—along with an increased violence of social origin—staged by those who are excluded from the system (Beck 2007: 11).

As can be seen, these two models, the only two existing ones to date, place Western democracies before an unsolvable and tragic dilemma: either paying the price of growing poverty with a higher unemployment rate—as happens in the first model—or tolerating a scandalous poverty rate with less unemployment—which takes place in the Anglo-Saxon model—though reducing it with precarious wages, with low productivity, with a minimum or insufficient coverage level and with higher inequality and crime rates (Beck 2007: 66). Explaining (which is seldom done by politicians, who insist on claiming that full employment policies are feasible instead) to youngsters, to women, to the long-term unemployed and to people above 45 years of age—the social segments with the highest unemployment rate—that these are the only two options available for states to solve their problems will definitely not offer them much hope. Without a doubt, both solutions are meagre and insufficient, and if we additionally take into account that they have already been applied since the 1980s, the impression is that the system as a whole seems incapable of proposing true alternatives, as if it were paralysed, as if it lacked creativity, as if it had collapsed and ultimately, as if it had reached the end of a stage.

The Characteristics of Work at Present

In any case, it is worth delving even deeper into the severity of the contemporary work crisis, describing some of its main characteristics (Galbraith 1984: 167 ff.; Sennett 2000: 19–145; Tezanos 2001: 22–146; Boltanski and Chiapello 2002: 299–395; Bauman 2003: 99–175; Innerarity 2004: 102–8; Beck 2006: 75 ff.; Beck 2007: 9–165; Beriain 2008: 142–164 and 204; Gratton 2012: 21; Roche Cárcel 2012: 144 ff.).

1. The transformation of the industrial and work society into the risk society probably constitutes the most outstanding peculiarity of our time. It needs to be remembered in this regard that risk, as defined by Ulrich Beck, consists in the measurable and quantifiable insecurity that reaches every field—economy, society and politics—and has the following dimensions: globalisation, ecology, digitisation, individualisation and the politicisation of work. Its most relevant consequences as far as work is concerned include lack of protection, discontinuity, imprecision, informality and, in short, the irruption of precariousness. Precarisation materialises through outsourcing and an increase in non-permanent work, temporary and part-time jobs,

all of which has to do with a twofold strategy followed by firms: a hiring policy which allows the employer to have complete freedom and a new policy regarding the company's structure which makes it possible for its owners to outsource labour and hide as such; in this way, they manage to avoid the constrictions of labour law.

Precariousness is additionally accompanied by the development of an economy based on insecurity and uncertainty, both of which draw a dark, blurred—and most probably, dangerous and highly risky—future. What really constitutes a novelty in this whole situation is the fact that the state and the economy pass the risks onto individuals and place the weight of market uncertainty on the salaried workers' shoulders. If one adds to this today's uncertainty representing a powerful force for individualisation which divides rather than unites, we will understand that danger is hovering over citizens' everyday life, filling it with a distressing and uncertain wait, or better said, with a risky feeling of despair.

2. Work is also defined by the 'despatialisation,' fragmentation and acceleration of time. Despatialisation finds its driving force in the existing contradiction between global capital and local work which has acquired a fragmentary nature worldwide. The paradox of this phenomenon lies in the fact that social proximity coexists with geographical distance; or expressed differently, that humans live and work locally isolated and globally connected. Thus, although capitalism has strengthened the value assigned to place and increased the desire to form part of a community, it has simultaneously encouraged the disappearance of barriers, the debordering, the deterritorialisation, the despatialisation of life's social and political components, as well as of production, and the consequent 'desocialisation' of work, which is leading to its virtualisation. As Marx was able to see, when—during the Industrial Revolution—work is considered a resource which can be separated from the person producing it, work becomes a legal fiction. But now, it has also largely lost its defined location in the factory, being situated in an ever-changing space or in a vague and disorganised 'non-place' where nothing other than concepts or ideas—or even worse, than the abstract benefits detached from the social aspect, from the capital-work-state contract—seems to take place any more. Work consequently transforms itself into something as virtual as the bits which travel at the speed of light inside computers and, in this respect,

it leads us once again to the disconnection of work from the human body and to its de-consideration as something mental, fictitious, invisible and liquid. Hence it seems at the very least illogical to check that, during a period characterised by a shortage of work and when the latter should be better valued, work does not acquire more solid features but rather more ethereal ones, cruelly fitting in with the prophetical sentence written by Shakespeare, Marx and Marshall Berman—'all that is solid vanishes into thin air'—referring to the modern world.

The deconstruction of the work space undoubtedly correlates with a new construction of time which has become disorganised, has accelerated its speed and is represented with a broken, metamorphosed arrow at a point which expresses the maximum and focused trust in a narcissistic present. As a cause or a result thereof, capital becomes more 'impatient' due to the desire for a rapid return, thus favouring dramatic and discontinuous changes in the belief that growth improves. We therefore think more on a short-term basis, which makes it more difficult for the human being—characterised by a slower biological nature—to assimilate the speed of the process, which in turn results—as will be seen below when referring to the last characteristic of work—in a corrosion of character, particularly when it comes to those aspects which bring humans together and grant them the feeling of a sustainable social self. In effect, a conflict arises now between a lasting aspect like character and a disarticulated experience of time which is preventing its consolidation and that of the lasting narrations which define it. This is completed with a tendency to make working hours more flexible, especially in large corporations, where fixed working timetables are less and less common. An example of this can be found in Toyota, where all idle times have been eliminated and the pace of work—or to put in another way, the intensity of activity with the same salary—has been maximised. At the same time, accumulated experience is hardly valued, stressing the contempt for the past or the disconnection from it and focusing on immediacy.

Work consequently becomes a slave to time, and more precisely, to the present, to the moment which tyrannises, dememorises and freezes our lives in a moment. But, does work not end up becoming a tyrant as a result too?

3. Flexibility, deregulation and informalisation constitute other aspects shaping work and result from an economic power system characterised by three elements: the discontinuous reinvention of institutions—

which has just been mentioned, the centralised concentration of power—to which I will refer below and the flexible specialisation of production. This last element has as its aim to achieve increasingly varied and quick products due to the instability of consumer demand, which has to do with the fact that the deregulation of labour relations allows for a quicker transformation of society's institutions.

4. The impact of new technologies along with the passing from the industrial, tertiary society to that of knowledge and information stands out as another significant characteristic of work. Four remarks need to be made in this regard. The first one is that the global market's link to new technologies represents the hallmark of contemporary capitalism, which is nothing other than the end of labour society, insofar as human beings are replaced by technologies. In fact, it is knowledge, not work, that currently expresses the main source of social wealth, but the knowledge society does not generate higher employment rates; what is more, it increases productivity without generating any jobs. The effects can be easily seen, because the machine-robot is making workers increasingly expendable, which adds to their alienation, to their social disappropriation and, in short, to their transformation into social 'non-subjects.'

The second aspect worthy of consideration is related to the so-called technological unemployment, which stems from a new economic growth model that does not generate jobs and, when it does, they are lower-quality ones. The great paradox is that greater wealth exists in technological societies—but also fewer and worse jobs.

The third remark has to do with the global context of employment and unemployment. It is a well-known fact that robotisation takes place at a faster pace than the appearance of new sources of work; and that the latter has not grown since the 1960s—when full employment is achieved—and even that an unemployment rate situated in the region of 30% has been maintained—in the twenty-first century.

Finally, the fourth focus of attention in what regards the impact caused by new technologies on work can be found in the overall consequences derived from the widespread introduction of the Internet: labour decentralisation, networked selling with a closer contact between producers and consumers, lower commercialisation costs, work organisation through networks, higher flexibility in contractual regulations, extension of new labour patterns—telework or outsourcing of self-employed workers, amongst others.

5. Another factor which shapes labour activity at present is what has come to be known as its 'Brazilianisation' (Beck 2007). Not in vain, we are on track to match the situation of South America, where barely 35% of the economically active population has some protection or aid from social security and where 40% of work has an informal nature. We have hitherto thought that Europe represented the apex of civilisation and that the aim was to universalise the world, to Westernise it. Precisely the opposite is happening, though: China and the emerging countries are ahead of us in economic terms, and so are Latin American countries when it comes to work modalities. As a collateral effect, this situation leads to a loss of self-esteem and of trust in Western values and abilities to effectively solve the major work-related problems we are faced with, yet another consequence of work despatialisation which in turn entails that of the territory, as well as a deterioration in the robustness of Western symbols. The desire to impose our values— very often by force, political messianism—has so far constituted a historical *leitmotif* for European and US foreign activity, and this is an intimate enemy of democracy (Todorov 2012: 35 ff.). In this sense, not seeing ourselves as the best may prove positive to temper our evangelising zeal, though definitely at a huge cost, since it places us at a clear disadvantage in terms of economy, labour and civilising efforts, without forgetting the implications and suffering for people.

6. Present-day work can likewise be described as hierarchy-based and uneven. Despite the growth of small- and medium-sized enterprises, networked organisations have increased too, to the detriment of the big firms typical of the industrial era. A greater and greater influence is also being exerted by large-sized coordinated economic ensembles (large corporations, groups, networked organisations of independent players and collaborations between companies and alliances). And, above all, the creation of oligopolies is progressing in every market, their presence and networks of collaborators expanding beyond their borders. An evolution has thus taken place from organisations with a pyramidal structure to others shaped around modern institutional networks, lighter on their base, and determined—as stated above—by weaker ties and defined by networked fragments and nodes, by a structure which no longer has the clarity of a pyramid—it is not simpler but actually more intricate— and by a top-to-bottom shapeless domination which becomes stronger as human ties weaken. Hence, even though a certain degree of

repudiation for authority supposedly manifests itself at the level of managers—heirs to May 68—and although they seek new—less classist and hierarchy-based and more participatory—labour activity methods, the actual outcome is not a disappearance of the structural hierarchisation which characterises the economy, but rather that the latter adapts to the new times. A passage is consequently taking place from a previous vertical economy to another more horizontal one. Those suffering the most in this economy are the individuals located at the base—significantly small—at the lower part, where an increasing number of people are forced to stay on the margins or pushed away—outside the labour world—and ultimately left aside from society and democracy too.

At the same time, a concentration of economic power is taking place, without centralisation, as a result of mergers; to such an extent that 200 large corporations are controlled by 150 individuals located in five countries. This concentration causes a huge economic and social distance. In this way, it is the most important entrepreneurs that control, run and manage the economic affairs—and more specifically, the macroeconomic ones—small entrepreneurs find it more and more difficult to survive in an environment of giants; and if the rich become richer and richer, the poor also become increasingly poor. It deserves to be highlighted in this respect that the last few years have been characterised by a decrease in wages and an increase in capital income. The concentration of power additionally entails an enormous danger, both for the labour world and for democracy itself. After all, the strength of trade unions is currently not comparable to that of such huge corporations, partly owing to their own mistakes but, above all, because of the successful practices used by firms to weaken those unions. The truth is that mass unionism has evolved to become more professional and less ideologised, this being a de-unionisation factor, as attested by the drop in membership figures. Furthermore, this weakening of unions has run parallel to the decrease in criticism against the capitalist enterprise and to the reduction in labour conflicts, which has resulted in an evident depreciation of unions' capacity both to negotiate and to defend the rights of their workers—the curtailing of such rights during the last few years does nothing but provide clear evidence thereof. The existence of a monopoly with so much power in so few hands does not exactly help at a time when economic power prevails over the political, to which must be added an intelligent invisibility strategy for this capital, which does not want to be photographed, which keeps business headquarters in various places, and which hides or makes it difficult to know where it pays its taxes and where it moves its profits.

The concentration of power is therefore giving rise to a new social hierarchisation. This is firstly due to the break-up of the existing ties between capital and work which were established during the industrial revolution, which remained valid until practically the 1980s and which brought about an economic, labour-related and institutional stability, together with a growing improvement of workers' labour conditions. Secondly, a dualisation arises between salaried work and the labour market: on one side, we have a stable, qualified workforce benefitting from a relatively high wage level and frequently unionised in large companies; on the other side, an unstable, poorly-qualified workforce hardly protected—and clearly excluded—in the small firms which deliver ancillary services. All of this triggers a previously unknown social polarisation between workers—those who have a job and those who do not—which replaces the older one existing between aristocracy and bourgeoisie, or between the latter and the proletariat. The middle class is not alien to this process either, since it is being eroded, due to the loss of quality in their jobs and of the wages associated with them, as well as to the higher tax rates demanded by the financial crisis.

It must also be borne in mind that both European and US firms have increased their productivity and competitiveness, but to the detriment of salaries and doing without more and more of the costs generated prior to employment (such as education and training) and after it (rebuilding of strengths, from wear and from ageing). These costs have been assumed by the Welfare State but, after its falling into decline, it can no longer foot the bill, which has caused the ruin of social capital. By way of example, electoral participation has decreased in the United States—only 30% of voters participate in elections—and a 'prison miracle' has taken place with figures of 500 inmates for every 100,000 grown-ups, in contrast to the 80 per 100,000 in Germany. Meanwhile, almost the same is happening in Europe, with the exception and perhaps only for the time being, of the data related to prisons and violence, and of those referring to political participation—considerably higher than the US figures. However, the danger of abstention in the coming elections is quite strong, coinciding with the growth of extremist positions in the political arena, as well as of populist, nationalist and far-right movements. For these reasons, it seems advisable for me to stress that the attack against the Welfare State and the neo-liberal and neo-conservative policies which have had such a disastrous social impact are being produced—as Adam Smith would put it—by invisible hands, yes, but not by fleshed or virtual beings; the virtuality of work stems from very specific interests and goals of real economic agents.

7. The last feature which describes contemporary labour activity in the West is its individualisation and the corrosion of character that comes with it. In fact, individuality grows in labour conditions and, particularly, in remunerations. Nevertheless, individuality also becomes visible in the deterioration of teamwork conditions, since that kind of work has become more superficial, in such a way that the—labour—community has turned into a 'fiction.' Likewise, the disintegration of the work community arises from the utilisation, in the same space, of workers coming from various firms and governed by different statutes, which leads to the dismantling and disorientation of collective action and, in short, to an individualisation of tasks.

We are not talking about a true individuality, a substantial one structured around singular ideas and emotions, though it is in fact a type of individualism which resembles the lonely activity of consumption and is consumed rather than lived. The worker's private and emotional life undoubtedly goes adrift because of the growing difficulty to reconcile personal and familial responsibilities with those related to work. Not in vain—as seen above—workers are being progressively and limitlessly forced to accept more flexible working hours, a full-availability status and a gradual increase in responsibility, additionally putting an enormous pressure on them to reach aims and goals, and to compete in an extremely cruel and inaccessible world where profits must be increasingly large and fast. Thus, work of course no longer personifies a pleasure, but rather a *tripalium*, an instrument of torture: we have advanced so little from the origin of the concept to the present day! Added to this, work does not provide an ethical model any more, insofar as a conflict arises between its values—a short-term purpose, an instrumental rationality based on goals and not on emotions, competitiveness, lack of solidarity—and the personal and family-related ones—obligations, honest behaviours, solidarity, empathy and understanding attitudes towards others.

This explains why the worker's character is corroding little by little, why work no longer constitutes an essential source for the shaping of personality, but quite the opposite. After all, as already pointed out above, if the character builds up on the basis of the lasting—long-term—aspects of our personal experience, a short-term-based approach to work which forgets the past, which does not take experience into account, which leaves emotions aside and which replaces human intelligence with a mechanical one, no longer makes it possible to shape character. In view of all the above, work is not legible, understandable for workers either, since they do not understand what they are doing or, at best, only do so superficially, which pushes workers to indifference and provides them with a fragile labour identity.

CREATIVE WORK IN THE NEW GLOBAL ECONOMY

On the Concepts of Creativity and Global Economy

This general context of work crisis develops within the current global economy which, strongly influenced by the New Information and Communication Technologies—social networks and the Internet, in particular—has stimulated and favoured creative activity. However, what I am going to try and discern here is whether the latter manages to reduce or alleviate the state of work crisis and whether it succeeds or not in improving the precarious situation that work is facing. With this aim, I will try to describe the role played by creativity in the global economy, additionally defining with some basic brushstrokes what I mean by 'global economy' and what creativity is all about.

The economy of globalisation shows a high degree of geographical dispersion and mobility while simultaneously being characterised by a territorial concentration of the resources used for service management and delivery purposes. Therefore, the more firms become globalised, the more their central functions grow (Sassen 2007: 80 ff.) and the more they help the cities where they settle down to assume the 'global' label. Nevertheless, a large city can only reach a global status through the availability of financial centres, the presence of international corporate venues, the development of business and trade management services, manufacturing centres, a well-developed transportation network, international tourism, a considerable number of inhabitants, and a multicultural mixture of national and foreign residents, as well as a concentration of artistic and scientific elites (García-Canclini 2005: 167).

In turn, creativity can be depicted as a new or valuable idea or action or as 'the formulation of new ideas and their application to produce original works of art and cultural products, functional creations, scientific inventions and techno-cultural innovations' (Boix and Lazzeretti 2012: 182–3).

Needless to say, innovation—that is, the translation of technology into inventions or new developments—has become the basic component to successfully compete in the economy of globalisation, determined by the New Information and Communication Technologies. This innovation has two essential features, though: immateriality and the democratic nature (Anuri 2001: 121–5). Indeed, 'the economy of access' (Rifkin 2000: 50), with its essentially cultural and virtual approach, its networks and access, as well as its concepts and ideas, has replaced the capitalism structured around industrial production and property.

Creative Cities and Creative Industries Generate New Social Inequalities

Economic globalisation and creativity therefore go hand in hand, since the former has facilitated the emergence of creative cities (Florida 2009: 74–213) in which economic growth has not been driven by specialisation, but rather by innovation and flexibility, along with geographical location, an essential factor in the global economy. This importance of the place, linked to its personality, is consequently what brings wealth. Here, in these creative cities, their core constitutes a 'new class of scientists, engineers, university lecturers, poets, actors, novelists, animators, artists, architects and designers, cultural workers, scientific thinkers, analysts and opinion leaders whose economic function consists in creating new ideas, new technologies and/or a new creative content' (Florida 2010: 8).

A booming creative, cultural or awareness industry concentrates in such creative cities (Boix and Lazzeretti 2012: 196), together with a 'creative class' to which capitalism has entrusted its own aesthetic reproduction in the new technological era (Delgado 2016: 73). Hence, as opposed to 'cultural industries,' the 'creative' ones have lost the cultural and democratic sense, because 'leisure is guided, and entertainment programmed' in them (Muñoz 2015: 222) and they have been exclusively oriented towards the context of markets and short-term profitability. All of this helps to understand why creativity has transformed itself into a highly economicist concept, as a result of which culture has been displaced in favour of creativity. This has happened more intensely during the current crisis period, since creativity has been confused with innovation, strengthening the economicist bias of politicians, placing the emphasis on technological determination, highlighting the lack of sensitivity towards culture and stressing the competitive vision of globalisation—which is not integrating, but disintegrating. Without forgetting that insisting on economicism instead of culture implies an irreparable democratic loss, insofar as culture represents the vital cement, the main value of democracy. That is why, in contrast with this profitable short-term-oriented culture, we should support cultural training per se and a series of cultural policies able to underpin social creativity from the base (Bustamante 1995: 18–23).

The new digital creative industries do not seem to have a predisposition to perform that task, though; or in any case, it could be admitted that they depend on an ambivalent and paradoxical panorama (Rodríguez Ferrándiz 2011: 151–155). In fact, they are favouring an overlap of the times and spaces for leisure and work, of an industrialisation, rationalisation and commercialisation of the former and of an informal look about the latter. Next to this, the conversion of the basic cultural product—the book, the record, the film, the video—into a digital file or into a document that can be accessed online, and its assimilation in a medium like the computer, leads—as in the New Technology industries—to such a radical dematerialisation, 'transfiguration' or 'transubstantiation' that it prevents us from referring to those new figures or substances as 'matter.' Hence, this transfiguration of cultural assets encourages a kind of creativity which is simultaneously democratic and non-democratic, and which consequently entails a creative and contemplative 'experimentation.'

Furthermore, the democratic aspect of the creative economy is more theoretical than real because, in practice, instead of creating equality, what it generates is a deep and growing inequality between the different nations and between individuals, marginalised and defined by a new form of illiteracy—related to the limited production, knowledge and use of technologies in this case (Anuri 2001: 121–5); or hugely enriched thanks to their creative talent. In this regard, Antonio Ariño precisely insists in his work *La Secesión de los ricos* [The Secession of the Rich] (2016: 62–94) on the fact that the creativity of the new technological and financial societies causes new inequalities, which explains why postmodern possessive individualism borrows the ideas of personal autonomy, merit and talent from the democratic movements of the 1960s (Boltanski and Chiapello 2002: 241 ff.) and accordingly legitimises the scandalous profits of a business elite and supports inequality.

Thus, Ariño (2016: 66–127) continues to point out, rich people are currently divided into four categories, namely: geeks, sheikhs, oligarchs and bankers. The first are geniuses in specific fields of engineering and computational science who achieve their status precisely thanks to their initiative, their inventiveness and their boldness. In turn, the high salaries and earnings of financiers have become the incentives needed to take risks and innovate and to increase their personal wealth almost endlessly. In addition to this, the 2008 crisis has encouraged the 'ultra-rich' to implement a geographical diversification of their investments and to develop new tax evasion strategies, thus building an ecosystem of mobile money which produces enormous technological, social and cultural innovations. Amongst these stand out relocated financial centres, along with spaces of technological innovation and inventiveness. As opposed to these privileged places, the peripheries of the capitalist system show a reality where poverty and the uneven distribution of income come as a result of the actual polarising logic which characterises the global economy (Amin 2002: 31).

In short, if the most decisive and controversial issue in democracy is probably the relationship between equality and freedom, between freedom and power (Flores D'Arcais 2013: 83), creativity does not seem to have positively influenced those ties; on the contrary, it has broken them, also making democracy and capitalism stand further apart too.

It can therefore be stated that, if the creativity of the global economy has opened an abyss between capitalism and democracy, that of cities and creative industries have done the same between economicism on one side, and culture and democracy on the other.

FINAL REFLECTIONS

As this chapter has enabled us to verify, the contemporary work crisis results from a deep polarisation and inequality stimulated by the global economy which, strongly influenced by the New Information and Communication Technologies, has encouraged and favoured creative activity. Nonetheless, creative activity has failed to reduce or alleviate the state of work crisis and has not managed to improve the precarious situation of work either. Present-day creative work has actually failed to reduce unemployment rates and has not even been able to substantially dignify the status of labour activity. One might expect creativity—so much in fashion during the 1980s and the 1990s and in the first years of the twenty-first century—to trigger a significant change in the enthronement of work as an essential activity of human beings, a significant one both individually and socially. However, we can check that creative work has not become the manna which miraculously rains on the thousands of unemployed people living on earth. Quite the opposite, creative work has brought new inequalities with it, showing the structural faults of a system, the capitalist one, which is deeply unfair by nature and no longer can offer an occupation—in quantitative and qualitative terms—to everyone who wants it; what is more, capitalism has apparently no interest in doing so because it pays more attention and focuses to a greater extent on obtaining increasingly large profits in gradually shorter and faster times.

Our research work has additionally served to verify that creative work is characterised by at least five essential aspects:

1. The same as work in general, it is structured around risk, flexibility and inequality.
2. It constitutes a competitive individual development factor and, as a corollary, a social fracture factor.
3. It is neither helping to remove the bad perception about the traditional concept of work nor contributing to a greater availability of spare time. What it does instead is—the same as contemporary capitalism—to merge business time with leisure time, work time with party time.
4. It is more based on innovation than on creativity strictly speaking, placing the emphasis not on the origin—the past—but on novelty—the future, focusing to a larger extent on the short term than on a structural transformation.
5. The creativity that it displays has mainly consolidated in social change but, by paying the most attention to those novelties which generate more profits, it has commoditised that change, merging it with the pace of goods. Hence it has not sought a social, reformist or revolutionary transformation, but rather increased economic profits for the leading industrial sectors, thus making them more powerful. In short, this explains the transformation of creativity into just another material resource—as Marx already saw—and into an instrument that largely contributes to inequality in the global capitalist system.

The creative economy has consequently widened the gap between market and state, between politics and economy, between capitalism and representative democracy, even activating the contradictions inherent to capitalism. In other words, it has worsened the crisis, the decline and collapse of democracy, in addition to generating new inequalities between the rich and the poor and between creative and non-creative states.

Finally, in my opinion, the present research work succeeded in confirming that the creative global economic system has commoditised creativity, emptying the latter of its meaning, and has empowered it with respect to culture, thus collaborating to deepen the crisis of representative democracies and its values, and most importantly for us, the crisis of work itself.

REFERENCES

Amin, S. (2002). *El capitalismo en la Era de la Globalización.* Buenos Aires: Paidós.

Anuri, D. (2001, November). La Democracia reforzada por la creatividad. *NUNTIUM,* 119–124.

Ariño, A. (2016). *La secesión de los ricos.* Barcelona: Galaxia Gutenberg.

Bauman, Z. (2003). *Modernidad líquida.* Buenos Aires: FCE.

Beck, U. (2006). *La sociedad del riesgo global.* Madrid: Siglo XXI.

Beck, U. (2007). *Un nuevo mundo feliz. La precariedad del trabajo en la era de la globalización.* Barcelona: Paidós.

Beriain, J. (2008). *Aceleración y tiranía del presente. La metamorfosis en las estructuras temporales de la modernidad.* Barcelona: Editorial Anthropos.

Boix, R., & Lazzeretti, L. (2012). Las industrias creativas en España: una panorámica. *Investigaciones Regionales, 22,* 181–206.

Boltanski, L., & Chiapello, É. (2002). *El nuevo espíritu del capitalismo.* Madrid: Akal.

Bustamante, E. (1995). De las industrias culturales al entretenimiento. La creatividad, la innovación...viejos y nuevos señuelos para la investigación de la cultura. *Diálogos. Revista Académica de la Federación Latinoamericana de Comunicación, 78,* 1–25.

Delgado, M. (2016). *Ciudadanismo. La reforma ética y estética del Capitalismo.* Madrid: Catarata.

Figueras, A. J., & Morero, H. A. (2013). La teoría del consumo y de los ciclos en Thorstein Veblen. *Revista de Economía Institucional, 15*(28), 159–182.

Flores D'Arcais, P. (2013). *¡Democracia! Libertad privada y libertad rebelde.* Barcelona: Galaxia Gutenberg-Círculo de Lectores.

Florida, R. (2009). *Las ciudades creativas. Por qué donde vives puede ser la decisión más importante de tu vida.* Barcelona: Paidós.

Florida, R. (2010). *La Clase Creativa. La transformación de la cultura del trabajo y el ocio en el siglo XXI.* Barcelona/Buenos Aires/México: Paidós.

Fraiman, J. A. (2015). *Algunas consideraciones sobre el concepto de trabajo en Karl Marx y el análisis crítico de Jürgen Habermas* (Vol. 25, pp. 235–245). Trabajo y Sociedad.

Galbraith, J. K. (1984). *La Era de la Incertidumbre.* Barcelona: Plaza & Janés.

García-Canclini, N. (2005). *La globalización imaginada.* Buenos Aires: Paidós.

Gratton, L. (2012). *Prepárate: el futuro del trabajo ya está aquí.* Barcelona: Galaxia Gutenberg-Círculo de Lectores.

Held, D. (1993). *Modelos de democracia.* Madrid: Alianza.

Hobsbawm, E. (2001). *Historia del Siglo XX.* Barcelona: Crítica.

Inglehart, R. (1991). *El cambio cultural en las sociedades industriales avanzadas.* Madrid: CIS.

Innerarity, D. (2004). *La sociedad invisible.* Madrid: Espasa Calpe.

Marx, K. (1985). *Trabajo asalariado y capital.* Barcelona: Planeta-Agostini.

Muñoz, B. (2015). *La dominación simbólica en la globalización. Una Teoría Crítica sobre la Postmodernidad.* Madrid: Fundamentos.

Naredo, J. M. (2002). Configuración y crisis del mito del trabajo. *Scripta Nova: Revista electrónica de geografía y ciencias sociales,* Extra Issue 6, 119.

Requejo Coll, F. (1990). *Las democracias. Democracia antigua, democracia liberal y Estado de Bienestar.* Barcelona: Ariel.

Rifkin, J. (2000). *La era del acceso. La revolución de la nueva economía.* Barcelona: Paidós.

Roche Cárcel, J. A. (2012). Tiempo líquido y cultura de la incertidumbre. *International Review of Sociology, 22*(1), 137–162.

Roche Cárcel, J. A. (2013). El incierto sentido del trabajo en la sociedad de riesgo global. *Barataria: revista castellano-manchega de ciencias sociales, 15,* 207–226.

Rodríguez Ferrándiz, R. (2011). De industrias culturales a industrias del ocio y creativas: los límites del "campo" cultural. *Revista Comunicar, 36, La televisión y sus nuevas expresiones, 18,* 149–156.

Sassen, S. (2007). *Una sociología de la globalización.* Buenos Aires: Katz.

Sennett, R. (2000). *La corrosión del carácter. Las consecuencias personales del trabajo en el nuevo capitalismo.* Barcelona: Anagrama.

Smith, A. (2007). *La riqueza de las naciones.* Madrid: Alianza editorial.

Sombart, W. (2009). *Lujo y capitalismo. Economía de la ostentación.* Madrid: Sequitur.

Tezanos, J. F. (2001). *El trabajo perdido. ¿Hacia una civilización postlaboral?* Madrid: Biblioteca Nueva.

Thaa, W. (2008). Democracia y crítica de la civilización en Max Weber y Hannah Arendt. *Revista española de ciencia política, 19,* 9–40.

Todorov, T. (2012). *Los enemigos íntimos de la democracia.* Barcelona: Galaxia Gutenberg-Círculo de Lectores.

Veblen, T. (2000). *Teoría de la clase ociosa.* Ediciones el aleph.com

Weber, M. (1997). *Sociología de la religión.* Bogotá: Fondo de Cultura Económica.

INDEX[1]

[1] Note: Page numbers followed by 'n' refer to notes.

© The Author(s) 2019
A. Scribano, P. Lisdero (eds.), *Digital Labour, Society and the Politics of Sensibilities*, https://doi.org/10.1007/978-3-030-12306-2

191

Printed by Printforce, the Netherlands